Paul and the Politics of Difference

Paul and the Politics of Difference

A Contextual Study of the Jewish-Gentile Difference
in Galatians and Romans

Jae Won Lee

☙PICKWICK *Publications* · Eugene, Oregon

PAUL AND THE POLITICS OF DIFFERENCE
A Contextual Study of the Jewish-Gentile Difference in Galatians and Romans

Copyright © 2014 Jae Won Lee. All rights reserved. Except for brief quotations in critical publications or reviews, no part of this book may be reproduced in any manner without prior written permission from the publisher. Write: Permissions. Wipf and Stock Publishers, 199 W. 8th Ave., Suite 3, Eugene, OR 97401.

Pickwick Publications
An Imprint of Wipf and Stock Publishers
199 W. 8th Ave., Suite 3
Eugene, OR 97401

www.wipfandstock.com

ISBN 13: 978-1-62564-824-2

Cataloguing-in-Publication Data

Lee, Jae Won

 Paul and the politics of difference : a contextual study of the Jewish-Gentile difference in Galatians and Romans / Jae Won Lee.

 xii + 192 p. ; 23 cm. Includes bibliographical references.

 ISBN 13: 978-1-62564-824-2

 1. Paul, the Apostle, Saint. 2. Bible. Galatians—Criticism, interpretation, etc. 3. Bible. Romans—Criticism, interpretation, etc. 4. Gentiles in the New Testament. I. Title.

BS2651 L41 2014

Manufactured in the U.S.A.   08/18/2014

In Memory of My Mother and Father

Contents

Acknowledgments | ix
Abbreviations | xi

1 Introduction | 1
2 Theoretical and Hermeneutical Perspectives on Difference | 29
3 Difference and Greco-Roman Meals | 70
4 Difference and Table-fellowship in Antioch (Gal 2:11–21) | 107
5 The "Weak" and the "Strong" at Table in Romans 14:1—15:13 | 136
6 Equality with Difference: Solidarity with the "Weak" | 162

Bibliography | 181

Acknowledgments

My doctoral dissertation on Paul and the Politics of Difference was an outcome out of my academic engagement in and struggle with a task to seek liberative potentials in the Bible, especially in the New Testament. Yet it was not until now that the dissertation has been shaped into a book. In this sense, this book represents only a beginning of my unfinished, ongoing task.

There are many people I wish to express my thanks for the personal friendship and intellectual companionship that I have shared with them for a long time in my life. But I would like to name only a few of them. As I reflect on my doctoral work at Union Theological Seminary in New York, I am enormously grateful to my dissertation advisor Brigitte Kahl for her wonderful support and her empire-critical biblical hermeneutics, and to Hal E. Taussig for his enthusiastic and critical guidance toward my engagement with the subject of Greco-Roman meals. My continuing academic relationships with them have helped me intensify my commitment to issues related to empire-critical biblical hermeneutics and the early Christian meal practices. I also would like to give my heart-felt thanks to my friends and colleagues in New York; Mary Boys, Kathy Talvacchia, Sue Pak, Seth Kasten, Mim Warden, and Eun Ja Lee for their strong support and remarkable friendship. My life in New York, in retrospect, compels me to remember constant encouragement and prayers that came to me from Korea, from thousands miles away; Soon Kyung Park, Kwang Sun Suh, Ae Young Kim, and Seung Hee Son.

I also would like express my deepest gratitude to Robert Brawley and David Rhoads for their support and intellectual companionship during my teaching at McCormick Theological Seminary. Their biblical scholarship, teaching, and friendship have been invaluable resource for my critical engagement and personal empowerment in my teaching. Their passionate

Acknowledgments

teaching for justice and mutuality remains both a profound inspiration and a significant challenge for my teaching and biblical scholarship.

I wish to give special thanks to K. C. Hanson, Matthew Wimer, Chris Spinks, and Laura Poncy of Wipf and Stock Publishers for all their efforts to bring my work into publication. Finally, I would like to give my most affectionate thanks to my sisters and brothers, my brothers-in-law and my sister-in-law, and all of my nieces and nephews. Despite "difference" that I might have introduced into my family, they never waivered their understanding, love, and care.

Abbreviations

Cicero
Fam.   *Epistulae ad familiares*
Sen.   *De senectute*

Juvenal
Sat.   *Satirae*

Lucian
Dial. meretr.   *Dialogi meretricii*
Symp.   *Symposium*

Cornelius Nepos
Praef.   *Praefatio*

Martial
Epigr.   *Epigrammata*

Plutarch
Quaest. conv. *Quaestiones conviviales*

Pliny the Younger
Ep.   *Epistulae*

1

Introduction

1. REVISITING THE ISSUE OF EQUALITY BETWEEN JEWS AND GENTILES

IN HIS SEMINAL ESSAY "Paul among Jews and Gentiles,"[1] Krister Stendahl declared that "the main lines of Pauline interpretation—and hence both conscious and unconscious reading and quoting of Paul by scholars and lay people alike—have for many centuries been out of touch with one of the most basic of the questions and concerns that shaped Paul's thinking in the first place: the relation between Jews and Gentiles."[2] Stendahl particularly tried to demonstrate that the doctrine of justification by faith "was hammered out by Paul for the very specific and limited purpose of defending the rights of Gentile converts to be full and genuine heirs to the promises of God to Israel."[3]

His grasp of the importance of the relation between Jews and Gentiles, however, did not provide a further investigation on the issue of equality between Jews and Gentiles beyond the effort to emphasize Paul's commitment to the religious rights of Gentiles as equal to Jews. The social and practical meaning of equality between Jews and Gentiles and its further

---

1. Stendahl, "Paul Among Jews and Gentiles." This essay is based on lectures delivered in 1963–1964.
2. Ibid., 1.
3. Ibid., 2; see esp. 23–40.

implications for the problems, tension, and conflicts which developed within early Christian communities were not taken into full consideration. Nevertheless, Stendahl's approach took a major step toward liberating Pauline theology from the Occidental Christian interpretation which imposed on Paul the later Western problem of the introspective conscience[4] as well as the anachronistic dichotomy between Judaism and Christianity.

Although Stendahl had substantial impact on subsequent scholarship, the full potential of this rediscovery of the "historical Paul" for post-colonial and liberation-oriented approaches to the origin(s) of the Christian movement has not yet been adequately explored. In Korean Christianity, for example, the concrete historical context of Paul's thoughts and praxis among Jews and Gentiles has been entirely lost and replaced by the Western Christian, time-and-place-less universalism, introspective individualism, and soteriological dogmatism. This has led the majority of Korean Christians to regard Christian faith as a means for an exclusively individual and otherworldly salvation. Since Christian faith has been understood as assuming a universal identity, the "Korean" identity in its concrete socio-political and cultural context did not make much difference to the meaning of being "Christian." As all human beings, according to the dominant interpretation of Paul's justification by faith alone, are sinners before God, it is believed that differences in social status, gender, ethnicity, and culture do not count.

Such a universal tendency, however, has had an enormous impact on the general role of Korean Christianity in the history of Korea. Here, I want to point out some negative aspects that Western theological universalism imprinted on the general ethos of Korean Christianity. First, it has contributed less to the transformation of and resistance against the structural injustice of domination and oppression than to the consolidation and maintenance of the status quo of the Korean society. The dimension of socio-political and communal embodiment of Christian faith has been subsumed by an individualized, a-historical, and a-cultural faith. Secondly, the identity of "Korean" Christianity has been assimilated into Western cultural universalism in such a way that the particularity of "Korean" identity in its specific socio-political and cultural history has been rendered insignificant and inferior to the universal "Christian" identity, which was actually no less than an Occidental or European identity. Ironically, but not

---

4. See Stendahl, "The Apostle Paul and the Introspective Conscience of the West," 78–98.

surprisingly, Christianity's assumed superiority over Judaism was translated into and identified with Christianity's superiority over other religions in Korea. In the Korean context, being "Christian" thus has not only been identified with being conservative toward socio-political transformation, but also with being exclusive toward traditional Korean religious and cultural heritage.

Although the social conservatism and religious exclusivism characteristic of a predominant form of Korean Christianity today requires a far more thorough investigation, the massive influence of the Western theological tradition cannot be underestimated. Especially, Western theological (soteriological) readings of Paul, more precisely of the doctrine of justification by faith, have to a great extent shaped the conservative general contour of Christian faith in Korea. Even the most progressive Christians in Korea are not quite free of the traditional interpretation of Paul. This may explain why Korean minjung theology—like most of Latin American liberation theology—while achieving a significant political reinterpretation of the praxis of the historical Jesus, has not attempted a corresponding new understanding of Paul.[5]

Recent New Testament scholarship has made significant contribution to the reassessment of assumptions, hypotheses, and social descriptions traditionally held especially regarding the origins of the early Christian movement and Judaism(s) of the first century Greco-Roman world. Particularly in the recent interpretation of Paul and the Christian movement associated with him, there have been some conspicuous shifts in interpretation which radically challenge the old pictures of Paul especially with respect to his relationship toward Judaism, the famous antithesis of Law-versus-Gospel, and the relationship between first-century Judaism and the Pauline Christianity.[6] To put it simply, the traditional image of the "dejudaized" Paul has been seriously challenged by some efforts of "rejudaizing" Paul, although the majority of Pauline scholarship continues to insist on the former.

---

5. In this regard, the work of Tamez, *The Amnesty of Grace* is a noteworthy exception. It is a reinterpretation and reconstruction of the doctrine of justification by faith from the standpoint of the poor and oppressed in Latin America. In the North American context, recently a few scholars have begun to pay attention to Paul's opposition to the Roman empire; Georgi, *Theocracy*; N. Elliott, *Liberating Paul*; and Horsley, ed., *Paul and Empire* and *Paul and Politics*.

6. Esp. E. P. Sanders, *Paul and Palestinian Judaism*; Dunn, "New Perspective on Paul"; Segal, *Paul the Convert*; Nanos, *The Mystery of Romans*; Boyarin, *A Radical Jew*; N. Elliott, *Liberating Paul*; Tamez, *The Amnesty of Grace*; and Horsley, ed., *Paul and Empire*.

At the heart of these changes lies the effort to challenge the long-held traditional Lutheran legacy of Paul as a theological opponent of Judaism. Above all, the doctrine of justification by faith, which was placed at the center of Paul's theology by the Protestant theological tradition, has been decentered and rightly contextualized. Following Stendahl's argument, scholars have acknowledged that Paul's main concern was not Luther's quest for a gracious God, but his own defense for the equal status of Gentile Christians, as well as a new vision of community which subverts the basic concepts of Roman Empire.[7] Furthermore, they discovered that the picture of Judaism drawn from Paul's supposed negative statements on the Jewish Law is fundamentally wrong, with no correspondence to the ordinary Jewish self-understanding of the relationship between God's grace and Jewish observance of law within the covenantal relationship. This discovery that first-century Judaism had nothing to do with the picture stereotyped as the religion of "legalistic work-righteousness" can be attributed to E. P. Sanders's extensive study of Paul and Palestinian Judaism,[8] which has received wide acceptance among Pauline scholars.[9]

While acknowledging valuable contributions to the interpretation of Paul's theology with more attention to the historical context of first-century Judaism, I take issue with the so-called "new perspective on Paul,"[10] asking how much it has brought a real shift of paradigm in the study of Paul. The new perspective on Paul basically tries to explain Paul's stance toward the Jewish law, specifically toward "works of the Law" against the background of "covenantal nomism" which was characterized by Sanders as the generally prevailing religious ethos in Palestinian Judaism.

The main argument derived from this perspective is that Paul opposed Jewish covenantal nomism understood in nationalistic terms—"covenantal nomism as restricting the covenant to those within the boundaries marked by the law, that is, to Jews and proselytes."[11] Although such an argument seeks to make Paul's theology intelligible to the covenantal context of first-century Judaism and to explore the social function of the Law, I would

---

7. See Horsley, ed., *Paul and Empire*.

8. E. P. Sanders, *Paul and Palestinian Judaism*.

9. E.g., Dunn, "New Perspective on Paul"; "Incident at Antioch"; Longenecker, *Eschatology and the Covenant*; Watson, *Paul, Judaism and the Gentiles*; Räisänen, *Paul and the Law*; Boyarin, *A Radical Jew*.

10. See Dunn, "New Perspective on Paul."

11. Dunn, "Theology of Galatians," 134–35.

argue that it remains limited to a primarily theological concern. It is still grounded on the supposed theological antithesis of Paul and Judaism. As Neil Elliott critically remarks, it "simply casts Bauer's old dialectic of 'Pauline universalism' versus 'Jewish particularism' in sociological terms."[12]

For many centuries since Paul left his letters to Western Christianity, theologians and scholars have been troubled by and preoccupied with a series of dichotomous formulae that they found crucial to Paul's theological doctrines such as law-gospel, flesh-spirit, works-faith, and so on. In order to avoid falling into another trap of the dichotomy of dejudaized Paul and rejudaized Paul, we need to problematize the definitions and nature of both terms of "dejudaized" and "rejudaized," and to be mindful once again of Paul among Jews and Gentiles as Krister Stendahl invoked.[13]

In this study, I challenge both the traditional interpretation of "dejudaized" Paul and the emerging reinvention of "rejudaized" Paul by revisiting and reassessing the problems involved in the Jew-Gentile difference in early Christian groups. I would argue that in both old and new interpretations of Paul, the differences between Jews and Gentiles are treated in rather simplistic, essentializing, and generalizing ways. Thus, I shall attempt to investigate the problems involved in the Jew-Gentile difference by relocating the issue into concrete socio-historical situations and discerning different and conflicting interests, tendencies and policies among different groups or members of the groups.

The question about equal status between Jews and Gentiles was one of the vexing issues among Pauline communities and has recaptured scholarly attention for the reinterpretation of Paul's theology and praxis. I revisit this familiar theme in Pauline scholarship by bringing a distinct angle to the fore, that is, the problem of equality and difference. At Paul's time it was closely linked with the relationship between Jews and Gentiles and played a crucial role in the historical development of early Christian self-understanding and social formation. Moreover, the problem of equality and difference has become a new focus of theoretical discourses within contemporary social criticisms and movements.

If, according to Elisabeth Schüssler Fiorenza, the vision of egalitarian community without injustice, subordination, and discrimination was a significant aspect of the early Christian faith and praxis (cf. Gal 3:26–28),[14] in

---

12. N. Elliott, *Liberating Paul*, 70.
13. Stendahl, *Paul among Jews and Gentiles*.
14. Schüssler Fiorenza, *In Memory of Her*, esp. 160–218.

Paul and the Politics of Difference

what ways were Christian congregations expected to practice such a vision of equality between Jews and Gentiles? Given the ethnic, socio-religious, and cultural differences between Jews and Gentiles, how could these differences be related to an egalitarian vision of faith that recognizes "neither Jew nor Gentile" (Gal 3:26–28)? How did Paul and other early Christians understand and practice this asserted equality between Jews and Gentiles?[15] How could and did Jewish Christians or Christian Jews understand the status of Gentile Christians? On the other hand, what could and did it mean to Gentile Christians that they were equal to their Jewish fellow believers? How did the understanding of equality intersect with experiences of difference between Jews and Gentiles within Christian communities?

One of my arguments in this study is that the problem of equality and difference between Jews and Gentiles cannot be treated simply in terms of abstract, theological principles such as Paul's opposition to Judaism and "Pauline universalism" versus "Jewish particularism." At the same time it cannot be understood merely as Paul's justification of the status of Gentile Christians,[16] or a matter of the diversity of first-century Judaism and early Christianity. There is a need for a more contextual approach to the dynamic, relational meaning of equality and difference between Jews and Gentiles by paying particular attention to the specific situation of each local Christian community within the first-century Jewish and Greco-Roman context. This implies that both "Jewishness" and "Gentileness" need to be contextually related to the problem of equality and difference with reference to emerging hierarchical social relations between Jews and Gentiles in the early Christian movement. Who defines "difference" as inferior and wrong, hence as "otherness" to be repressed and excluded? Who claims "difference" as equal-but-different and emancipatory, hence as "identity" to be reclaimed and included? Under what political, social, religious, and cultural conditions? These questions crucial to the issue of equality (identity) and difference are not only relevant to the contemporary politics of difference, but also imperative for a fresh approach to the problem of equality and difference in early Christian communities of Jews and Gentiles.

---

15. Cf. Gal 3:26–28; Rom 3:29–30; 1 Cor 7:19.

16. Following Stendahl, especially John Gager and Lloyd Gaston overly emphasized this one-sided interpretation of the relation between Jews and Gentiles. See Gager, *Origins of Anti-Semitism*; Gaston, *Paul and the Torah*.

2. REVIEW OF LITERATURE

In the current interpretation of Paul and Pauline movement(s), I discern two different positions dealing with the issue of equality/difference between Jews and Gentiles within early Christian communities. At the risk of schematization, I define the first position as "equality without difference," and the second position as "equality with difference." A few scholars whose works are representative of different approaches and foci will be selectively reviewed.

2.1. Equality without Difference

(a) E. P. Sanders

As pointed out above, according to the traditional approach stemming from the Reformation, Paul attacked the idea that salvation can be earned by acts of obedience to the Law, as held by his Jewish or Jewish Christian opponents. Paul has thus been interpreted as a theological opponent of Judaism, whereby Judaism itself has been characterized as a religion of "works-righteousness." In his *Paul and Palestinian Judaism* E. P. Sanders made a fundamental challenge to such a stereotyped presentation of Judaism.

Sanders argues that Palestinian Judaism of 200 BCE to 200 CE should be understood principally within the context of the relationship between law and covenant. Based on a thorough investigation of the Jewish material relevant to that context, Sanders highlights a basic element of the Judaism of the period, which stands in direct opposition to the picture of Judaism described in the traditional interpretation of Paul: "In all the literature surveyed, *obedience maintains one's position in the covenant, but it does not earn God's grace as such*."[17]

Defining the basic character of the Jewish observance as "covenantal nomism," Sanders asserts that it was "the basic *type* of religion, *pervasive* in Palestine before 70 and known by Jesus and Paul."[18] Throughout his work, Sanders argues that the Judaism of the first century cannot be characterized as "petty legalism, self-serving and self-deceiving casuistry, and a mixture of arrogance and lack of confidence in God,"[19] and that it is misleading to

---

17. E. P. Sanders, *Paul and Palestinian Judaism*, 420 (emphasis original).
18. Ibid., 422–26 (emphasis original).
19. Ibid., 427.

link Paul's negative statements against the Law with such a characterization. As Daniel Boyarin's deliberate comment on Sanders's undisputable contribution says, "He has laid the foundations for a reading which neither slanders Judaism nor slanders Paul by making his account of Judaism a slander."[20]

In order to explain Paul's attitude toward the Law, Sanders finds an alternative in his understanding of Paul's Christological soteriology: In Jesus Christ God has provided the salvation for all who believe, whether Jew or Gentile. Sanders continues to argue that for Paul "Righteousness *cannot* be by law, *since it is by faith*, not since doing the law leads to boasting."[21] He also says that "The promise *cannot* be inherited on the basis of keeping the law, because that would exclude Gentiles. But Gentiles *cannot* be excluded, for God has appointed Christ as Lord of the whole world and as savior of all who believe, and has especially called and appointed Paul as apostle to the Gentiles."[22] Thus, the antithesis of faith and law itself is not changed at all. Rather its ground is argued from a different perspective. Here, it is important to note that in his understanding of Paul's "by faith, not by law" Sanders seeks to combine Paul's Christological soteriology with the issue of Gentile inclusion, although the logical priority is given to the former and it is not accounted for how the two are tightly connected. Sanders draws the issue of Gentile inclusion principally from his understanding of Paul's Christological universalism, that is, "Christ as savior of *all*." But that universalism, Sanders argues, is only possible through faith in Christ, and therefore it is exclusivistic universalism, in the sense of "not by law."

One of the problems with Sanders's soteriological interpretation of Paul is that Paul's position is rendered as inexplicable within the context of covenantal nomism of the first-century Judaism which Sanders has presented so convincingly. At the same time Paul's position remains unique when compared with the views of other Jewish Christians. As Sanders himself recognizes, if other Jewish Christians also had faith in Christ and believed that they are saved by faith, then soteriological Christology does not seem to be an appropriate explanatory framework to account for different views, tendencies, and strategies with respect to issues involved in difference between Jews and Gentiles within the early Christian communities.

20. Boyarin, *A Radical Jew*, 47.
21. E. P. Sanders, *Paul and Palestinian Judaism*, 484.
22. Ibid., 489–90 (emphasis original).

As a consequence, it is not surprising to see that Sanders deals with the practical dimension of the issue of Gentile inclusion and the equal fellowship between Jews and Gentiles within the Christian community in terms of "matter of behaviors" with respect to the Jewish law. According to Sanders, when the question is not about an entry requirement, Paul regarded important aspects of the law as "indifferent" or "optional," especially the requirement of circumcision, special days, and special food.[23] Sanders further argues that such a principle of "tolerance" toward the Jewish laws did not work in actual interaction between Jews and Gentiles within the Christian community. Sanders offers this reason: "If Jewish and Gentile Christians were to eat together, one would have to decide whether to live as a Jew or as a Gentile . . . The Antioch incident would seem to show that, if Jews were present, Paul would expect them not to observe the Jewish dietary laws."[24]

Did Paul really view the Jewish particularities embodying the Jewish way of life as the obstacle to Christian unity? Sanders presents the picture of Paul as a Jew who eventually "viewed it as the only behavior in accord with the truth of the gospel to live as a Gentile,"[25] for the sake of unity and equality for the Gentiles.

I will try to problematize his assumption that the observance of the Jewish laws is the only criterion that determines the "difference" between Jews and Gentiles. Sanders's discussion of the practical dimension of the equal fellowship of Jews and Gentiles almost necessarily evades a proper treatment of Rom 14:1—15:13, where, contrary to Sanders's view, Jews are expected to continue their practices.

(b) James D. G. Dunn

James D. G. Dunn fully accepts Sanders's basic understanding of Judaism's covenantal nomism by which obedience of the law was characterized as "maintaining" the covenantal relationship with God, not as a means of "entering" the covenant.[26] While generally agreeing with Sanders's description of the first-century Judaism, Dunn rightly observes the methodological limitation of Sanders's work: "The most surprising feature of Sanders' writing, however, is that he himself has failed to take the opportunity his own

23. E. P. Sanders, *Paul, the Law, and the Jewish People*, 113–14.
24. Ibid., 177.
25. Ibid., 178.
26. Dunn, "New Perspective on Paul," 186.

ground-breaking work offered. Instead of trying to explore how far Paul's theology could be explicated in relation to Judaism's 'covenantal nomism,' he remained more impressed by the *difference* between Paul's pattern of religious thought and that of first-century Judaism."[27]

Thus, Dunn's main intention is to demonstrate how Paul and other Jewish Christians might be related to the covenantal nomism of first-century Judaism. Dunn finds the key clue from his exegetical elaboration on the textual and sociological meaning of the term "works of the law" in Galatians. Dunn observes that within the historical context of Judaism and the mind-set of the first-century Jews, the notion of "works of the law" became the fundamental identity marker, or boundary marker which distinguishes the Jews as God's covenant people from Gentiles and others. As such it refers to the observance of particular laws like circumcision, food laws and Sabbath.

Dunn points out that at a certain juncture of the historical development of early Christian movement(s), particularly at the Antioch incident, Paul came to see a problem involved in "covenantal nomism." In terms of "justification by faith in Jesus Christ," not "justification by faith" which reflects a basic Jewish understanding, Paul objects to the idea that "God's justification depends on 'covenantal nomism.'"[28] In attacking "justification by works of the law," Paul attacks a particular understanding of the covenant, that is, a "nationalistic or racial" understanding of the covenant. Dunn presents this as the precise point where Paul the Jew distanced himself from his fellow Jews and other Jewish Christians.

Regarding Dunn's contribution, at least two points need to be mentioned for my study. First, Dunn gave considerable weight to the historical significance of justification by faith in Jesus by relating it closely to covenantal nomism. He attempted to deal with the issue of covenantal nomism within the historical development of early Christian movement(s), taking into considerations when and how the issue became a matter of conflict between Paul and his fellow Jewish Christians. Second, Dunn brought the issue of identity to the discussion of justification by faith, making the issue of covenantal nomism a common ground for comparing different approaches among early Christian groups toward the problem of emerging Christian self-identity.

---

27. Ibid., 186 (emphasis original).
28. Ibid., 195.

Introduction

Yet, there are some debatable points in Dunn's work. First, in his work Dunn consistently argues that Paul attacked the nationalistic, racial, and ethnic expression of covenantal nomism. However, Dunn does not seem to offer an understandable motivation for Paul's criticism of the nationalistic identity of the covenant, apart from the explanation that Paul understood Jesus' death and resurrection as the fulfillment of the covenant which transcends the ethnic boundaries of the covenant. But Dunn does not provide an explanation of why Paul understood Jesus' death and resurrection as transcending the ethnic boundaries of the covenant. Second, as far as the issue of identity is concerned, Dunn's approach appears to be more or less static. Although he rightly deals with the "social function of the law" in his discussion of the relationship of Paul to covenantal nomism, it still remains a question of whether Paul should be interpreted as totally denying the national identity of covenantal nomism in terms of Jewishness.

(c) Alan F. Segal

In *Paul the Convert: The Apostolate and Apostasy of Saul the Pharisee*,[29] Alan Segal presents a great deal of discussion on the problem of Jew-Gentile difference in Paul and early Christian communities. Segal appropriately locates the issue within the diverse context of first-century Judaism and identifies the crux of the problem with the question of ritual distinctions between Jews and Gentiles within early Christian groups as a Jewish apocalyptic sectarian movement. An important aspect of Segal's contribution lies in the complex way he articulates the significance of Paul's conversion experience in its personal and social effects for the understanding of the meaning of law and faith in Paul, his commitment to Gentile Christian communities, and consequently his position about the Jew-Gentile difference.

Dissociating his position from the traditional approaches to theological and psychological aspects of Paul's conversion, Segal urges us to see both personal and social aspects of Paul's conversion experience as integral to Paul's articulation of a new meaning of faith in Christ and its social consequences for Paul and his Gentile Christians. Segal also stresses that Paul's own personal conversion experience is tightly linked to his postconversion experience in the Gentile community. This double-edged—both personal and communal—experience is, according to Segal, what led Paul to attain a new understanding of "faith." Thus, Segal says: "Faith means more to Paul

29. Segal, *Paul the Convert*.

than remaining faithful and steadfast to the covenant. It is not something that Judaism or Jewish Christianity exhibits, but it *is* inherent in gentile Christianity. The paradigm for this type of religion is Paul's own conversion from the surety of his Pharisaic observances to the freedom and uncertainties of his gentile Christianity."[30]

Although Segal often uses somewhat totalizing words such as "Jewish Christianity" and "gentile Christianity" in describing different social formations of the early Christian movement, and tends to see them as separate entities, he is certainly rejecting the conventional understanding of Paul's conversion as a change in religion, that is, conversion from one religion (Judaism) to another religion (Christianity). Rather, Segal emphasizes that to Paul conversion means a "radical change in the community to which Paul give allegiance,"[31] and that by faith Paul talks about the centrality of faith for defining a new community to which he was converted. The new community is based on "the experience of transformation into the spirit through faith, which lives without the obligations of Torah."[32] According to Segal, this new faith means to Paul a radical revaluing the meaning of the observance of Jewish law, for he was once faithfully committed as a Pharisaic Jew.

Segal rightly insists that Paul's statements and arguments regarding the opposition of law and faith be considered as being derived not from any abstract theology, but from his experience with Gentile Christian congregations based upon his own conversion experience: "He is advocating a new definition of community in which the performance of the special laws of Judaism does not figure. This new definition is an attempt to enfranchise the community in which he lives, the community in which he learned the value and meaning of his religious conversion."[33]

Further, challenging the traditional approaches to the Pauline law-faith antithesis, Segal pinpoints the origin and core of the opposition of law and faith in the following statement: "The vexing issue of the ritual status of gentiles—and not their salvation or even philosophical issues of universalism or particularism or the value of the works' righteousness—directly occasions Paul's meditations on law.[34]

30. Ibid., 121 (Segal's emphasis).
31. Ibid.
32. Ibid., 122.
33. Ibid., 124.
34. Ibid., 125.

Introduction

While Segal basically agrees with the argument of Stendahl, Gaston, and Gager that Paul made negative statements about Jewish law mainly for the defense of the religious rights of the Gentiles, he takes a different position from their assertion that Torah remains in effect for Jews in terms of "two separate paths—salvation for gentiles in Christianity and for Jews in Torah."[35] I agree with Segal's position, inasmuch as it underscores the central importance of faith in Christ for the definition of a new community of believers (*both Jews and Gentiles*)[36] within Judaism.

Yet, Segal's argument moves beyond this. Based on his reading of Galatians 2, especially Gal 2:15–16, Segal argues for the exclusive value of faith in Paul, meaning that faith excludes Torah for all—not only for Gentiles but also for Jews.[37] Interpreting the faith-law opposition Paul articulated in Gal 2:15–16 in soteriological terms, Segal argues that to Paul "ceremonial Torah is of no significance for salvation for *anyone*."[38] This is the point at which Segal differs from the Stendahl-Gaston-Gager position. According to Segal, since Jewish ceremonial law has no soteriological significance for all, Paul considers the observance of ceremonial law irrelevant to anyone. This leads Segal to suggest that Paul might have given up observing the ceremonial laws and even encouraged Jewish Christians to do so.[39] Thus, Segal maintains that Paul, as a consequence of his conversion experience and his commitment to his Gentile Christian communities, advocates the irrelevance of ceremonial Torah for salvation and promotes the eradication of ritual distinction between Jews and Gentiles. Segal explains this as Paul's consistent "ideological" position toward Jewish ceremonial law that functioned to differentiate Jews from Gentiles.[40] As far as Segal's focus on such an ideological position is concerned, it might not be wrong to associate his interpretation with the category of "equality without difference."

However, regarding the practical dimension of Paul's position toward Jewish ceremonial law and the Jew-Gentile difference Segal presents an

---

35. Ibid., 130.

36. Whereas Segal seems to overemphasize the Gentile composition of the community to which Paul was converted, I prefer to see more mixed nature of both Jews and Gentiles such as in the Antiochene community.

37. Segal, *Paul the Convert*, 130–33.

38. Ibid., 132 (emphasis original).

39. Cf. ibid., 130, 210. "There can be no doubt that Paul himself has not only preached the end of ceremonial laws, he has given up his adherence to them, though obviously not to their ethical impulse and statutes" (210).

40. See ibid., 201–18.

interesting argument, which allows much more complexity and flexibility for Paul's policy. Segal deals with the practical issues of circumcision and dietary laws within the early Christian communities more contextually and from a Jewish legal perspective, focusing on the importance of unity between Jewish and Gentile Christians or Paul's vision of a new, unified Christian community.[41] Mainly drawing on Paul's statements in 1 Cor 7:17–20 and 1 Cor 9:20–22 as well as the story about Paul's practice of vows in Acts 18:18 and Acts 21:17–26, Segal argues that Paul often changed his practice regarding Jewish ceremonial law and made occasional compromises for the sake of church unity, but without violating his ideological principle of freedom from Jewish ceremonial law.

Paul's overriding concern for the unity of church, Segal argues, enabled him to make "a generous or diplomatic accommodation to the circumcised gentiles and Jews within Christianity, but it is not a compromise in principle."[42] Segal makes a distinction between Paul's ideological principle (= the abolition of Jewish ceremonial laws) and his policy of magnanimity (= accommodation to *Jewish Christians*):[43] "From Paul's perspective the accommodation is a kind of magnanimity. He outlines two axioms, an ideological position of strength and a diplomatic principle of conciliation."[44] Thus, Segal's discussion of Paul's practice and accommodating policy seems to be determined by his understanding of Paul's ideological principle. That is why Segal refers to Paul's practice as a "compromise," assessing it in light of Paul's ideological principle, as Segal asserts: "When salvation itself is not the issue, and especially when church unity *is* the issue, Paul, however, seems ready to accommodate . . . Although this is a compromise ritual position, Paul is not compromising his ideological position. Since Paul believes that his ritual is of no importance for salvation, whether he observes it or not is irrelevant. He chooses not to exercise his freedom to ignore them."[45]

Furthermore, although Segal tries to show how Paul accommodates himself to different situations to maintain unity between Jews and Gentiles within the Christian communities, Paul's compromise is explained basically in terms of his own accommodation to "the feelings of the circumcised

---

41. See ibid., 201–28, 224–53.
42. Ibid., 214.
43. Ibid., esp. 210–18 (my emphasis).
44. Ibid., 236.
45. Ibid., 239 (emphasis original).

gentiles and Jews within Christianity."[46] Segal seems to give less attention to the dynamic and social relations underlying the problems involved in the Jew-Gentile difference and especially varying patterns of Jew-Gentile hierarchical relations within/between the communities. Recognizing Segal's comprehensive discussion on the issue of Jewish ceremonial law within the early Christian communities and his contextual approach to Paul's practice toward the ceremonial law, I intend to deal with Paul's practice by relating the problem of Jew-Gentile difference within early Christian communities to the issue of social hierarchical relations. This means an attempt to focus on the concrete contexts before and after the Jerusalem conference and the Antioch incident, the relationship between the Jerusalem church and the Antioch church, and differences in Jew-Gentile relations between the community at Antioch and the community in Rome.

(d) Elizabeth A. Castelli

Elizabeth A. Castelli's book *Imitating Paul: A Discourse of Power*[47] is a critical engagement with Paul's discourse of mimesis from the postmodern perspective on the problematic of sameness (identity) and difference. Although Castelli's book does not deal with my question concerning equality and difference between Jews and Gentiles, her work deserves a special recognition in relation to the theoretical framework she has introduced to Pauline studies. As shall be discussed in the following chapter, the theoretical and hermeneutical considerations of my study have some resonance with Castelli's critique of "the economy of sameness" as "the construction of the foil of the other as a cultural necessity" in Western culture and the master discourses of Western Christianity.[48] Castelli's study of Paul's discourse of mimesis can be considered as a significant work which initiated the project of critical appropriation of postmodern discourses into the arena of Pauline studies. Within a similar cultural critical framework, Daniel Boyarin brought his own "Jewish" question for his interpretive critique of Paul's universalism in the general contour of Pauline discourses. My use of postmodern language and notions such as "discourse," "social formation," and "identity/difference" in this study is in part indebted to Castelli's contribution.[49]

46. Ibid., 214.
47. Castelli, *Imitating Paul*.
48. Ibid., 41.
49. For the definitions of such terms, see ibid., 51–56. As shall be discussed below,

Paul and the Politics of Difference

Stressing that Paul occupies an "important place in the master narratives of Western culture," Castelli interrogates how Paul's discourse of mimesis as "the drive toward sameness" contributes to the construction of the "the hegemony of identity" in Western culture.[50] Given her focus on the problem of sameness and difference, Castelli understandably takes up Paul's discourse of imitation, because imitation on the linguistic level stands on the side of sameness and identity. On this point, Castelli writes: "Mimesis presupposes a valorization of sameness over against difference. Certain conceptual equations accompany this move: unity and harmony are associated with sameness while difference is attributed characteristics of diffusion, disorder, and discord."[51]

Further, Castelli emphasizes the social implications articulated in the mimetic relationship in terms of a hierarchical relationship, the privileged status of a person or a model, and the role of authority. Thus, Castelli's interpretive goal is to investigate how Paul's rhetoric of mimesis ideologically functions as a discourse of power and as such establishes a certain set of hierarchical social relations in early Christian social formation. This enables Castelli to deploy particularly Michel Foucault's theoretical notions and discourses on "power" and "truth/claim to truth."

In her reading of Paul's discourse of mimesis Castelli emphasizes Paul's "privileged position" as "the one who speaks" and the role of his authority within early Christian communities. Paul's discourse on mimesis, according to Castelli, "constructs the early communities within a hierarchical economy of sameness which both appropriates the members of the early communities and reinscribes Paul's privileged position as natural."[52] Consequently, Castelli's reading of Paul's discourse of mimesis concludes that it is "a demand for the erasure of difference,"[53] which has contributed to "the broader Western enactment of sameness and resistance to difference."[54]

While appreciating Castelli's theoretical frameworks and interpretive agendas in her critique of the economy of sameness, my approach to identity/difference will show some differences in the interpretive agenda,

---

my appropriation of postmodern critique of "the logic of identity" and the meaning of "difference" draws on Young's work, *Justice and the Politics of Difference*.

50. Castelli, *Imitating Paul*, 17.
51. Ibid., 16.
52. Ibid., 117.
53. Ibid., 124.
54. Ibid., 127.

emphasis, and strategy, and therefore a different reading of Paul's politics of difference. First, although I also consider hierarchical relations an important interpretive lens in my reading of Paul's discourse, I put more emphasis on hierarchical relations between Jews and Gentiles within Paul's communities, rather than on Paul's privileged position toward his communities. Second, although I acknowledge the significance of the social and reading effects of Christian discourses such as Paul's discourse, I do not see why textual effects must be separated from the issue of "intentionality" of texts (authors), so far as "the claim to truth" is perceived as "intentional," not "self-evident" (as Castelli argues).[55] Further, I claim that "the gap between intent and effect" invites readers to discern its historical and ideological complicities, rather than rendering the author's intention irrelevant. What is more important for my concern is to frame the question in terms of "reading effects for whom?" Third, in approaching the problem of sameness and difference, my study is more concerned with the relations of "equality" to "sameness" and "difference." I do not think that the notions of equality and unity are identical with "sameness," thus categorically repressing difference. These questions and related issues shall be discussed in the following chapter of this study.

(e) Daniel Boyarin

A Radical Jew: Paul and the Politics of Identity is the product of Daniel Boyarin's own wrestling with Pauline (Christian) universalism from the cultural critical perspective of a contemporary Jew. Boyarin's reading of Paul is a radical challenge to Western Christian universalism which has been "a powerful force for coercive discourses of sameness, denying the rights of Jews, women, and others to retain their differences."[56] Bringing the specific question of Jewish difference and other differences, Boyarin situates his work within the intellectual climate of the contemporary critical and cultural studies. What motivates his work is the cultural critical stance he takes against the Christian universalism "which deprives those who have historically grounded identities in those material signifiers of the power to speak for themselves and remain different."[57] He asks the same question that I brought to this study and with which I am struggling, that

---

55. For Castelli's position on these issues, see ibid., 119–21.
56. Boyarin, *A Radical Jew*, 233.
57. Ibid., 220.

is, "Are the specificities of human identity, the differences, of value, or are they only an obstacle in the striving for justice and liberation?"[58] However, Paul's politics of difference that my work aims to offer as an answer to the question shall be strikingly different from Paul's universalism as Boyarin sees and rejects it as flawed.

From the outset, Boyarin starts with his basic assumption that "Paul was motivated by a Hellenistic desire for the One, which among other things produced an ideal of a universal human essence, beyond difference and hierarchy."[59] Paul's passionate concern for the oneness of humanity was accomplished, according to Boyarin, by the interpretive means of "the radically dualist and allegorical hermeneutic" Paul developed. Throughout his book, Boyarin persistently argues that Paul's universalism of "neither Jew nor Gentile" is meant to be the erasure of not only Jew-Gentile difference but also all human cultural specificities. Despite the significance of the cultural critical hermeneutics Boyarin brings to the Pauline discourse, his reading of Paul far too much equates Paul's universalism with Western Christian imperialist universalism, or at least the post-Pauline development. The significant historical change of time and power is not taken into full consideration.

Boyarin's presuppositions that Paul's universalism was motivated by a Hellenistic ideal of a universal human being beyond difference and hierarchy and that Paul sought to eradicate all human cultural particularities and differences, particularly Jewish difference, are problematic. Although Boyarin regards Paul's discourse as an inner-Jewish cultural discourse, he fails to apply this convincingly to the actual reading of Paul's text and context. "Jewish difference" is mostly discussed as Jewish self-identity within the framework of later Jewish-Christian relations, not that of Jew-Gentile relations at the time of Paul.

It should be acknowledged that the early Christian groups represented in Paul's discourse did not yet form a religious entity separate from Judaism, nor did they obtain any social and political power as to define or devalue the Jewish cultural and ethnic practices as "difference," although such a nascent tendency could become visible within certain groups as reflected in Romans. Who defines "difference" as "otherness" to be excluded and who claims "difference" as "self-identity" becomes crucial for the contextual and

---

58. Ibid., 3.
59. Ibid., 7.

Introduction

relational understanding of the meaning of "difference" in antiquity and our postmodern society as well.

Since here I problematize Boyarin's definition of the term "Jewish difference" and its applicability to Paul and his communities, I feel compelled to make definitional and conceptual clarifications on terms I use in my work, such as "Christian," "Christians," Jewish Christian," and "Gentile Christian." Although the proper use of the terms "Jewish Christians" and "Gentile Christians" has been disputed,[60] the use of the adjective "Christian" and "Christians" is generally taken for granted among New Testament scholarship. As I pointed out, if the early Jewish messianic and apocalyptic groups in Palestine and the Diaspora with which Paul and other Jews and Gentiles associated did not yet belong to a religious entity separate from Judaism, i.e., what has become "Christianity" in later time, the question here is whether the use of the term "Christian" in referring to such groups and the members is appropriate.

Further, the ambiguity and difficulty involved in the use of the term "Christian" becomes more complicated when we need to characterize the nature of such communities within the larger framework of Jewish communities. In other words, to what extent did Pauline communities or the early Jewish sectarian communities which had a belief in Jesus Christ as the Jewish messiah associate themselves with the surrounding Jewish synagogue or household communities and at the same time dissociate themselves from those larger Jewish groups? Despite its importance, the historical complexity and the paucity of historical evidence related to this question does not allow us any clear answer.

Given that during the pre-70 CE period no follower of Jesus, including Paul, identified him/herself as a "Christian" in the sense of what we call later "Christianity" separate from Rabbinic Judaism, I concede that my use of "Christian" is definitely anachronistic.[61] However, despite a considerable—though unidentifiable—degree of affinity between Pauline communities and Jewish synagogue communities in the Diaspora, whenever there is need to differentiate the former from the latter I use the term "Christian" to refer to the Pauline communities, such as early "Christian" communities or Pauline "Christian" communities. Even in that case, my

60. For example, see Malina, "Jewish Christianity or Christian Judaism," 46–56; Nanos, *The Mystery of Romans*, 21 n. 1.

61. In Acts 11:26 the author of Luke-Acts retrospectively, about thirty years after, refers to the members of the Antiochene community as "Christians" (οἱ Χριστιανοί), and the term nowhere occurs in Paul who exclusively talks about Jews and Gentiles.

use of the term "Christian" precludes any implication of the later phenomenon of a complete break between the Christian ἐκκλησία and the Jewish συναγωγή. Rather, my emphasis is on the "associative" and "analytical" use of the term "Christian." This refers to the community's association with "Christ" in differentiation from other communities on the one hand, and to Jews and Gentiles within the community in differentiation from other Jews and Gentiles outside the community on the other hand. A flexible use of the term "Christian" articulated in this way will be pertinent to the use of other terms such as "inter-Jewish," "intra-Jewish," "inner-Christian," and "intramural."[62]

Regarding the conventional use of "Jewish Christians" and "Gentile Christians," some scholars prefer the terms "Christian Jews" and "Christian Gentiles," emphasizing that at least before 70 CE Christianity was not a separate religion from Judaism. In that case, the term "Jewish Christians" is perceived as bi-religious rather than ethnico-religious. However, I do not think that a bi-religious meaning fits the term "Gentile Christians." I believe that, given the early pre-70 CE period of historical ambiguity and uncertainty, "Jewish Christians" and "Christian Jews" are interchangeable in application. Considering the intramural character of Jewish-Gentile relations within Pauline communities, I prefer to use "*Jewish* Christians" and "*Gentile* Christians" as ethnico-religious terms—not too rigidly, though.[63]

---

62. For the use of these terminologies by other scholars, see chapter 4 n. 1 below.

63. After my dissertation was completed, some scholars have taken issue with the translation of Ἰουδαῖος and Ἰουδαῖοι as "Jew" and "Jews" with regard to historical, theological, and ethical problems: e.g., see Esler, *Conflict and Identity in Romans*, esp. 62–76; Cohen, *The Beginnings of Jewishness*, esp. 69–139; and J. H. Elliott, "Jesus the Israelite," 119–54. While Cohen argues for the relevance of the use of Jew/Jewish for Ἰουδαῖος after 100 BCE with its shifting religious meaning, Esler and Elliott have made persuasive arguments that the term Ἰουδαῖοι used in the time of New Testament should be translated as "Judeans," not "Jews." Further, Elliott has made a compelling case that "Israelite" "(Ἰσραηλίτης)" is the inside term preferred as their self-identification by the people of Israel, including Jesus and Paul, while Ἰουδαῖος ("Judean") is the term with which the outsiders referred to those who were affiliated with the land of Judea, Jerusalem, and temple.

Although I made explicit the anachronistic problem of the use of the term "Christian" in studying the New Testament texts, I have not dealt with the similar problem embedded in the use of terms "Jew" and "Jewish." While in this work I have stressed the ethnico-religious and social differences within different Christ groups in the Diaspora and opposed essentialist approaches to Jew(Judean)-Gentile relations, I concede that I am following the conventional terminology of "Jew" and "Jewish," but not the traditional interpretations.

2.2. Equality with Difference

(a) Peter J. Tomson

Peter J. Tomson[64] aims to trace and argue for the pervasiveness of halakha in Paul's letters and thought. He acutely observes that "the abandonment of the traditional Protestant view of justification as the heart of Paul has resulted in the re-adoption of the Patristic hypothesis that Paul's main concern is the practical annulment of the Jewish law."[65] Tomson attempts to challenge such a position and argue that the Jewish Law at the practical levels remained valid for Paul as well as other Jewish Christians.

According to Tomson, Paul should not be understood as the one who separated Christianity from Judaism by eradicating the practical, halakhic distinction between Jews and Gentiles. Rather, it is argued that Paul remained a practicing Jew even after he was converted to the Christian movement. On the other hand, Tomson continues to argue that Paul's consistent position was that those Gentiles who joined the new Jewish sectarian movement did not have to become Jewish proselytes by receiving circumcision. Tomson grounds his argument for Paul's pluralism on his interpretation of 1 Cor 7:17–24.

As for the issue of table-fellowship in Galatians and Romans, Tomson takes a different position from the dominant one in Pauline scholarship which underlines the discrepancy in Paul's attitude toward Jewish Law. Tomson argues that Paul pleads for pluralism for the sake of the unity of each church without asking Jews to abandon the observance of the Jewish laws. With careful attention to different situations reflected in Galatians and Romans, Tomson elucidates how Paul tries to maintain the goal of co-existence of Jews and Gentiles through his "pluralist"—not inconsistent—position toward Jewish law in each community, arguing that in Galatians, including the Antioch incident, Paul urged tolerance toward Gentiles, whereas in Romans toward "delicate" Jews.[66] The theme of "unity" stands out in Tomson's interpretation of Paul's "pluralist position" as in Sanders and Segal, but he comes to a different conclusion.

However, some points need to be made for further study of the issue. (1) Tomson does not seem to give any explicit explanation for the thrust of co-existence of Jews and Gentiles apart from the unity of church

64. Tomson, *Paul and the Jewish Law*.
65. Ibid., 237.
66. Ibid., 222–29, 236–44.

or pluralism which allows different lifestyles for both Jews and Gentiles. (2) Consequently, it is not surprising to see that Tomson attributes to Paul a pluralism in its very "neutral rationale,"[67] that is, lacking a specific perspective, although Tomson admits that Paul's pluralism does not mean "indifference" to the Jewish law. That is why Tomson explains the rationale underlying Paul's position in dealing with the difference between Jews and Gentiles at table-fellowship in terms of popular ethos of pluralism at Paul's time represented by Cynico-Stoic and later Rabbinic traditions.[68] (3) Hence, Tomson's discussion on the meaning of "difference" is fundamentally based on the halakhic difference between Jews and Gentiles and the conclusion he draws is, as Tomson himself admits, a re-adoption of the so-called Paul's *status quo* theory, meaning that "as long as we stay in the flesh the Law remains in force."[69]

(b) Mark D. Nanos:

Mark D. Nanos's *The Mystery of Romans* is one of the most provocative works among recent studies of Paul's letter to the Romans.[70] His reading of Romans is an attempt to challenge the traditional Lutheran interpretation of Paul and its lingering legacies in the contemporary Pauline scholarship. Nanos's reading of Paul, his message and intentions in Romans, strikingly differs from that of the majority of the Pauline scholars. One of the main points in his argument is that for Paul, gospel means "a Law-observant one for Jews and a Law-respectful one for gentiles."[71]

In defense of a very Jewish Paul, Nanos presupposes the thoroughly Jewish context of Paul and his mission to Gentiles and the formation of early Christian communities. The Jewish context that Nanos explores for his reading of Paul is rather circumscribed to some general aspects of the historical context of Jews and Jewish communities in Diaspora. Nanos emphasizes, among others, the role of the synagogue in the Jewish community, the presence of "God-fearing" Gentiles and their relations to the halakha

---

67. Ibid., 250.
68. Ibid., 245–54.
69. Ibid., 237. For a different reading of 1 Cor 7:17–20, see Segal, *Paul the Convert*, 214–15.
70. Nanos, *The Mystery of Romans*.
71. Ibid., 23 and *passim*.

Introduction

operative in the category of "righteous Gentiles."[72] Nanos applies the full implications of these factors to his reading of Paul's message in Romans by relating them to the implied audience (Christian Gentiles), the tension between the "weak" and the "strong," and the issue of equality and difference between Jews and Gentiles.

One of the most provocative arguments Nanos makes is that he identifies the "weak" in Romans with non-Christian Jews rather than Jewish Christians and the "strong" as Gentile Christians.[73] According to Nanos, the traditional identification of the "weak" in Romans with the Jewish Christians is problematic, because in that case scholars are passing judgment on the continuous practice of Jewish laws on the part of Jewish Christians as if it were "deficient in faith."[74] Nanos sees such judgment as the very judgment Paul opposed to in Rom 14:3.[75] Although Nanos's identification of the "weak" with non-Christian Jews as a solution for such a dilemma appears to be appealing, it reveals some ambiguity and weakness. For example, if we follow Nanos's proposal regarding the identity of the "weak" and the "strong," we need to imagine a Christian group in Rome which had much undifferentiated association with non-Christian Jews, Christian Jews, non-Christian Gentile God-fearers, and Christian "righteous Gentiles" within the larger Jewish community. Moreover, it is hard to understand how Christian Gentiles—they must have been in a minority position within the Jewish community, albeit in a majority position over Jewish Christians—could be tempted to disregard and despise non-Christian Jews and the rules of behavior which righteous Gentiles were expected to observe. In my view, the identity of the weak and the strong as Jewish Christians and Gentile Christians in Rome can still work for the same argument that Nanos makes.

Throughout his reading of Romans and Galatians as well, Nanos discusses the relationship between Jews and Gentiles and Paul's position toward them by considering the principle of universal "monotheism" (that is, the One God of Israel is also the One God of the nations) as integral to Paul's conviction and arguments.[76] According to Nanos, on the basis of such "monotheism" Paul insisted that (1) Jews should not become like

---

72. See ibid., 41–84.

73. See ibid., 85–165 (Chapter 3: "Who were the 'Weak' and the 'Strong' in Rome?"), esp. 119–59.

74. Ibid., 88–95.

75. Ibid., 103–19.

76. Ibid., esp. 179–201.

Gentiles, by giving up the very practices that make them Jews, and that (2) Gentiles should not become Jews by adopting circumcision, but respect the minimal requirements expected of "righteous gentiles." This is how Nanos explores the meaning of Paul's understanding of the equality between Jews and Gentiles in Christ in terms of an "equal, but different" principle: "They are different, *Jews* and Gentiles—yet *equal* in Christ."[77] Nanos endeavors to demonstrate that such "monotheism" promoted the "equal, but different" principle without devaluing the meaningful validity of the Jewish law and customs on the part of Jews and Jewish Christians, and that this very monotheism was equally operating for Paul's position in his confrontation with Peter at Antioch (Gal 2:11–21).

Nanos's exegesis of the Antioch incident, however, turns out to be somewhat problematic. Although I accept Nanos's challenge to the dominant scholarly view that Paul's concern for equality between Jews and Gentiles was motivated by and/or resulted in the abrogation of differences among them, his discussion of the issue remains too theological, heavily drawing on the theme of "monotheism." The study of Paul and his politics of equality/difference needs a further consideration of the concrete historical context of each local community within a broader Roman imperial context in which Jewish and Pauline communities were situated.

3. THEORETICAL AND HERMENEUTICAL CONSIDERATIONS AND READING STRATEGY OF THIS STUDY

In the preceding section, I have sketched briefly two contrasting interpretive trends in current interpretation of Paul with regard to the issue of equality/difference between Jews and Gentiles. Both trends commonly acknowledge that Paul's attitude toward Jewish Law has much to do with the issue of equal status of Jews and Gentiles within the Christian community, rather than with the critique of Jewish legalism. But, does equality or justice necessarily mean the denial or limitation of Jewish and Gentile difference?

According to the first position, Paul's devaluation of the validity of the Jewish Law in theory and/or in practice was motivated by and/or resulted in the eradication of differences between Jews and Gentiles. Scholars who belong to this category sought to explain Paul's position under the rubric

---

77. Ibid., 286 (emphasis original).

of "universalism," although they use different terms with slightly different emphases. A fundamental problem with this position is the nature of universalism it imposes on Paul. No doubt, the ideal of universalism and social unity that transcends differences and thereby reproduces cultural imperialist relations of domination and oppression should be challenged and dismantled. But, does Paul in Galatians and Romans promote such a universalism?

On the other hand, the second position contends that Paul, like his other Jewish fellows, remained a Torah-observant Jew. Not only did he not urge Jews to abandon their practice of the Jewish Laws, but further encouraged Gentiles to accommodate to the Jewish laws. Thus, the co-existence of Jews and Gentiles which Paul advocated is characterized by the principle of "pluralism" in the sense that Jews remain Jews and Gentiles remain Gentiles. Who would have opposed such a neutral pluralism, if that was Paul's position? The argument for such a neutral pluralism seems to undermine both historical and ideological complexity involved in the issue in question.

In order to search for equality and difference between Jews and Gentiles, I will make connections with the contemporary theoretical and hermeneutical context of Paul's day in which the discourse on equality and difference had become an emerging issue, and by making explicit my social location from which I engage the contemporary politics of difference as well as the Pauline discourse on equality and difference. Secondly, I contextualize the Pauline discourse on equality and difference between Jews and Gentiles by situating it into a proper *Sitz im Leben*, that is, the setting of table-fellowship within Pauline Christian communities (Gal 2:11–21 and Rom 14:1—15:13). Furthermore, I shall recontextualize the practice of table-fellowship at early Christian meals within the larger cultural milieu of Greco-Roman meal practice.

The way of posing questions regarding the issue of equality and difference between Jews and Gentiles, the scholarly interpretation of Paul's universalism, and its implications have some resonance with the contemporary critical discourse on the politics of identity/difference. Thus, in chapter 2 of this study, I shall attempt a dialogical and critical engagement with the current social criticisms on the politics of difference, particularly taking into consideration postmodern, feminist, and postcolonial perspectives on "difference." Furthermore, such an engagement will be made by bringing a distinct perspective from my own Korean context, that is, a liberation-oriented *minjung* perspective in order to see how different approaches to the politics of difference intersect with the similarities and dissimilarities of one another.

In particular, in order to problematize dualistic, binary terms and conceptions, including the very terms "Jews and Gentiles" in Pauline discourse and Pauline scholarship, I will pay attention to the postmodern criticism of Western philosophical and theoretical discourse on "the logic of identity"[78] which serves to deny and repress difference. On the other hand, my approach to the problem of equality and difference is to a certain extent motivated by and has affinity with the recent issue of "competing paradigms of liberation."[79] The ideal of liberation as the elimination of group difference has been recently challenged by social movements of the oppressed. The politics of difference which asserts group difference has been promoted by these social movements. What is at stake here is the meaning of social "difference" within the context of equality/justice. The focus on the meaning of social and political "difference" will be further discussed in my reappropriation of feminist and postcolonial perspectives on "difference." The primary meaning of "difference" as denied, marginalized, and alienated identity within hierarchical power relations in terms of class, gender, race, and empire will be explored and appropriated.

Scholars, following Stendahl's argument, have acknowledged that the thrust of Paul's justification by faith was not Luther's quest for a gracious God, but Paul's concern for the equal status of Gentile Christians. Yet, it has not been sufficiently explored how the issue of equality and difference between Jews and Gentiles in Paul and the early Christian movement is closely linked to the specific setting of "table-fellowship" of Jews and Gentiles, as it is shown from different perspectives, e.g., in Galatians (Gal 2:11–14), Romans (Rom 14:1—15:13) and Acts (Acts 10, 11, 15).[80] Preparing for my exegetical and interpretive reading of two meal texts in Gal 2:1–21 and Rom 14:1—15:13 in chapters 4 and 5, I shall discuss in chapter

---

78. For an excellent theoretical elaboration of the post-modern discourse on identity/difference within the framework of social justice, see Young, *Justice and the Politics of Difference*. For "the logic of identity," see esp. 96–121.

79. Ibid., esp. 156–73.

80. Considering that the problems involved in the Corinthian meal settings are not directly related to the issue of Jew-Gentile equality and difference, I will not deal with the Corinthian situation throughout this study. For the Corinthian problems, see Theissen, "The Strong and the Week"; Theissen, "Social Integration"; Gooch, *Dangerous Food*; Horsley, "1 Corinthians." For imperial context, see esp. Price, *Rituals and Power*.

3 the significance of Greco-Roman meal practice as an important setting for table-fellowship in early Christian communities.

Greco-Roman common meals as a social institution provided the cultural milieu for social and religious activities of various groups, clubs, and associations in the first-century Roman world, including Jewish and early Christian gatherings. The practice of table-fellowship represents an important context in which members of early Christian communities embodied their faith in concrete, communal, and interactive ways within their specific historical situations. It was a communal space where especially the ideal of equality between Jews and Gentiles could be tested in the face of mutual difference. I will affirm this emphasis by examining how differences in social status, class, and gender were structurally arranged and displayed at Greco-Roman meals and how the tension between social equality and social difference was dealt with at rhetorical and practical levels in relation to common meals. Furthermore, in order to explore diverse ways of dealing with and negotiating those social differences at meals, including Paul's position toward the differences between Jews and Gentiles at common meals, I shall discuss how the logic and dynamic of Greco-Roman meals intersects with the logic and dynamics of ritual in general.

Recognizing that the early Christian meal practice was a primary *Sitz im Leben* in which Jew-Gentile difference was problematized, debated, and negotiated within the process of early Christian social formation, in chapters 4 and 5 I will focus my exegetical and interpretive work on the two texts (Gal 2:11–21 and Rom 14:1—15:13) which allow us a glimpse of the early Christian table-fellowship trouble with the Jew-Gentile difference at different communities of different social hierarchical relations. Along with the theoretical and hermeneutical perspectives I bring to the familiar texts, a socio-historical and socio-rhetorical reading will be guiding my reading and interpretation of Paul's dealing with the differences between Jews and Gentiles.

One of the main arguments in this study is that by dealing with the contextual meanings of contingent differences between Jews and Gentiles within the particularities of different communities and by negotiating those differences within the framework of equality-versus-difference, Paul actually presents a coherent politics of difference, which is embodied in both his practices and theological argumentations. I would contend that Paul's practices related to the issue of the Jew-Gentile difference at the early Christian community meals exemplify such a politics of difference.

Furthermore, I will argue that while Paul's practice acted out at the Antioch incident (Gal 2:11–21) represents his concern for and defense of the Gentile difference, Paul's rhetorical practice in negotiating the Jew-Gentile difference between the "weak" and the "strong" at Christian meal practice in Rome (Rom 14:1—15:13) represents his concern for and defense of the Jewish difference.

Would it be possible to suggest that Paul might have an emancipatory and egalitarian understanding of "universalism" and "unity" when he wrestled with the vision of community of "neither Jews nor Gentiles" (cf. Gal 3:26–28)? Then, the question will become crucial: "universalism or pluralism—from whose perspective?" With this question in mind, this study aims to offer an alternative reading of "neither Jews nor Gentiles" in Paul's politics of difference and its implication.

2

Theoretical and Hermeneutical Perspectives on Difference

QUESTIONS AND PROBLEMS INVOLVING difference in class, gender, race, and culture are embedded in efforts to understand the meaning of human existence, individually and collectively, and to transform injustice and inequality in society into justice and equality. Especially at the turn into the 21st century the question of difference has become a contested issue in contemporary theory and in social movements. Biblical scholarship has also tackled the question of difference with diverse concerns and reading strategies. Moreover, an increasing number of scholars in the areas of New Testament and Christian origins have approached difference in terms of social status, class, and gender in early Christian communities with groundbreaking sensitivity.

This chapter focuses on some features of contemporary theories, which I first engage in dialogue, and then consequently centers on the hermeneutical perspective from which I examine difference in Galatians and Romans. I investigate diverse perspectives on difference in postmodern, feminist, and postcolonial criticism and bring them into dialogue with a Korean *minjung* perspective in order to determine how these perspectives reinforce, correct, redirect, or extend each other. An exhaustive account of these theories lies beyond my purposes in that my aim is to highlight critical concerns, practical issues, and political agendas in discursive practices concerning identity and difference.

1. POSTMODERN DISCOURSE ON DIFFERENCE

1.1. Deconstructing the Dichotomy

Modern conventional thinking about difference developed under the colossal influence of Western thought and tradition, especially under the banner of the Enlightenment. What kinds of fundamental tendencies can be detected in conventional thinking about difference as it has developed under the influence of the Enlightenment? More specifically, how have we been taught and tamed in thinking about difference—particularly difference in gender, class, race, religion, and culture? In its broad sense postmodernism is an attempt to grapple with such questions. The term "postmodern" cannot be reduced to a simple definition but nevertheless designates a general condition of contemporary Western civilization and a distinct discursive practice responding to the crisis of modernity.[1]

Among the wide-ranging critiques of modernity, the modern understanding of the self and subjectivity, the idea of history as linear and progressive, and the modernist separation of art and mass culture have drawn considerable attention. My concerns concentrate on the postmodern discourse on the problematic of identity and difference, particularly in the sphere of postmodern deconstruction. The emergence of postmodern discourse on "difference" itself is a sizeable project that would require a historical and critical analysis of the relationships between modernism and postmodernism, lies beyond what is needed in this chapter. For my purposes it is suitable to limit the discussion to some aspects of postmodern criticism of foundationalism and essentialism in the Western philosophical tradition.

---

1. Despite the wide use of the term "postmodernism," the range of meanings is broad, elusive, and often confusing. Particularly in the intellectual context in the United States, it is used as an appropriation of the theories of postwar Europe, especially French poststructuralism represented by Derrida, Deleuze, Foucault, and Lyotard. Of these only Lyotard refers directly to such theories as postmodernism. Although Lyotard is often resorted to in the discussion of the postmodern condition, Derrida has received the lion's share of attention in the discussion of the postmodern focus on "difference and Otherness," and Foucault for his articulation of relations between knowledge and power. See, e.g., Lyotard, *The Postmodern Condition*; Derrida, *Writing and Difference*. On the term postmodernism and its meaning see esp. Jameson, *Postmodernism*; Hutcheon, "A Postmodern Problematics" and *The Politics of Post-Modernism*; Huyssen, "Mapping the Postmodern." For a collective engagement with postmodernism by biblical scholars see The Bible and Culture Collective; George Aichele, et al., *The Postmodern Bible*.

Theoretical and Hermeneutical Perspectives on Difference

In order to understand the postmodern turn on difference, it is vital to grasp the postmodern critique of objectivism, which is tightly linked to its critique of the modern construct of the self and subjectivity. Indeed, the postmodern challenge to modern objectivism amounts to a major contribution which other contemporary modes of critical thinking accept and appropriate with little objection. Although the critique of objectivism is not a postmodern invention, postmodern criticism of the modern concept of truth and knowledge has become its signature characteristic because of its radical attacks on traditional philosophical underpinnings. If modern objectivism represents "the attempt to reveal general, all-encompassing principles which can lay bare the basic features of natural and social reality," the postmodern challenge to the norm of objectivity that has been dominant in Western academic environments not only accepts "earlier historicist claims about the inevitable 'situatedness' of human thought within culture" and the value-laden aspect of any theoretical inquiry of interpretation, but further focuses on "the very criteria by which claims to knowledge are legitimized."[2]

A fundamental belief that constituted the spirit of the Enlightenment was that truth about an object or of a text could be ascertained by means of observation and objective reasoning, that is, by an impartial subject, who was distant, at least with respect to rational thinking, from the particularities of the social context in which both the subject and the object are positioned. The strong certainty of so-called transcendental or impartial reason led to the understanding of the subject or self as being detached and abstracted from the particularities of situation, feeling, body, affiliation, and point of view. The result, as Cornel West accurately notes, was "to isolate early modern European culture into separate spheres of goodness, truth and beauty—and morality, science and art—reinforcing meanwhile the role of philosophy as a tribunal of pure reason for the claims of culture."[3]

As a critical response to an epistemological crisis at the turn into the 21st century, postmodernism challenged the very anchors of foundationalism and essentialism underlying the Western philosophical tradition, especially as it is embedded in the scientific paradigm of the Enlightenment. The emergence of powerful postmodern discourse corresponds to the phenomenon that with the demise of European modernism the authority of

---

2. Nicholson, "Introduction," 3.
3. West, "Race and Modernity," 68.

science—in many ways similar to the authority of the church in the age of the Enlightenment—was losing its foundational moorings.

Postmodern attacks on the certainty, the primacy of the subject, and the totalizing paradigm in modern philosophical and scientific discourses continue to deepen and expand, affirming Lyotard's definition of postmodern "as incredulity toward metanarratives" as the "apparatus of legitimation."[4] This process of demythologizing science and deconstructing the subject is part of a larger context in which the postmodern turn has generated an emphasis on plurality, ambiguity, and difference, all of which are clearly echoed by the joint authorship of *The Postmodern Bible*: "The postmodern critique of the Enlightenment legacy seeks to make us more sensitive to differences, better able to think about incommensurability and change, and aware of the socially constructed character of knowledge and the various means of production . . . It also attempts to engage in indeterminacy, chaos, and ambiguity—not as failures of modernity but as its inevitable other side."[5]

There is no doubt that postmodern criticism has had crucial and emancipatory impact on other critical theory, including feminism, literary criticism, and postcolonialism. For example, in arguing for the prospect of a postmodern feminism, Nancy Fraser and Linda Nicholson have stressed the importance of the postmodern critique of foundationalism and essentialism in the service of integrating the strengths and eliminating the weaknesses of both postmodernism and feminism: "Postmodernists offer sophisticated and persuasive criticisms of foundationalism and essentialism, but their conceptions of social criticism tend to be anemic. Feminists offer robust concepts of social criticism, but they tend to lapse into foundationalism and essentialism."[6]

Postmodern discourse on difference unveils what is called "the logic of identity"[7] or "the economy of sameness,"[8] which has governed West-

---

4. Lyotard, *The Postmodern Condition*, 36–37.

5. The Bible and Culture Collective, *The Postmodern Bible*, 10.

6. Fraser and Nicholson, "Social Criticism without Philosophy," 20.

7. Following Theodor Adorno and resonating with Derrida's critique of a metaphysics of presence, Iris Marion Young singles out the universalizing, essentializing, and totalizing tendencies in the Western philosophical tradition as the logic of identity, and contrasts it with the politics of difference, for which she argues (*Justice and the Politics of Difference*). For her critique of the logic of identity, including the ideal of impartiality, see esp. 96–112.

8. Castelli, *Imitating Paul*, 124–36.

ern philosophy and culture. The logic of identity refers to a drive toward unity—an urge that denies and represses difference. In exposing and challenging the logic of identity, the postmodern project of deconstruction has uncovered the construct of binary oppositions that have been built into the Western philosophical tradition. These binary polarities are characterized by dichotomies such as mind/body, spirit/flesh, male/female, universal/particular, white/black (color), same (identity)/differences, center/margin, Christian/Jewish (heathen), and Occidental/Oriental. The crux of the Western logic of identity lies in that inasmuch as the first side of the dichotomy is privileged over the second side, the second is relegated to the category of inferiority. Furthermore, these binary polarities are structured in correlation with good/bad, inside (inclusion)/outside (exclusion), and self (us)/other (them).

In particular, Derrida's version of deconstruction—an influential current of thought among academics in the United States—has made a salutary contribution to the critique of the logic of identity. Focusing on the political power of rhetorical operations in binary oppositions (such as those mentioned above), Derrida has revealed how these operations sustain hierarchical world views by devaluing the second terms as something subsumed under the first. He draws special attention to the opposition of speech and writing, exposing how in the intellectual history of the West, speech has almost always been privileged over writing.[9] According to Derrida, speech has always been the paradigm not only for every form of presence but also for every form of truth. Western theological or philosophical fundamentals such as God, being, essence, existence, substance, subject, object, consciousness are constructed by "the metaphysics of presence" or "logocentrism."[10] Thus Derrida's critique of the metaphysics of presence gears his deconstruction towards what is suppressed in texts or omitted from them. Yet insofar as the meaning of difference in Derrida's deconstruction can be understood as "an emphatic affirmation of Saussure's dictum that language is a network of differences,"[11] the concern for "otherness and difference" is focused on linguistic or textual alterity or deviant modalities. In such a deconstructionist project "the play of difference," with

---

9. Derrida, *Margins of Philosophy*, 94. Derrida does not mean to inscribe writing over speech, which would reinscribe hierarchy.

10. Derrida, *Of Grammatology*, 79: "Logocentrism is an ethnocentric metaphysics. It is related to the history of the West."

11. The Bible and Culture Collective, *The Postmodern Bible*, 124.

much of its focus on notions of discontinuity, delay, deferral, heterogeneity, and alterity, is privileged over "the politics of difference."

Despite its thorough criticism of totalizing, essentializing, and dualistic logic in modern discourse, and its significant impact on certain feminist approaches to gender difference, deconstructionist postmodernism has evoked serious critique among theorists, including feminists. Questions have been raised regarding its deconstruction of the self, the meaning of difference, and its limitations as a social criticism. For example, Christine Di Stefano questions the motives and consequences of the postmodern deconstruction of the self. She asks provocatively: "Why is it, just as the moment in Western history when previously silenced populations have begun to speak for themselves and on behalf of their subjectivities, that the concept of the subject and the possibility of discovering/creating a liberating 'truth' become suspect?"[12]

In her feminist critique of postmodernism, Di Stefano argues that "postmodernism expresses the claims and needs of a constituency (white, privileged men of the industrial West) that has already had an Enlightenment for itself and that is now ready and willing to subject that legacy to critical scrutiny."[13] I suggest that the argument holds not only for feminism but can be extended to the Third World or postcolonial critique of postmodernism, to which I return below. Unlike postmodern Westerners the Third World cannot afford a deconstructed self and the deferral of coherence and the truth of their claims. In other words, for them to adopt such a position is to weaken what is not yet strong.

Calling for a critical appropriation of postmodernism for feminism, Linda Nicholson cautions prudently against "a nominalist ontology and an individualist politics" that might result from the radical postmodern efforts to abandon generalizations, theories, and subjectivity, and the consequent version of difference: "To invoke the ideal of endless difference is for feminism either to self-destruct or to finally accept an ontology of abstract individualism."[14] Further, Susan Bordo warns that the critique of the modernist "view from nowhere" should not lead to the equally problematic "view from everywhere."[15]

---

12. Di Stefano, "Dilemmas of Difference," 75.
13. Ibid.
14. Nicholson, "Introduction," in *Feminist/Postmodernism*, 8.
15. Bordo, "Feminism." Cf. Young, *Justice and the Politics of Difference*, 99–107.

In his discussion of the new cultural politics of difference in the United States, especially among African American movements, Cornel West catches the potential deficiency in postmodernism: "The major shortcoming of Derrida's deconstructive project is that it puts a premium on a sophisticated ironic consciousness that tends to preclude and foreclose analyses that guide action with purpose."[16] Fraser and Nicholson are in close agreement when they say that "there is no place in Lyotard's universe for critique of broad-based relations of dominance and subordination along lines like gender, race, and class."[17]

But beyond this kind of debate, I emphasize that postmodernism should not extrapolate difference and otherness to mere abstractions (this is precisely what is deconstructed by radical alterity beyond essentialism), and thus in order to evade this possibility, the discourse on difference needs to be historically specific and politically engaged. In other words, difference itself needs to be value-laden, socially loaded, and ideologically charged. As such, difference is to be negotiated within specific social contexts through particular human agents. Iris Marion Young's relational and contextual understanding of difference is an especially constructive way of appropriating the postmodern discourse on difference into a specific history and politics, and I now turn to an appreciative discussion of her work.

1.2. The Politics of Difference

Iris Marion Young, a political theorist and feminist critic, situates the postmodern concern for difference in concrete, though diverse, and practical contexts of social action and group dynamics, profoundly embedding difference in the broader context of justice and emancipation. Among the various critical issues with which Young deals in *Justice and the Politics of Difference*, her take on difference deserves special attention. Although she follows the postmodern critique of the logic of identity, Young goes beyond the potential danger of abstract play on difference by taking into consideration both concrete instances and multiple situations of oppression among groups struggling for emancipation.

Young challenges "an ideal of justice that defines liberation as the transcendence of group difference," because it is tantamount to "an ideal of assimilation." Instead she proposes a different approach to justice and

16. West, "New Cultural Politics," 132.
17. Fraser and Nicholson, "Social Criticism without Philosophy," 23.

liberation in terms of an "emancipatory politics of difference," which affirms and promotes group difference.[18] Recognizing the challenges to notions of rising above difference, which come from a variety of social movements, including feminism, to the effect that "a positive self-definition of group difference is in fact more liberatory,"[19] Young offers a political theoretical explanation of why ignoring or transcending group difference is problematic and even contributes to oppression.

Young emphasizes an important but often unnoticed point, namely, that affirming group difference involves a reconception of the meaning of equality: "The assimilationist ideal assumes that equal social status for all persons requires treating everyone according to the same principles, rules, and standards. A politics of difference argues, on the other hand, that equality as the participation and inclusion of all groups sometimes requires different treatment for oppressed or disadvantaged groups."[20]

While recognizing that the ideal of liberation as the elimination of group difference—especially privileged difference—has been enormously important in the history of emancipatory politics, Young explains why a politics of difference needs to be promoted rather than the assimilationist ideal. First, "blindness to difference" is problematic, for it "disadvantages groups whose experience, culture, and socialized capacities differ from those of privileged groups."[21] This is primarily so because in the assimilationist strategy "the privileged groups implicitly define the standards according to which all will be measured."[22]

Second, promoting the allegedly universal rules, standards, and norms which actually represent the interests of privileged groups, the dominant groups normally become blind to their own specificity. Thus, blindness to difference "perpetuates cultural imperialism by allowing norms of expressing the point of view and experience of privileged groups to appear neutral and universal."[23] What is obscured is "the value-laden nature of their own starting points and their power to ignore their own horizon of ignorance."[24]

---

18. Young, *Justice and the Politics of Difference*, 157.
19. Ibid.
20. Ibid., 158.
21. Ibid., 164.
22. Ibid.
23. Ibid., 165.
24. Ferguson, "Resisting the Veil of Privilege," 100.

Third, the assimilationist strategy contributes both to the "denigration of groups that deviate from an allegedly neutral standard" and to "an internalized devaluation by members of those groups themselves."[25] This last point is related to the question of how marginalized groups can reclaim and reconstitute their positive sense of difference.

In the context of promoting a politics of difference rather than the assimilationist ideal, Young conceptualizes two distinct understandings of difference. One is an essentializing concept of difference, and the other is a relational view. According to the essentializing understanding, difference is defined by the privileged group as "absolute otherness," "exclusion," and "opposition," through which differences within groups in society are essentialized, repressed and denied.[26] By way of contrast, the politics of difference perceives group difference as "relations of similarity and dissimilarity that can be reduced to neither coextensive identity nor nonoverlapping otherness."[27] She further asserts that such a relational and contextual understanding of difference "relativizes the previously universal position of privileged groups," undermines the essentializing assumptions of difference, and further allows oppressed groups to seek to "seize the power of naming difference itself."[28]

Finally, Young concludes about the power of the politics of difference: "Groups experiencing cultural imperialism have found themselves objectified and marked as a devalued essence from the outside, by a dominant culture they are excluded from making. The assertion of a positive sense of group difference by these groups is emancipatory because it reclaims the definition of the group by the group, as a creation and construction, rather than a given essence."[29]

On the one hand, the deconstructionist approach of postmodernism facilitates the disruption of hierarchical structure and power in textual constructs and the discovery of the suppressed other within texts. On the other, the politics of difference as Young has expressed it makes it possible to recognize unquestioned assumptions underlying conceptualizations of identity and difference and to arrive at new understandings of identity in terms of relationships rather than in essentializing characteristics. Although Young's

---

25. Young, *Justice and the Politics of Difference*, 165.
26. Ibid., 169–70.
27. Ibid., 171.
28. Ibid.
29. Ibid., 172.

proposals are largely shaped by postmodernism, she offers something beyond the postmodern neglect of social and political agendas.

2. FEMINIST DISCOURSE ON DIFFERENCE

Western feminism, the complexities of its historical development notwithstanding, emerged as both discursive and practical movements which undertook the problems of a hierarchical male/female dichotomy and of female "otherness" (difference). Especially in the United States feminist activism and discourse started as resistance against hierarchical social structures shaped by male supremacy and dominance, and was influenced by the Civil Rights movement and other group activism against social injustice and inequality.

Although the awareness of and suffering from social inequality between men and women gave rise to feminist consciousness among (initially white middle-class) women, subsequent feminism, in diverse forms, encountered problems generated from within, such as the problem of sex/gender difference, the problem of essentialism in defining "being woman," and the problem of differences among women. The purpose of this section is not to survey the development of Western feminist thought or to review major trends in current theory and theology. The discussion is rather focused and its aim modest. Its purpose is to consider how equality viewed as sameness in universal and essentialist terms has been uncovered and questioned, and how equality has been recovered as feminists have struggled with differences of gender, race, and class.

2.1. The Problem of Equality and Sameness

In order to claim equal status and attain equal treatment, women involved in the first stages of feminist movements denounced women's difference prescribed by the social hierarchy of male and female dichotomy. Difference at this point was not determined by feminist themselves. Neither did feminists reclaim difference as a basis for erasing social discrimination. What may be called "the rationalist position" in feminism underscored that "'difference' has been used to legitimize the unequal treatment of women, and therefore difference was repudiated theoretically and practically in order for women to assume their rightful place in society as the non-differentiated equals of men."[30] Until the mid 1970s the ideal of sexual liberation perceived as the elimination of gender difference guided feminist efforts to uncover, attack, and dismantle the male domination which was upholding male/female oppositions and related binary polarities (e.g., universal/particular, public/private, mental/emotional).[31] To be sure, these efforts made considerable contributions to the advancement of (some) women's socio-economic status and political position in American society.

Nonetheless, the very effort of disclosing, rejecting, and correcting the universal mastery of males under the banner of equality was eventually challenged from within the feminist movement itself. Latent in these processes was the acquiescence to male norms as the launching pad for promoting women's rights and the devaluation of female identity apart from the male/female dichotomy. Feminist theory thus acknowledged that its claim of equality was grounded upon the concept of "sameness" and the assumption of male norms as universal. In the early 1980s especially white feminist theory began to focus on "difference" primarily in terms of sex/gender. This shift was a significant move enabling women to affirm, reclaim, and even celebrate the positive meaning of difference as determined by women themselves.[32] Consequently, white feminist theorists and theologians turned to the task of defining what constitutes "woman" or female subjectivity and expended substantial energy on elaborating and dealing with the dichotomy of sex/gender difference.[33] Linda Gordon succinctly catches this complex situation when she comments that gender as a social construction "was used both to criticize the 'artificial' male/female dichoto-

---

30. Di Stefano, "Dilemmas of Difference," 67. This position has been termed "romantic feminism" or "the androgynous strain in feminism" or "humanist feminism" by Rosemary Ruether, Linda Gordon, and Ellen Armour respectively. This position, which sought to reduce gender difference, was dominant in the nineteenth century and in the twentieth century until the late 1970s. "Humanist feminism is thus analogous to an ideal of assimilation in identifying sexual equality with gender blindness, with measuring women and men according to the same standards and treating them in the same way" (Young, *Justice and the Politics of Difference*, 161).

31. See Miles, "Feminist Radicalism"; Young, "Humanism."

32. For the creation of the women's culture that burst forth in the United States by the mid 1970s see esp. Jaggar, *Feminist Politics and Human Nature*, 275–86.

33. Among white feminist theologians two leading figures were Mary Daly and Rosemary Ruether. See Daly, *Beyond God the Father*; *Gyn/Ecology*; *Pure Lust*; Ruether, *New Woman/New Earth*; *Sexism and God-Talk*. Among white feminist theorists see Spelman, *Inessential Woman*; Butler, *Gender Trouble*. For a helpful discussion on the problem of women's identity see Armour, *Deconstruction*, 7–44.

my and to valorize the previously devalued female side of the dichotomy."[34] The course of the debate about whether female subjectivity is grounded in biology or in a social construct turned in favor of the latter by conceptualizing gender difference as a central category for women's identity.

In this process of intentional avoidance of sameness as circumscribing equality, two interrelated issues emerged as problematic. The first was that feminism's gesture of distancing itself from grounding equality in sameness while embracing difference failed to dismantle the traditionally assumed dichotomy of equality-versus-difference. It actually sustained this traditional dichotomy by gravitating to the "different" side of the binary opposition. Thus, feminism's focus on gender difference, contrary to its intention, helped render the notion of equality very elusive. Over against this conundrum, Joan W. Scott took up the issue of equality-versus-difference and attempted to deconstruct the established dichotomy by using poststructuralist theory. Scott claimed that the debate about equality-versus-difference among (U. S.) feminists was "created to offer a choice to feminists, of either endorsing 'equality' or its presumed antithesis 'difference.'"[35] But then Scott called into question the validity of the presumed antithesis arguing that "the antithesis itself hides the interdependence of the two terms, for equality is not the elimination of difference, and difference does not preclude equality."[36] Her resolution is "the unmasking of the power relationship constructed by posing equality as the antithesis of difference and the refusal of its consequent dichotomous construction of political choices."[37]

The second problem is related primarily to the question of essentialism, which African American feminists/womanists and Third World feminists have raised in the face of the views of white feminists on gender difference. This deserves a more elaborate discussion to which I now turn.

2.2. Gender Difference and the Problem of Essentialism

In sum, since the late 1970s feminism has adopted the notion of gender and has taken a further step to dissociate itself from the problem of sameness underlying the ideal of equality in liberal humanist feminism. On the one hand, the emphasis on gender as a social construct rather than a

---

34. Gordon, "Trouble with Difference," unpublished paper, 2.
35. J. W. Scott, "Deconstructing Equality-versus-Difference," 38.
36. Ibid.
37. Ibid., 44.

biological essence enabled feminists to uncover and challenge the social construction of gender norms which elevates maleness as normative in the socio-political and economic hegemony of male domination. Maleness as normative relegates female difference to "other." Although the cause and motivation of protest was not limited to gender oppression, feminist critics showed tendencies to identify the main enemy of women's oppression with the patriarchal structure which perpetuates forms of social injustice and discrimination on the basis of gender difference. Accordingly, with their discourse centered on the binary opposition of male/female, feminists manifested a propensity to privilege gender difference over other differences such as race and class. For example, viewing women's femaleness as their defining essence, Mary Daly states: "Women who accept false inclusion among the fathers and sons are easily polarized against other women on the basis of ethnic, national, class, religious and other male-defined differences, applauding the defeat of 'enemy' women."[38] To a certain degree, this already, even implicitly, prefigures the dangerous assumption and creation of "an essential woman" among white feminist theorist and the problem involving the concept of woman.

A trend known as cultural feminism has devoted much energy to defining femaleness both in comparison with and as an alternative to maleness.[39] Although the move to reclaim long-suppressed female identity/difference, empowered women in many aspects of their public activity, the initial passion for equality was diluted, that is, the political stance against male supremacy and dominance. The more women's natural, traditional characteristics were valorized, the more essentialized gender difference became. Moreover, the hidden assumption was that women share an essence that transcends socio-economic status, historical and cultural location, and other particularities. "In the depoliticized celebration of femaleness, gender becomes non-relational."[40] Too much stress on gender difference rendered differences of race and class—inseparable from gender oppression—invisible and irrelevant.

At this juncture the fundamental question raised by African American feminists comes to the fore: Which woman is the subject? White feminist

---

38. Daly, *Gyn/Ecology*, 365.

39. Mary Daly and Adrienne Rich have been influential proponents of this trend. See Daly, *Gyn/Ecology*; Rich, *Of Woman Born*. For a critique of cultural feminism from the viewpoint of poststructuralist theory, see Alcoff, "Cultural Feminism."

40. Gordon, "Trouble with Difference," 3.

theorists and theologians quickly acknowledged the validity of the critiques of their failure to deal with race as an integral factor in the oppression of women.[41] The central issue in feminist theory in the 1980s became the universalizing and homogenizing of women. In effect this was "the problem of essentialism"—another form of the problem of sameness in understanding gender difference, no longer, as in the first stage of feminism, sameness as the prerequisite for equality with men but now sameness among women. When white feminist recognized the problem of universalizing and homogenizing women as a barrier to acknowledging diversity, their theory shifted toward unearthing and eradicating essentialism. The situation of Western feminist discourse was ironic and paradoxical: "The gender-difference emphasis, which arose to protest the male universal, had produced its own universal that in turn produced a new kind of difference talk: about differences *among* women."[42] The question, then, is: To what extent is the discourse on multiplicity and diversity, which current feminism promotes, liberatory?

2.3. Differences among Women and the Problem of Diversity

African American feminists and womanist theologians began to challenge white feminists' use of "men" and "women" as monolithic terms and their blindness to the difference race makes for gender.[43] In effect, their critique was that white feminists made their own "(middle-class white) woman" the representative of the "true" woman as a raceless, classless woman. African American women adopted another aspect of the black/white binary opposition in order to distinguish the experiences of black women from those of white women and to reclaim a distinctive culture of African American women.

On the one hand, the dichotomy of black/white expressed the sociohistorical reality of hierarchical relationships between white and black women and the oppression of the latter. On the other, the return to the black/white polarity opened the possibility for other versions of women, that is, difference among women to emerge as a site of contention. Thus

---

41. See esp. the critiques of hooks, *Ain't I a Woman*; David, *Women, Race, and Class*.

42. Gordon, "Trouble with Difference," 4.

43. See esp. Williams, "The Color of Feminism"; Williams, "Speaking the Black Woman's Tongue"; and Williams, *Sisters in the Wilderness*. See also Grant, *White Women's Christ*; C. J. Sanders, "Womanist Theology/Feminist Theology."

other women of color challenged the tendency of African American feminists to use exclusionary categories of black and white.[44] Furthermore, some women issued calls for the inclusion of differences in sexual preferences and family forms in the politics of women's difference.[45]

As diverse women, who had once been marginalized, began to raise their own voices in the face of tendencies to homogenize the nature of women's identity and to be reductionistic about the causes of the oppression of women, talk about multiple differences and diversity among women became much more prominent in the feminist movements of the 1990s. This parallels closely the phenomenon that diversity or pluralism has become fashionable in other fields of academia in the postmodern and global era. Feminist/womanist theorists, often drawing on poststructuralist theories, are far more disposed toward models of diversity over binary models. The more they talk about differentiated differences among various groups of women, the more inclusive, they think, are their theories.

As current feminist discourse moves toward the politics of inclusion under the rubrics of diversity and multiplicity, few scholars have attended to the weaknesses lying veiled under the emphasis on diversity. For example, white feminist theorists and theologians are inclined to include racial differences in their discussions of diversity among women. Yet, as Ellen Armour noted, they "tend to see race and class oppressions as increasing the quantity of oppression but not its quality."[46] Failing to see whiteness as well as blackness as a racial mark, white feminist may talk about racial differences only when black women or women of color merit special mention. Historical and socio-economic relations underlying and determining the hierarchical, racial difference between white women and women assigned to other racial constructs are overlooked. In short, configurations of power among women receive insufficient notice. As Linda Gordon perceptively notes, "One of the weaknesses of 'difference' and 'diversity' as concepts is that they seem to suggest solutions through mere addition, without looking at the patterns of relationships."[47] The danger of a one-dimensional

---

44. Mohanty, "Under Western Eyes"; Oduyoye, "Reflections."

45. E.g., see Butler, *Gender Trouble*; *Bodies that Matter*.

46. Armour, *Deconstruction*, 20.

47. Gordon, "Trouble with Difference," 6. Similarly, Ann Ferguson underscores "the nonadditive embeddedness of our particular gender identities" ("Resisting the Veil of Privilege").

emphasis on diversity is to encourage "additive thinking" in terms of the plurality of quantities rather than in terms of relational qualities.

3. POSTCOLONIAL PERSPECTIVE ON DIFFERENCE

As discussed above, postmodern criticism seeks to deconstruct the logic of Western hegemony of Western thoughts and discourse which serve to repress the discourse of difference. Similarly, feminists/womanist criticism dismantles the hierarchical social construction of gender which renders women's difference (in spite of all its diversity) as "other." Even so, it might be fair to say that both postmodernism and feminism originated in a Western critical environment, and both are also inevitably circumscribed by Western concerns. It is precisely at this point that I want to draw attention to a recent critical stance called "postcolonialism" and the difference it makes to the discourse of difference.

Since it is not my intention to perform a comprehensive review of current state of postcolonial studies, my dialogue with postcolonial perspectives centers on three key points that are relevant to my project: (1) the meaning of "difference" in postcolonialism; (2) the urgent need to relocate the discourse on difference in its appropriate context of justice; and (3) the potential promise of postcolonial criticism for biblical studies.

Before considering the meaning of "difference" in postcolonialism, I need to say some words about the term "postcolonial" and problems involving its use in postcolonial theories. Like other "post-" words, postcolonialism does not allow us a unified and monolithic definition. It is primarily because different countries in Africa and Asia have experienced different natures and forms of colonial domination at different historical stages. As Susan V. Gallager puts it, "Colonialism shows different faces in different parts of the globe, and its progeny come in different shapes, colors, and dimensions. Any discussion of postcolonialism, then, is a discussion of the difference and multiplicity as well as of the commonality of oppression and injustice."[48]

There has been some discussion regarding the proper appropriation of the term "postcolonial" mainly due to a dual sense that the term carries with it. On the one hand the word "post-" carries the sense of something which is after colonialism, and on the other hand it is related to the interpretation

---

48. Gallagher, *Postcolonial Literature*, 7–8.

of its relationship to colonialism.[49] Although, viewed historically, the forms of colonialism as the conquest and direct control of other people's land by the former European empires are over, "if colonialism is a way of maintaining an unequal international relation of economic and political power . . . then no doubt we have not fully transcended the colonial."[50] While postcolonialism is unquestionably connected to former colonial situations, it is not just about historical periodization of colonialism/post-colonialism.

3.1. Postcolonial Understanding of Difference

Postcolonialism emerged as a political challenge to so-called Western orientalism, which refers to ways the West construed and represented the Orient for its own interests in colonizing the culture of the subjected people in order to consolidate its political and economic colonization. Postcolonialism unveils how this construction and representation resulted in a "denied or alienated subjectivity" of the other who has not only experienced colonization but also possesses a distinct political agenda and theory of agency.[51] The meaning of difference is thus construed critically within the historical and global context of colonial imperial domination imposed by the West. Unlike postmodernism, postcolonialism takes seriously not only the role of the empire in constructing the marginalized other but also the significance of "subjectivity," "representation," and "history." Dealing with the question of definition of the subject in postmodernism, Mishra and Hodge stress the diverging political agendas in postmodernism and postcolonialism respectively: "If for postmodernism the object of analysis is the subject as defined by humanism, with its essentialism and mistaken historical verities, its unities and transcendental presence, then for post-colonialism the object is the imperialist subject, the colonized as formed by the processes of imperialism."[52]

---

49. See the articles in Williams and Chrisman, eds., *Colonial Discourse and Post-Colonial Theory*.

50. Williams and Chrisman, "Introduction," 4.

51. See Tiffin, "Introduction"; Slemon, "Modernism's Last Post"; Hutcheon, "Circling the Downspout of Empire": "The Post-colonial, like the feminist, is a dismantling but also constructive political enterprise insofar as it implies a theory of agency and social change that the post-modern deconstructive impulse lacks" (183).

52. Mishra and Hodge, "What Is Post(-)colonialism?" 281.

Paul and the Politics of Difference

Such difference between postmodernism and postcolonialism should not be overlooked in spite of similar strategies and forms of discourse noticeable among poststructuralism, postmodernism, and postcolonialism. Like postmodernist and poststructuralist criticism, much postcolonial literature is committed to dismantling, unmasking, or questioning the concepts of hierarchy and otherness. It is understandable that the relationship of three "posts"—poststructuralism, postmodernism, and postcolonialism—is energetically debated within critical conversation about postcolonial literature today.[53] For example, as a critique of the process of the Western discursive construction of power and knowledge about the Other, postcolonial theory highlights a set of binary concepts such as center/periphery, self/other, and colonial/post-colonial. The deconstruction of hierarchical relations grounded on such oppositions certainly points to one of similarities in the writing strategies deployed by postmodern and postcolonial analyses.

Nevertheless, postcolonialism parts company with postmodernism especially in terms of its political agenda.[54] This is primarily due to the origins of commitments (or lack thereof) from distinct socio-historical locations. In other words, most postcolonial writers hold that deconstruction as such cannot be the goal of their postcolonial discursive practice. As a case in point, Susan Gallagher explains: "In their more postmodern works, the unmasking and dismantling of authority is merely a strategy, a means of fulfilling a political agenda to retrieve identity in the face of cultural imperialism. By questioning colonial authority, post-colonial writers do not necessarily question *all* authority. Rather, they set out to dismantle a specific historically grounded discourse in the hopes of demonstrating that an alternative discourse is possible."[55]

Thus, in a way that is similar to feminist/womanist discourse on difference, postcolonialism takes "difference" to be first and foremost about a "subjectivity" which is denied or rendered alien by colonial and imperial discourse. At the same time, difference is about a subjectivity which is an identity and agency to be affirmed and asserted as alternatives to the representations of colonialism. As such, the question of difference in a

---

53. For a general sketch on this issue see Williams and Chrisman, "Introduction."

54. See During, "Postmodernism or Postcolonialism?"; Gallagher, *Postcolonial Literature*; Tiffin, "Post-Colonialism, Post-Modernism"; Mishra and Hodge, "What Is Post(-)colonialism?"

55. Gallagher, *Postcolonial Literature*, 14 (her emphasis).

postcolonial perspective is closely related to the significance of history and representation, particularly the submerged history and representation of suppressed people. To this extent postcolonial theory considers history and historical agency indispensable. This radical perspective pushes justice to the fore, even though justice often emerges in terms of the binary formulation colonial/postcolonial.

There is no doubt that the postcolonial project of refocusing the question of subjectivity is not an easy one, nor does it suggest any monolithic forms. Within postcolonial theory there is a strong tendency to highlight the notion of "hybridity" in approaching and articulating the issue of postcolonial identity. Coined, elaborated, and popularized by Homi Bhabha,[56] hybridity is one of the most frequently occurring and significant terms in postcolonial theory. Bhabha uses the term as a way of dismantling "the binary logic through which identities of difference are often constructed—Black/White, Self/Other"—and suggesting that "interstitial passage[s] between fixed identifications open . . . up the possibility of a cultural hybridity that entertains differences without an assumed or imposed hierarchy."[57] Hybridity thus emphasizes the complexity involved in postcolonial identity and the representation of difference: "Terms of cultural engagement, whether antagonistic or affiliative, are produced performatively. The representation of difference must not be hastily read as the reflection of *pre-given* ethnic or cultural traits set in the fixed tablet of tradition. The social articulation of difference, from the minority perspective, is a complex, on-going negotiation that seeks to authorize cultural hybridities that emerge in moments of historical transformation."[58]

Such emphasis on the notion of hybridity as well as the syncretic nature of postcolonial societies, cultures, and discourses represent a kind of resistance against "a movement toward nativism, a futile, romantic attempt to return to a pristine, pre-colonial culture," which is also another form of resistance against the identities imposed by colonial domination and discourses on subjected people.

Hybridity is quite appealing to postcolonialists who are interested in the dynamics of cultural interaction and engagement between the colonizer and the colonized. Yet, it should not be overlooked that the mode of hybridity is a specific response arising out of a specific form of historical

56. Bhabha, *The Location of Culture*.
57. Ibid., 4.
58. Ibid., 32.

colonization. In other words, hybridity is most compatible with situations involving (white) settler colonies rather than in locations where colonizers did not settle. Despite the wide-ranging appeal of hybridity in postcolonial studies, the undifferentiated adoption of it begs the question—assuming its validity before making any analyses of particular historical conditions. Problematizing the importance of hybridity in postcolonialism's complicity with postmodernism and further calling for "an adequate materialist theory of postcolonialism," Mishra and Hodge have made a sharp critique on "a model of the construction of meaning which advances . . . hybridity over purity, syncretism over difference, pluralism over essentialism":

> The paradigmatic postcolonial text is the West Indian novel which is elevated, implicitly, to the position of pre-eminence: all postcolonial literatures aspire to the condition of the West Indian, and the achievements of West Indian writers are read back into the settler traditions. But the West Indian paradigm is just not applicable to a country like Australia for instance, either historically or linguistically . . . All uncritical adulation of pluralism which leads, finally, to post-colonialism becoming the liberal Australian version of multi-culturalism, then produces concepts such as "hybridity" and "syncretism" as the theoretical "dominants" of postcolonial society.[59]

All this reminds us of some caution that while remaining faithful to its pronounced "committed criticism" to decolonizing the colonial discourses, the postcolonial study of "difference" should never lose sight of historical specificities and power relations determinative of different colonial/postcolonial (imperial) conditions, as well as diverse (even conflicting) strategies responsive to different contexts.

3.2. Postcolonial Reading of the Bible

Although there have been some anticipatory developments, postcolonialism's approach has emerged as a new hermeneutical challenge in biblical studies.[60] Postcolonial readings of the Bible exhibit three distinctive but

---

59. Mishra and Hodge, "What Is Post(-)colonialism?" 286–87.

60. Especially in the Two-Thirds world, liberation-oriented biblical interpretation prepared the way for the emergence of postcolonial readings of the Bible. Thus, postcolonial criticism should be a specific ideological articulation of liberation-oriented criticism rather than a substitute for it. For postcolonial readings see the essays in *Semeia* 75 (1996), ed. R. S. Sugirtharajah; and Sugirtharajah, *Asian Biblical Hermeneutics*.

interrelated aspects: the name postcolonial itself, its political commitment, and its reading posture.

First, scholars who claim their readings of the Bible as "postcolonial" have made themselves more or less associated with postcolonial theory that I briefly discussed above. Those scholars are not deeply concerned with some of the contested issues among postcolonial theorists, for instance, problems of terminology and the relationship between postcolonialism and postmodernism/poststructuralism. Rather, as Susan Gallagher notes, most scholars understand postcolonialism "less as a historical marker than a political or philosophical marker, *post* as in *opposed* to a certain practice called *colonialism*."[61] Thus, an Asian postcolonial biblical scholar, R. S. Sugirtharajah writes on the relationship between postcolonialism and biblical studies: "Postcolonialism is roughly defined as scrutinizing and exposing colonial domination and power as these are embodied in biblical texts and in interpretations, and as searching for alternative hermeneutics while thus overturning and dismantling colonial perspectives."[62]

In appropriating postcolonial discourses, reading strategies, and political positions, scholars committed to postcolonial interpretation call attention to the reality or shadow of empire or colonialism both in the formation of biblical texts and in the history of interpretation. With respect to difference, postcolonial readings of the Bible locate the question in a global framework of imperialism of the past and the present. In other words, in postcolonial reading, difference is primarily about the other as produced and represented by and for the benefit of Western imperialism. Further, postcolonial biblical scholars strive to reclaim and rehabilitate marginalized discourses and denigrated identities. But unlike postmodern critics, they pursue this task in association with liberation-oriented Two-Thirds world perspectives.

Second, by introducing postcolonialism into the biblical criticism, the practitioners of postcolonial reading of the Bible present explicitly or implicitly its ethics of interpretation as critically focus on imperialism, neo-imperialism, and Eurocentrism. As Musa W. Dube, a Botswana feminist biblical scholar of southern Africa, defines, "By its practice and its goals, imperialism is a relationship of subordination and domination between different nations and lands, which actively suppresses diversity and promotes

---

61. Gallagher, "Mapping the Hybrid World," 230 (her emphasis).
62. Sugirtharajah, "Biblical Studies after the Empire," 16.

a few universal standards for the benefit of those in power."[63] What is distinctive in postcolonial biblical criticism is that it does not stop at merely defining imperialism, or describing the realities of empires relevant to both ancient and contemporary worlds. Postcolonial biblical scholars are compelled to bring imperialism and the reality of empire to the front, and to resist imperial domination through biblical criticism. As Kwok Pui-Lan remarked in her review essay of a *Semeia* volume on postcolonial criticism, "These diverse authors demonstrate that the introduction of postcolonial discourse into biblical criticism offers new avenues to interrogate the Bible as a cultural product, the formation of canon, and the politics of biblical interpretation."[64]

Thus, postcolonial reading of the Bible claims to be an "oppositional" reading to the cultural and discursive domination of colonialism and imperialism. For example, Sugirtharajah takes issue with Eurocentrism for his central task, contending that "Postcoloniality involves the once-colonized 'Others' insisting on taking their place as historical subjects. Unlike other current theoretical practices such as feminism and structuralism, postcolonial discourse is not about the West, but about the colonized 'Other.'"[65] Accordingly Sugirtharajah presents the project of oppositional postcolonialism as involving the search for protesting voices.

Furthermore, such oppositional perspective enables Dube to take a rigorous position to investigate "imperializing texts," which she defines as "those literary works that propound values and representations that authorize expansionist tendencies grounded on unequal international/racial relations," and to "decolonize" those imperializing text, including the Bible.[66] Dube's reading for decolonization involves "awareness of imperialism's exploitative forces and its various strategies of domination, the conscious adaptation of strategies for resisting imperial domination, as well as the search for alternative ways of liberating interdependence between nations, races, genders, economies, and cultures."[67] Thus, Dube has well demonstrated the political commitment involving postcolonial reading of the Bible: "Reading the Bible and other cultural texts for decolonization is, therefore, imperative for those who are committed to the struggle for

---

63. Dube, "Reading for Decolonization," 38.
64. Kwok Pui-Lan, "Response," 212.
65. Sugirtharajah, *Asian Biblical Hermeneutics*, 16.
66. Dube, "Reading for Decolonization," 38.
67. Ibid.

liberation. Why the Bible is a usable text in imperial projects and how it should be read in the light of its role are central questions to the process of decolonization and the struggle for liberation."[68] Given the ideological nature of the committed criticism pronounced by postcolonial biblical critics, I would say that what postcolonial biblical criticism has undertaken and seeks to offer is not (and should not be) merely to add yet another different reading to the diversity of readings which becomes fashionable and much celebrated in postmodern, North American biblical scholarship.

Third, as for its reading posture, postcolonial biblical criticism takes up a dual reading project of deconstruction (decolonization) toward reconstruction (liberation) as a common goal, albeit diverse emphases in reading strategies. Scholars are concerned to interrogate, debunk, and decolonize the effects of empire and forms of imperial complicity in the process of scriptural production,[69] the formation of canon,[70] and the history of biblical scholarship.[71] At the same time, they endeavor to search for and offer alternative readings by recuperating marginal figures in the texts and reconstruing the meanings of submerged voices,[72] or by dismantling the hierarchical structure of imperializing texts,[73] or by questioning the imperialist tendencies of Western biblical studies.[74]

For my concerns, I want to focus on two points, which especially Sugirtharajah and Horsley have made clear and which relate to what I already articulated in the Introduction. The first point is about the problem of the relationship between Christianity and other faiths on which both Western imperialism and Eurocentric biblical interpretation have exercised much impact. In his critical review of Christian discourse and commentary writings in colonial India, Sugitharajah points out that there is a striking analogy between "Western construction of the Orient" and "Christianity's relation to other faiths" in those commentaries.[75] Sugirtharajah protested that those commentaries served to establish "a theological hierarchy with Christianity at the top and other religions placed underneath it as imper-

---

68. Ibid., 44.
69. E.g., Dube, "Reading for Decolonization."
70. E.g., Berquist, "Imperial Motives."
71. E.g., Horsley, "Submerged Biblical Histories."
72. E.g., Perkinson, "A Canaanitic Word."
73. E.g., Dube, "Reading for Decolonization."
74. E.g., Horsley, "Submerged Biblical Histories."
75. Sugirtharajah, "Imperial Critical Commentaries," 88.

fect and inferior" by loading imperial agendas (in India under the British colonization) along with binary distinctions, in identifying Christianity in relation to other religions: "Christians and heathens, believers, and unbelievers, 'us' and 'them.' The construction of the demonized 'other' serves to validate the superiority of the Christian faith . . . The effect of all this is to establish British dominance and to provide the moral imperative for imperial intervention, subjugation and the prolongation of the British presence in a heathen land."[76]

Furthermore, Sugirtharajah well demonstrated how commentators in support of imperial domination advocated "a pietistic and personal form of Christian faith rather than a Christian concern for the uplifting and betterment of the underprivileged,"[77] which eventually led to the effect of perpetuating the exclusivist Christian faith claiming Christianity as "the only pointer to God."[78] This situation can be almost universally applied to Asian countries, including Korea, where Western European Christianity was imported into multi-religious environments. As I will discuss this problem in consideration of the reality of Korean Christianity below, the exclusivist insistence on Christian faith is one of the most fundamental problems which stands in the way of the transformation of Korean Christianity and society.

The second point is related to what Richard Horsley has called for in his endorsing emergent postcolonial readings of the Bible. Horsley particularly invokes the role of biblical studies in general as "one of many products of modern Western imperial culture and its 'orientalism.'"[79] Similar to Sugirtharajah, Horsley criticizes biblical scholarship's construction of "a parochial-political and legalistic-ritualistic 'Judaism' as an Other-religion over against true, universal and purely spiritual religion; Western European Christianity."[80] According to Horsley, such a misrepresentation of Judaism and Christianity of the first century reveals a lack of concern in biblical studies for taking into serious account the reality of Roman empire, eventually leading biblical studies to "depoliticize" particular books (e.g., the Gospel of Mark) and the authors (e.g., Paul) or movements that produced them.[81] Although Horsley, as a Western biblical scholar, is somehow cau-

---

76. Ibid., 89.
77. Ibid., 92.
78. Ibid., 93.
79. Horsley, "Submerged Biblical Histories," 154.
80. Ibid.
81. Ibid., 154–55.

tious in using the term postcolonial, he aligns his consistent self-critical, liberation-oriented biblical criticism with the significance of postcolonial reading of the Bible. Underscoring an analogous relationship between the Roman Empire and modern empires, Horsley suggests a reading posture against the traditional interpretations of biblical scholarship: "A postcolonial (and anti-imperial) biblical studies includes in its agenda the emancipation of previously submerged or distorted histories of the movements that produced the literature that was later included in the Bible—partly by avoiding, opposing, and replacing the essentialist and depoliticizing categories and approaches of imperial Western biblical studies."[82]

Furthermore, Horsley argues that modern New Testament studies submerged Jewish people's history and aspirations primarily by reading the Gospels and Paul's letters as "the founding documents of Western Christianity, as the beginnings of the history of Western Christian civilization" rather than "the literature of peoples subjected to a Western empire."[83] This leads Horsley to propose an alternative, postcolonial reading of Paul: "The most significant way in which a postcolonial reading of Paul disrupts the standard essentialist, individualistic and depoliticized Augustinian-Lutheran Paul, consists in the rediscovery of the anti-imperial stance and program evident in his letter—for those with 'eyes to see.'"[84]

I would argue that such a point should be taken as an important reminder even for scholars who have launched the project of decolonizing imperialist biblical texts.[85] There is no doubt that the Bible is now a contested site as it was throughout the complex process of its formation and interpretation. Certainly, it should be acknowledged that the Bible contains not only liberating texts but also imperializing texts. Precisely because of this, how one relates the reality of empire to biblical texts becomes crucial in categorizing certain texts as either liberating or imperializing. Besides, it would beg further questions if postcolonial reading strategies for decolo-

82. Ibid., 155.
83. Ibid.
84. Ibid., 167–68.
85. Perhaps the most highly developed work on biblical interpretation from this postcolonial perspective is the extensive "African Americans and the Bible" project by Vincent Wimbush. Although one may argue that the African American cultural perspective differs somewhat from the postcolonial perspective, for the purpose of this dissertation, Wimbush's work represents a profoundly articulated and committed example of biblical interpretation outside the Eurocentric domination. See Wimbush's edited volume, *African Americans and the Bible* and the works cited therein.

nization follow postmodern reading gestures by focusing unduly on imperializing reading effects of the biblical texts without attempting to make distinctions between imperialist biblical texts in original, socio-historical contexts and the imperialist (mis)interpretation of biblical texts for imperial agendas.

4. DIFFERENCE AND THE PERSPECTIVE OF MINJUNG THEOLOGY IN KOREA

Up to now I wanted to elaborate the relational and contextual understanding of the notion of difference and the socio-political significance of difference as the site of oppression, struggle, and resistance in relation to gender, class, race, and empire. Now I turn to my own context by focusing on the development of minjung theology as a Korean Christian movement for the transformation of Korean society. On the one hand, although I myself was engaged in the movement of minjung theology, my social location of residing in the United States over the past two decades has unfortunately prevented me from making direct and continuing involvement with the development of minjung theology. Thus, in this section I do not intend to bring to discussion all the diverse, profound theological themes that minjung theology has developed especially during the 1990s.

On the other hand, I have become more conscious of the importance of the reunification of Korea than I was in Korea. The suffering of Korean minjung and minjung as the subjects of history cannot be fully explained and discussed without taking into serious account the past and present reality of the divided Korea by and under the imperial power of the United States.[86] How to bring about the reunification of Korea in spite of differences in ideology and political systems has become the most urgent task for reclaiming the political and cultural identity of Korean nation and Korean minjung.

Therefore, I will focus my discussion here on the understanding of the minjung as the subjects of history in minjung theology in consideration of some shifts in emphasis. In addition, I will discuss some hermeneutical issues that have been raised in minjung theology's emphasis on reading the Bible from the perspective of the minjung.

---

86. For a thorough investigation of the socio-political, international, and imperial relations involved in the Korean War, see Cumings, *The Origin of the Korean War*.

4.1. Minjung Theology as a Praxis-oriented Theology

Like other liberation theologies in Latin America and South Africa, and feminist, womaninst, and black theologies in the United States, minjung theology—a Korean liberation theology in the continent of Asia—emerged as a theology of practice in the midst of the social crisis of Korean society in 1970s. Minjung theology started as a critical theological reflection on the socio-political and economic reality which overdetermined the brutal reality of the exploited and oppressed among Korean people, minjung. As such, minjung theology entailed the practical concern which takes the preferential option for the socially oppressed and marginalized. The most profound contribution of minjung theology lies at its rediscovery of the minjung as the subjects of history in Korean society and its commitment to doing theology from the perspective of minjung.

First of all, a definitional explanation of the term "minjung" is necessary. Suh Kwang Sun gives a good English translation and interpretation of the definition of the term:

> "Minjung" is a Korean word, but is a combination of two Chinese characters "min" and "jung." "Min" may be translated as "people" and "jung" as "the mass." Thus "minjung" means "the mass of the people, or mass, or just the people." But when we try to translate it into English, "mass" is not adequate for our theological purpose; and "the people" is politically dangerous in anti-Communist Korea, because it has become a Communist word. Although "the people of God" may seem to be the most safe and perhaps neutral expression both in Korean and English, theologically and politically "minjung" cannot be translated into "the people of God."[87]

Certainly the last sentence of the quotation emphasizes the theological and political context in which the term minjung has come to gain a specific connotation at a specific historical moment, or in which minjung theologians as well as various minjung movement have begun to rediscover and appreciate anew the reality and meaning of minjung. There is no doubt that from the beginning of Korean history, and particularly since the very beginning of the twentieth century, there were always minjung, the political and economic reality of minjung, and their struggles in the midst of the vicissitudes of the Korean history. However, what minjung theology discovered can be understood in terms of the self-critical reflection on

---

87. K. S. Suh, "A Biographical Sketch," 16.

how theologians and the Korean church have contributed to rendering the Korean minjung invisible, voiceless, and insignificant. In other words, the minjung had remained, so to speak, as "Other" to the founders of minjung theology before their blindness was changed by the minjung of the 1970s. Actually, it is true that to the majority of Korean theologians and the Korean Christians minjung still remain as "Other," or "difference," because they insist that Christian theology or discourse is about the universal human being rather than particular minjung and/or women. They insist that the difference of minjung and/or women does not make any difference for their understanding of Christian life or reading of the Bible as the Word of God.

How, then, could minjung theologians experience the so-called "Copernican" conversion[88] in doing theology? What made their eyes to open wide to the sufferings and struggles of the Korean minjung? Although it cannot be absolutely denied that some significant similar phenomena in world history, such as liberation theology in Latin America and minjung theology in Korea, could have a certain degree of interaction and mutual impact, minjung theology in Korea, as Suh Kwang Sun asserts, should not be viewed "a Korean expression either of liberation theology imported from Latin America or of theological writings coming from West European and North American communities."[89] This does not mean to say that minjung theology is superior to liberation theology in Latin America, nor to say that minjung theology is totally new kind of theology.

What enabled the first-generation minjung theologians to encounter a totally new momentum in doing theology was the death of a young laborer, Jeon Tae Il, who immolated himself to death to resist the oppressive political and economic reality of the Korean society in 1970s, and the subsequent outburst of minjung movements. Jeon Tae Il's suicide shocked not only the labor movement but also other social movements including student movements and religious movements in Korea, and actually ignited the remarkable movement for human rights and democracy in the 1970s. Shocked by such an event, a few theologians opened their eyes to the socio-political, economic reality of Korean society under the military regime, came to discover that it is the minjung who are able to transform society and history as the subjects of history, and began to do theology from what they had discovered.

---

88. C. N. Kim, "The Significance of Minjung," 108.
89. Ibid., 16.

Over the last three decades, the historical development of minjung theology has exhibited three major phases relative to each decade. It has been acknowledged that the genealogy of minjung theology can be explained by the ways it has responded to changing historical situations of Korean society as well as the development of popular minjung social movements. Thus three generations of minjung theologians are roughly categorized in terms of minjung theology in 1970s, 1980s, and 1990s.[90] Of course, both minjung theologians and activists of the minjung church movement have been living over the three decades (except Suh Nam Dong and Ahn Byung Mu), thus the periodization of minjung theology does not exclude some overlaps in personal theological activities and theological themes. Yet due to the significant shifts in emphasis and strategy, the issue of continuity and discontinuity within such a trajectory of minjung theology has been a focus of discussion.

4.2. Minjung as the Subject of History

Who are the minjung? This has been one of the central questions to which minjung theologians have devoted much theological reflections and theoretical considerations since the beginning of minjung theology. Again, it should be emphasized that minjung theology did not start with the question of who the minjung are from purely academic and theoretical concerns and purposes.

Based on his experience of the suffering and struggle of the Korean minjung in the 1970s, Ahn Byung Mu engaged in the study of the historical Jesus. Ahn drew special attention to the presence and usage of ὄχλος in the gospel of Mark, arguing that the ὄχλος in Mark reflect and represent the ὄχλος at the time of the historical Jesus.[91] Ahn characterized the ὄχλος in Mark as the people who gathered around Jesus. These people were the so-called sinners and the tax collectors, who stood condemned in their society, and the sick. The ὄχλος in Mark were differentiated from λάος used especially for "God's people" (Hebrew, ʿam), as well as from the disciples. It goes

---

90. Although this self-referential categorization is generally accepted and widely talked among minjung theologians as well as other theologians, it cannot be attributed to a specific minjung theologian. Such a categorization came to exist when minjung theologians needed to make differentiations retrospectively and prospectively as they encountered different challenges in the development of minjung movement in general and minjung theology movement in particular.

91. Ahn, "Jesus and the Minjung."

without saying that these people were contrasted with the ruling class from Jerusalem who attacked and criticized Jesus as their enemy. According to Ahn, both the ὄχλος in the context of the historical Jesus and the ὄχλος in the context of Mark refer to the people who were exploited, oppressed, and marginalized in the total process of political, economic, and cultural distributions of the society.

Furthermore, Ahn asserted that the ὄχλος were the bearers of social suffering and the one who desperately needed and yearned for liberation, and that they were the subjects of the Jesus-event.[92] Here, Ahn defined the Jesus-event primarily as a minjung event in Galilee which Jesus brought into history together with minjung. As such, the Jesus-event continued and continues to be represented and performed in the midst of and through Korean minjung event(s). Ahn described such a phenomenon of reoccurring minjung events in history by using the metaphor of a volcanic chain. In other words, minjung event is like a volcanic chain which runs through without cessation, but explodes and ejects at certain historical junctures. In that way, Ahn identified the Jesus-event which occurred in the first-century Palestine with minjung event(s) in the Korean society of the 1970s.

Although Ahn's understanding of the minjung presupposed sociopolitical, economic, and cultural categories as shown in his analysis of the term of ὄχλος in Mark, he refused to identify the minjung in terms of sociological categories. Instead, he insisted that the minjung cannot be determined by sociological categories or identified with any specified social class, asserting that the historical dynamics that the notion of minjung carries precludes any theorization of it. Thus, Ahn defined the primary role of minjung theology as the theology of "witness" which is committed to re-telling the forgotten, suppressed, and forbidden stories of the minjung's sufferings and struggles, concentrating his biblical interpretation on

---

92. In his study of the historical Jesus, Ahn coined the term of "Jesus-event" and popularized it among minjung theologians. Although it seems that the notion of "Jesus-event" can be related to the German biblical scholars of the so-called New Quest of the historical Jesus, such as Ernst Käsemann, Günter Bornkamm, and Willi Marxsen, Ahn, who actually studied in Germany, never mentioned it. In fact, Ahn's use of "Jesus-event" has some resonance with Marxen's use of *"die Sache Jesu."* See Marxen, *The Beginnings*. Yet, Ahn used the term "Jesus-event," equivalent to "Jesus-movement," as an important hermeneutical key to the understanding of the Jesus movement from the perspective of minjung. While Marxsen used *"die Sache Jesu"* in order to seek the continuity between the earthly Jesus and the risen Lord, Ahn focused on "Jesus-event" to highlight the discontinuity between the historical Jesus and the Christ in Kerygma (or, Christ of theological proclamation).

recovering the stories of minjung in Galilee and the stories of Jesus who lived with the minjung, in the midst of the minjung.

On the other hand, some theologians tried to understand and articulate the experience of the minjung by drawing attention to Shamanism, one of the indigenous popular religions in Korea, and traditional minjung culture, and "*han*." Han is a Koran word which denotes an accumulation of suppressed and condensed experiences of oppression. *Han* of Korean minjung has been rooted in the long, multilayered history of the suffering of Korean minjung and nation: particularly the history of a century since the beginning of the twentieth century covering the political trajectory of colonization, neo-colonization, the division of the nation, the pro-USA, anti-communist dictatorial regime in South Korea, Park Jong Hee's military coup and his long-term dictatorship, the 5.18 Kwang Ju Massacre and the Kwang Ju Minjung Struggle. Especially Suh Nam Dong was inspired by a resistant poet Kim Chi Ha, who wrote many poems with the theme of *han* by depicting the vivid reality of the *han* of Korean minjung, and adopted the motif of "*han*" as an important theological motif for his doing theology from the perspective of minjung. Recognizing that *han* of Korean people has been deeply embedded in and shaped by the socio-biography of Korean minjung in history, Suh depicted its characteristics as follows:

> (1) Koreans have suffered numerous invasions by surrounding powerful nations so that the very existence of the Korean nation has come to be understood as *han*. (2) Koreans have continually suffered the tyranny of the rulers so that they think of their existence as *baeksong*. (3) Also, under Confucianism's strict imposition of laws and customs discriminating against women, the existence of women was *han* itself. (4) At a certain point in Korean history, about half of the population were registered as hereditary slaves and were treated as property rather than as people of the nation. These four may be called the fourfold *han* of Korean people. Indeed, as the poet Ko Eun exclaims, "We Koreans were born from the womb of *han* and brought up in the womb of *han*."[93]

Although the categories such as class, status, gender, and empire are not explicitly used, those categories are certainly implied in Suh Nam Dong's understanding of the genesis of the *han* of Korean minjung. Suh further elaborated on both passive and positive ways in which *han* has functioned

---

93. N. D. Suh, "Toward a Theology of Han." See also A. S. Park, *The Wounded Heart of God*.

within the cultural and political reality of Korean minjung. As "an underlying feeling of Koran people," *han* is "a dominant feeling of defeat, resignation, and nothingness. On the other, it is a feeling with a tenacity of will for life which comes to weaker beings. The first aspect can sometimes be sublimated to great artistic expressions and the second aspect could erupt as the energy for a revolution or rebellion."[94] According to Suh, the God of the Bible is the one who redeems, atones, and liberates minjung—both of the Bible and of Korean people—from their *han*. To minjung, liberation means being delivered from *han*. While the term "sin" is the language used by the ruling class people and the Western theology, sin amounts to *han* to the eyes of the minjung.

Suh Nam Dong's profound theological imagination drawing upon the theme of *han* allowed him to articulate what he called "a theology of confluence (conjunction)." Although Suh did not give a clear definition of the concept of "confluence," the latter refers to the event that different traditions become confluent, and further to the method which makes it possible. "Confluence" is presented as a theological paradigm by which Suh sought to explain the ways which the two currents of tradition, that is, the current of minjung tradition of the Bible and Christianity and that of political and cultural tradition of Korean minjung, become confluent. Here, "confluence" is viewed as being related to two dimensions, the dimension of social, political, and economic liberation and the dimension of cultural and religious identity. Suh redefined it as the task of theology to witness and interpret "confluence": it is the role of political theology to witness and interpret the confluence that occurs on the socio-political dimension, while it is the role of cultural theology to witness to and interpret such confluence that occurs on the cultural-religious dimension. What minjung theology is trying to do is to witness to and interpret the confluence which occurs on these two socio-political and cultural-religious dimensions.

While reflecting theologically and responding to the sufferings and struggles of the Korean minjung in the 1970s, Ahn Byung Mu focused on interpreting the historical significance of the Jesus-event as minjung event(s), Suh Nam Dong paid much attention to the various traditions of Korean minjung such as folk stories, songs, mask dances, poems, novels, and so on. Despite differences in approach and focus, both Ahn and Suh shared the common hermeneutical starting point that the minjung are the

---

94. Ibid., 58.

subjects of history for the transformation of society, and laid the foundation for the subsequent development of minjung theology.

4.3. Differences among Minjung Theologians

Although the second or younger generation of minjung theologians in the 1980s adopted the fundamental theological premises laid out by the theologians of the first generation, the radical change of social situation of the Korean society as well as the growth of various minjung movements in 1980s impelled the theologians to respond to the new challenge responsibly. Especially, the 5.18 Kwang Ju Minjung Struggle in 1980, which was the Kwang Ju minjung's tenacious resistance against Kwang Ju Massacre by the Korean government aided by the U.S. military intervention, became another watershed in the history of the Korean minjung movement. Minjung movement activists including students, laborers, and farmers were eager to adopt available social transformation theories and praxis theories. Particularly social theories representative of eastern European Marxism had great appeal to them. A growing consciousness was that the conflicts and contradictions of the Korean society of the 1980s were not only caused by the oppressive military dictatorship of the Korean government, but also conditioned by the multi-layered oppressive forces of the imperialism, neo-colonialism, world capitalism of the United States in which the Korean capitalistic society was incorporated.

Younger minjung theologians also felt the need to reappropriate praxis theories in order to more correctly grasp the structural contradictions of Korean society and to develop minjung theology as a theoretically well-grounded praxis theory. A number of articles written by minjung theologians during the 1980s and the early 1990s are critical efforts to theologically elaborate on the various issues raised within the elevated phase of the Korean minjung movements, for example, in terms of "a theology of *mul* (that is, material),"[95] "the sub-structure of historical revelation,"[96] "the epistemological revolution with respect to the issues of material and class,"[97] "a biblical foundation for minjung theology's theory of minjung,"[98] and so on. To put it simply, the ideological critical approaches to the concept of

95. Kang, *The Theology of Mul*.
96. N. D. Suh, *In Search of Minjung Theology*.
97. Ahn, "The Jesus Movement and *Mul*."
98. J. H. Kim, "Minjung as the Subject of History."

minjung, the socio-political and economic reality of biblical minjung, and other biblical, theological themes were preferred and spread rapidly among minjung theologians.

Simultaneously, it was time for an increasing awareness of the tragic reality of our divided nation which was rightly viewed as a product of the U.S. imperial strategy for securing its hegemony over the region of East-North Asia. Accordingly, minjung theologians began to draw attention to the significance of the concept of *minjok* (that is, nation) and its implications for the praxis of minjung theology, especially for the praxis of reunification of Korean nation. In this context, while recognizing the undeniable contribution made by the minjung theology in the 1970s, Park Soon Kyung, the most prominent reunification theologian in Korea, made a sharp criticism: "The minjung theology in the 1970s presupposes anti-Communist Christianity and the ideal of the bourgeois human rights democracy, and thus setting up the historical momentum of the reality of minjung on that period. Consequently, the concept of minjung in minjung theology was not sufficient to integrate the modern history of Korean people and envision a new horizon for the future of Korean nation."[99]

Persistently claiming that the threefold concept of *minjok-minjung-women* should be treated as both the subjects and the main theme of the theology for national reunification, Park points out:

> Yet, considered the situation of division in which the imperial domination of Korea operates as the main source for the internal social contradictions of Korea, and considered the world situation in which the East is being absorbed into the West, the issue of the national reunification, by which our national sovereignty and subjectivity can be reclaimed, should be treated as the first and foremost task. *Minjok* as the subjects of reunification is the very subject of the Korean national liberation and at the same time is the short-cut to solve the problems involved the reality of minjung.[100]

Along with all these efforts, in the late 1990s another practical problem was raised by a few theologians in relation to the context of the minjung church movement. It was indicated as a problem that the theories, concepts, and languages that the minjung theologians of the 1980s used in terms of social scientific and ideological critical approaches were too

99. S. K. Park, "National Reunification," 56.
100. Ibid., 57.

foreign and unintelligible to the majority of minjung who belonged to minjung churches. Despite the appropriateness of such problematization, some of reactionary attempts to uncritically readopt the traditional languages and Christian religiosity turned out to be problematic when they assumed merely reactionary tendencies or obscured the necessity of the transformative praxis entailed in minjung theology. In addition, the disintegration of the socialist countries in the Eastern Europe and the ostensible transient economic growth in Korea has caused a kind of social anomie characterizing the confusion of theory and praxis.

However, the economic situation of Korean society at the turn of this century was determined by its subjection to international economic injustice done in the name of the IMF management system and to international violence and oppression done under the disguise of "globalization," that is, the transnational and imperial hegemony of Western monetary capitalism.[101] This should be discerned as "a sign of the time" which strongly warns against any delusion that the era of minjung is over, now begins the era of citizens differentiated from minjung. Furthermore, while it seems justifiable to reconceptualize the concept of minjung in more flexible, dynamic, and relational ways by considering not only the socio-economic aspect of oppression but also the cultural-political aspect of oppression,[102] such an effort should not be falling into the danger of diluting or obscuring the continuing social and theological struggles to reclaim the national identity of one Korea by recognizing the differences between South and North.

---

101. Since the Korean government accepted the IMF management system in December of 1997, several economists in Korea characterized the current economic situation as being subject to the neo-imperialism of the international banking capital. There have been a number of articles which have dealt with the deteriorating economic reality of Korean society as well as minjung. I did not have access to any article written in English by Korean economists. But, for the general economic situation that some Third World countries are facing under the IMF management system, see Chossudovsky, *Globalization of Poverty*. For an analysis of the Korean case, see his article in *The Economist* (December 13, 1997). Chossudovsky, who teaches economics at the University of Ottawa in Canada, recently visited Korea and presented a very similar analysis of the current economic reality of Korean society in an article entitled "Recolonization of Korea."

102. J. H. Kim, "A Genealogical Understanding," 6–29. This article is an attempt to articulate the historical and theological development by appropriating Foucault's theoretical discourses.

4.4. Hermeneutical Implications for This Study

It cannot be denied that minjung theology has discovered and taken the realities of the minjung, that is, the sufferings and struggles of the minjung in the Korean history and culture as a hermeneutical starting point for its theological praxis for the liberation of minjung. Such a hermeneutical principle has been unquestioned and continued to be sustained and developed. Foregrounding minjung as the hermeneutical key, minjung theologians were able to make two crucial points. On the one hand, by claiming that the minjung are the subjects of history, minjung theologians have come to see and affirm that minjung have what Latin American libration theology called "the epistemological privilege of the poor."[103] Closely related to the first point, the second point is that minjung theologians redefined the meaning of doing theology as a "preferential option for minjung,"[104] which is also called "the partiality for minjung."[105] In other words, minjung theology is a committed theology which takes sides with the oppressed, exploited, and marginalized people in Korea. These hermeneutical grids demonstrate the remarkable similarities found in other liberation theologies, especially in Latin America and South Africa, although each theology has come out of its particular historical and cultural context.

As for the relationship between minjung theology and the Bible, what is the most striking is that enormous efforts have been concentrated on rediscovering the relationship between Jesus and minjung in the first-century Galilee and the meaning of the Jesus event (movements) as the minjung movement for the kingdom of God in this world. It would not be too bold to say that apart from works of reinterpreting the exodus event in the Hebrew Bible, most studies of the New Testament in minjung theology have been devoted to reconstructing the study of the historical Jesus from the perspective of minjung. Some factors which contributed to this state can be detected. Above all, Ahn Byung Mu as one of the founding minjung theologians and a New Testament scholar came to have great influence on new studies of the historical Jesus, which is quite different from the renewed quest for the historical Jesus among North American scholarship during the last decades.

---

103. Segundo, *The Liberation of Theology*.

104. See Kang, "A New Search for Theological Hermeneutic"; C. N. Kim, "The Significance of Minjung."

105. J. H. Kim, "Minjung as the Subject of History," 21–47.

Theoretical and Hermeneutical Perspectives on Difference

More importantly, another factor is related to the critical stance of minjung theology toward the conservative understanding of the Bible prevailing in the majority of Korean churches and Christians. Kim Chang Nack points out three kinds of the use of the Bible that minjung theology should reject: the use of the Bible as the proof for doctrinal justification; the use of the Bible for the purpose of mere consolation and pious life style; and the use of the Bible as an answer for existential question.[106] Individualistic, pietistic, doctrinal, introspective, ahistorical, and apolitical understandings of the Bible have been overwhelmingly dominant in the Korean church with great focus on the Christ of faith. The understanding of religion as an entity separate from politics has also served to consolidate the Korean church's complicity in anti-communist ideology strongly promoted by the military regimes in Korea.

Thus, it is understandable that biblical scholars following the lead of Ahn Byung Mu have sought to distance the meaning of the historical Jesus and the Jesus movement from the early Christian understanding of the Christ of the kerygma. Their agenda was to underscore the political hermeneutics involved in the Jesus movement as minjung movement and to liberate Korean Christians (therefore, Jesus and the Bible) from enslavement to the individualistic, universalizing, and apolitical Western Christianity and biblical interpretations.

Based upon such hermeneutical assumptions, some scholars have focused on the problematic of Western historical criticism in order to pursue a biblical hermeneutics of minjung theology.[107] The critique of the Western historical criticism by minjung theologians was centered on its idealist epistemological framework and the claim of value-free objectivity. Hence, scholars have adopted biblical criticisms such as socio-historical, and sociological, and particularly materialistic approaches to the Bible. Yet, it should be pointed out that much more elaboration in terms of methods and reading strategies is needed for a biblical hermeneutics of minjung theology. Particularly, there are methodological problems entailed in minjung theology's reading of the political hermeneutics of the historical Jesus. I agree with Ched Myers's remark in his analysis of the liberation hermeneutics of Latin American theologians, although he acknowledges its significant contributions and strong influence upon his political reading of the Gospel of Mark: "Ironically, the very strength of liberation hermeneutics has mired it

---

106. C. N. Kim, "The Significance of Minjung," 150–51.
107. See especially the articles of Kim and Kang in n. 104 above.

in methodological problems. Although rightly rejecting the existentializing hermeneutics of Western biblical scholarship, their attempts to 'rehabilitate the historical Jesus' have tended to repeat the mistakes of earlier historicist studies."[108] Myers goes on to say that "the problem of historicism is central to a political hermeneutics that would be historically grounded, but no real solution has been offered by liberation theology."[109]

Myer's criticism may be equally applied to minjung theology's emphasis upon and reading of the historical Jesus. For example, despite his professed theoretical break with the positivistic approach underlying Western biblical scholarship of the historical Jesus—including both the "old" and the "new" quests, Ahn's reconstruction of the historical praxis of Jesus repeats the "new quest" which attempted a "historical reconstruction by trying to rigorously separate 'kerygma' from 'history.'"[110] Ahn does not use the notion of historicity in terms of historicity or authenticity of texts. Instead, Ahn differentiates the Jesus event from kerygma. On the one hand, by the Jesus event is meant certain events related to Jesus' public and collective (with the minjung of the first-century Palestine) activities, for example, such as Jesus' suffering and being executed. On the other hand, by kerygma is meant the early church's interpretation on the meaning of Jesus' death and resurrection. According to Ahn, the reason why the priority should be given to "history" over "kerygma" is that the kerygma has dehistoricized the Jesus-event mainly for the apologetic sake of ecclesiastical survival or apostolic authority.[111] Furthermore, Ahn has proposed a hypothesis that the main bearers of the Jesus event tradition were the very minjung who followed Jesus and witnessed Jesus' activities, and that the minjung passed on the Jesus event tradition (not the kerygma tradition) by telling stories in the form of "rumors." However insightful it may be, Ahn's reconstruction of the historical Jesus reveals a tendency of universalizing in that the diverse traditions about the historical Jesus were treated as if they represented a uniform tradition of minjung.

What is more important is that the dichotomy between the Jesus event tradition (= the Jesus movement) and the kerygma tradition (= early Christian communities, including Paul) is an unwarranted oversimplification. We

---

108. Myers, *Binding the Strong Man*, 464.

109. Ibid., 465.

110. Ibid. Myers defines such attempt as "insistence upon distinguishing the prepaschal and postpaschal tradition—the new quest in a new guise."

111. Ahn, "The Body of Transmission," 229–55.

need to differentiate the significance of early Christian kerygmatic formulations from what has been established later in the "tradition of theological hermeneutics," where "the *kerygma* thus becomes the domain of abstract thought or 'spiritual' reflection—that is, the domain of the theologians!"[112] Biblical scholars of minjung theology tend to interpret Paul's sayings or thoughts separately from his activities, which stands in contradiction to their approach to the historical Jesus. Sharing some of the widespread assumptions about Paul's thought they tend to hear Paul's voice as the voice of oppression, not as that of liberation. As Neil Elliott remarks, "The Paul we hear has been thoroughly depoliticized, the social and political dimensions of his work have been suppressed, and a narrow band of theological tones has been amplified, even to the point where a phrases like 'the politics of Paul' may strike us immediately as nonsensical."[113]

Although Paul never used the term ὄχλος in his letters, it cannot be denied that there were so many people, whom Paul often identifies as those who were treated unequally and differently because of their differences in race, class, and gender. Whether minjung theologians call them "minjung" or not, they constituted the majority of the cell communities to which Paul and his fellow workers ministered in the midst of the Roman imperial power. Moreover, the heterogeneous composition and historical particularities of the Pauline communities call us for a relational and contextual—but, not relativistic—understanding of "difference." In this vein, it should be critically interrogated whether Paul's extending inclusivity and reciprocity beyond the Jewish people, particularly through the meal practice of table fellowship, can be interpreted within the well-established scholarly framework of Christian "universalism" versus Jewish "particularism" and "ethnocentrism." The problem is that both scholars who are in favor of Paul and those who are challenging Paul ground their interpretations of Paul upon such a universalizing and essentializing framework. It has eventually served not only for "the dejudaization of Paul" but also for "the theological marginalization of Paul's politics."[114]

In the final analysis, if theologians and biblical scholars of minjung theology in Korea, like theologians of liberation in other contexts, correctly have come to redefine the starting point and meaning of doing theology as the practical reflection upon the concrete historical reality of the oppressed

---

112. Myers, *Binding the Strong Man*, 9.
113. N. Elliott, *Liberating Paul*, 57.
114. Especially see ibid., 55–90.

and poor, is it not the time for minjung theologians to seriously ask whether Paul was not doing something similar?

If Paul strenuously struggled for reconciliation and unity between Jew and Gentile among the early Christians within the first-century Roman imperial context, is it not the time to attend to Paul's politics of difference so that South-Korean Christians may be empowered to participate in the struggle for reunification of Korea by recognizing the difference between North and South, by building solidarity with the people of North Korea, and thus by reclaiming our national identity divided and suppressed within the imperial context of the last century?

CONCLUSION

I have sketched some of current theoretical and hermeneutical frameworks which need to be discussed with respect to the issue of "difference." Postmodern critique of the logic of identity offers a radical criticism against the mastery of hierarchy underlying Western philosophical tradition and culture. It has problematized and unearthed a Western philosophical framework in which certain categories of notions and groups of people were attributed, subjected, and suppressed as "difference," or the "Other." The particular targets were the tendency of universalizing the self and that of essentializing the other in the Western philosophical discourses. The undisputable contribution of the postmodern criticism is that it has drawn attention to the significance of the historical contingency in all forms of knowledge and culture. The question of "difference" lies at the center of the postmodern respect of "the particular and the local." However, the postmodernist deconstruction of "the grand narratives" of Western history and decentering of the subject does not allow much room for the difference that a denied subjectivity can make.

On the other hand, Iris Marion Young's critical articulation of the politics of difference is helpful in reminding us of the differential meanings of difference, that is, essentializing difference and emancipatory difference. An emancipatory politics of difference challenges an ideal of justice that defines liberation as the transcendence of group difference, and it affirms group difference. I have pointed out that such a politics of difference requires a relational and contextual understanding of difference, which I will appropriate for the study of the Jew-Gentile difference within Pauline communities with focus on Galatians and Romans. Then the question is, relational and contextual to what?

I drew attention to feminist and postcolonial approaches to the problem of difference in order to highlight the political agendas and implications involved in the discourses on difference. In feminist discourses, gender difference is regarded both as the main cause of patriarchal and sexist oppression of women and at the same time the main resource for the struggle for women's liberation. By foregrounding the agency of a denied subjectivity, that is, women as difference, the feminist/womanist criticism has moved the issue of difference into the realms of social and political action. Yet, the problematic of universalism and essentialism inherent within the feminist discourses revealed that gender difference cannot be dealt with separately from other differences such as race and class.

Postcolonialism has brought the reality of empire to the fore, challenging any Western claim to "universality" in colonial forms of knowledge and culture. Thus, like feminism, postcolonialism is committed to work to assert and affirm a denied or alienated subjectivity, and submerged history and culture. Drawing on the postcolonial framework, biblical scholars seek to decolonize the imperialist assumption that the Bible and biblical interpretations are innocent of the oppression and violence done by the empires in ancient and modern worlds. Blindness to the matter of "empire" with respect to the Bible and biblical interpretations has served to re-colonize the minds and spirits of a once colonized or subjugated people.

Furthermore, considering my own particular context I tried to rearticulate the question of "difference" in connection with the historical sufferings of Korean minjung and their political struggles for justice and liberation. Like feminism and postcolonialism, talking about difference in Korean context is about minjung as the subjects of history in the divided nation. Minjung, the oppressed and poor in Korea, encompass the differences in class, race, gender, and empire. This demonstrates that the emancipatory politics of difference involves a complex, dynamic, and ongoing process of noticing and negotiating differences with respect to race, class, gender, and empire. Drawing upon the theoretical and hermeneutical considerations I have discussed in this chapter, and recognizing that the Bible becomes a site of struggles for an identity and for self-determination, I will devote the following chapters to the study of the Jew-Gentile difference as it evolved within Pauline communities.

3

Difference and Greco-Roman Meals

DESPITE THE ENORMOUS CONCERN among scholars of early Christianity(ies) for the social context of various social and theological forms of diverse Christian groups, it is a recent phenomenon that serious attention has been drawn to meal practices in which members of early Christian groups engaged. Emphasis on meal practice as an immediate and important context of early Christian social formation derives from, or is related to, at least two aspects of which recent scholarship has become more aware in efforts to re-imagine the beginnings of early Christianity.[1]

The first aspect has to do with the existence of various associations in the first-century Greco-Roman world. It is known that between the individual and the Roman state there were a considerable number of associations, e.g., collegia, clubs, guilds, philosophical schools, which were formed to meet various needs of the members of such groups. Members of these groups gathered regularly for their interests and purposes. In this regard, early Christian groups, particularly those within the social map of the Mediterranean world, do not appear to be uniquely different from other associations. The emergence of voluntary associations during the historical period when early Christian groups began to appear is a social phenomenon

---

1. For the scholarship on early Christian meal practice see Smith, "Social Obligation"; Smith, *From Symposium to Eucharist*; Smith and Taussig, *Many Tables*; Taussig, *In the Beginning Was the Meal*; Corley, *Private Women*; Theissen, *Social Setting*; Jewett, "Tenement Churches"; Klinghardt, *Gemeinschaftsmahl*; Taussig, "Dealing under the Table"; Lampe, "The Eucharist"; Mack, *Who Wrote the New Testament?*, 75–79; Crossan, *The Birth of Christianity*, 423–80.

Difference and Greco-Roman Meals

which allows one to see at least an analogous relationship between the early Christian groups and other voluntary associations, even if the relationship does not mean that one derives from the other.[2] Of course this does not mean that early Christian movements were a totally Hellenistic phenomenon, separate from Jewish origins. Rather, it emphasizes the comparative similarities which first-century Jewish and early Christian groups shared with other Greco-Roman social and religious groups, and which led their social formation to appear in the eyes of their neighbors and outsiders as comparable to various clubs and associations.

The second aspect is closely, but not exclusively, related to the first. It has been recognized that the most common feature in gathering at those social and religious associations, including Christian and Jewish groups, was common meals.[3] In fact, the common meal tradition itself was deeply and widely embedded in the social and cultural milieu of Greco-Roman societies. The common meal tradition or the Greco-Roman banquet tradition was "a complex and important social institution" in the ancient world to be adopted, accommodated, and assimilated into a variety of different contexts with different interpretations.[4]

On the basis of available textual evidence, this chapter demonstrates how social differences among those who participated in meals were noticed, marked, and further negotiated. Although the so-called Greco-Roman symposia literature contains discourse on egalitarian, homogeneous table-fellowship in a somewhat idealized manner, it betrays that in practice formal meals were often structured by hierarchies of class and gender in Greco-Roman society. For example, Greco-Roman banquet customs exhibit differences in posture and position, and in the portions and quality of food distributed at meals. What types of posture and order of seating were

---

2. For the renewed attention to the phenomenon of voluntary associations as a comparative socio-cultural context for the study of social realities of Jewish and early Christian groups in the first centuries of the Mediterranean world, see especially articles in Kloppenborg and Wilson, eds., *Voluntary Associations*.

3. Although first-century Jewish meal custom might manifest specific differences, I consider Jewish meal practice to be part of the broader Greco-Roman common meal tradition, and that as such Jewish meal practices largely followed the general formal patterns of Greco-Roman meals. This consideration is based upon the work of Dennis Smith, Matthias Klinghardt, and Hal Taussig on the Greco-Roman meal tradition, which will be reviewed in this chapter. Thus, Jewish meal traditions will not be discussed as a separate topic. Rather, my discussion of Jewish meal traditions will be centered on the issue of Jewish-Gentile difference at table-fellowship in the following two chapters.

4. Smith and Taussig, *Many Tables*, 21–23.

people supposed to assume at meals? Who reclines or sits where? Who gets more or finer food? All such considerations mattered in the production of a part of social construct. Such differences at meals not only reflect social differences marked by the social categories of status, class, and gender, but also often contradict the convivial fellowship of equality, harmony, and unity that is highly valued and stressed in the symposia literature such as Plutarch's Table-Talk. Before we deal with the issue of "difference" at meals, we need to look briefly at how the ideal of equality is depicted and discussed in some literary materials.

1. EQUALITY AND MEAL

What do people expect at a common meal? What can a common meal provide for the participants? It is axiomatic that when people gather for a communal meal, they want to eat with good cheer and conviviality. This was true in antiquity as well as in the modern world. Though usually taken for granted, it is important to note that meals tend to invite people to expect something different from what they experience in ordinary social relations. Certainly, it has something to do with the function of common meals to promote a horizontal or egalitarian ethos. Greco-Roman literature on table-fellowship enables us to grasp such a horizontal ethos by providing discourses on "proper meals" (συμποτικά) in its somewhat idealized literary construct. Even satire literature such as Lucian's *Symposium* affords us the opportunity to glimpse a proper meal, paradoxically, through its sharp criticism of the excesses of banquet customs. Furthermore, a small number of communities, like the Epicurian school and the Jewish Therapeutic society, engaged in social experiments of the communal nature of the ideal meal. Their actual community meals exhibit a kind of social equality.

Although the Greco-Roman banquet custom did not derive from a direct concern for social equality, one way to look at this issue at meals is to consider main themes promoted in the literary construction of "a proper meal." Above all, the portraits of the proper meal characterize the essential elements as (1) the communal nature of meal fellowship, (2) the meal as promoting friendship, and (3) the lowering of social barriers.[5] These elements are implicitly, sometimes even explicitly, related to the question of social equality.

---

5. See Smith, "Social Obligation," 39–73; D'Arm, "Roman Convivium," 308–20.

First, the Greco-Roman symposia literature profiles ideal meals in various ways to emphasize and define the communal nature of table-fellowship. There is no doubt that the communal nature of meals serves to promote social bonding and community solidarity among participants. The communal nature of the meal was often defined in terms of the symbolism of "common participation (ἡ συμποτικὴ κοινωνία)" at the table.[6] The general symbolism of common participation was expressed by common sharing of the wine bowl or a common food platter, and common participation was also emphasized in proper conversation, which was considered an indispensable part of the Greco-Roman symposium. Thus Plutarch says: "Indeed, just as the wine must be common to all, so too the conversation must be one in which all will share."[7]

Certainly the symbolism of common participation, often associated with the metaphor of "one" or "oneness," is a general and broad concept. It could extend to other aspects of meal practice including the order of seating and the quality and quantity of food. Thus, it is not surprising that the symbolism of common participation presupposes a sense of social equality, occasionally triggering debates among participants over these issues. For example in Plutarch, at the table Timon raises his voice in defense of social equality against "transferring empty fame and vanity from agora and theatre to the symposium": "If in other matters we are to preserve equality among men, why not begin with this first and accustom them to take their places with each other without vanity and ostentation, because they understand as soon as they enter the door that *the dinner is a democratic affair* and has no outstanding place like an acropolis where the rich man is to recline and lord it over meaner folk?"[8]

Here Timon advocates social equality with respect to the order of seating. The meal is characterized as an outstandingly communal place for the practice of equality in striking contrast to other places which privilege hierarchical social differences. Juvenal also draws upon a full range of equality language in describing a convivial gathering attended by the consul Lateranus: "There is indeed equal liberty, shared cups, no separate couch for any nor table set apart for any."[9] Again, equality is tightly linked to the communal nature of meals expressed by shared implements and facilities.

6. Plutarch, *Quaest. conv.* 615A.
7. Ibid., 614E.
8. Ibid. (my emphasis).
9. Juvenal, *Sat.* 8.177–78.

Second, as Dennis Smith and others have noted, terms such as φιλία, φιλοφροσύνη, εὐνοία, κοινωνία, and other similar terms are used to characterize the communal nature of table fellowship.[10] The friend-making character of the table (τὸ φιλοποιὸν τῆς τραπέζης) is described as follows: "A guest comes to share not only meat, wine, and dessert, but conversation, fun, and the amicability that leads to friendship."[11] This also is reminiscent of what Cicero says to his close and cultivated friend who had given up attending dinner parties in order to persuade him to change his mind:

> Really, Paetus, I advise you, as something which I regard as relevant to happiness, to spend time in honest, pleasant, and friendly company. Nothing becomes life better, or is more in harmony with its happy living. I am not thinking of physical pleasure, but of community life and habit and of mental recreation, of which familiar conversation is the most effective agent; and conversation is at its most agreeable at dinner-parties. In this respect our countrymen are wiser that the Greeks. They use words meaning literally "co-drinkings" or "co-dinings" (*symposia, syndeipna*) but we say "co-livings" (*convivial*) because at dinner-parties more than anywhere else life is lived in company.[12]

Rather than language expressive of equality, Cicero uses terms such as happiness, harmony, and pleasure, thus making explicit the link between *convivia* and *amicitia*. It is difficult, however, to know the extent to which the friendship-making character of the dinner party actually provided equal social relations among the co-diners.

Third, Smith shows how expressions of friendship at the table in the Greco-Roman philosophical tradition function as a source for ethics, inasmuch as instances of friendship define "the nature of the social obligation of the participants in the meal toward one another."[13] Thus, under the rubric of friendship at the table, aspects of meal etiquette and corresponding social obligation could be discussed in the setting of a meal.[14] To illustrate, there are discussions about the proper seating position and proper

---

10. Smith, "Social Obligation," 51; Klinghardt, *Gemeinschaftsmahl*, 153–74.
11. Plutarch, *Quaest. conv.* 660B.
12. Cicero, *Fam.* 9.24.3.
13. Smith, "Social Obligation," 51.
14. Ibid., 49–52.

Difference and Greco-Roman Meals

distribution of food in which emphasis falls on the ethical principles of φιλοφροσύνη and ἡδονή.[15]

The symbolism of common participation and the topic of friendship in Greco-Roman symposia literature do not necessarily presuppose the ideal of equality, though they could often imply it. Aspects of social bonding and social obligation were certainly operative and served to establish a sense of unity at a common meal. Although this helps to interpret common meal practice as an entity to itself apart from social reality outside the meal, tension between social stratification and social equality was virtually constant at common meals. Moreover, the common meal tradition could function as a replication of social reality outside of meals by encoding social differences in rank and status of the participants.[16] Tensions between equality and difference at meals were not entirely solved even in communities that show tendencies toward the ideal of social equality.

In a treatise entitled *On the Contemplative Life*, the first-century CE Jewish philosopher Philo of Alexandria gives a lengthy descript of a Jewish monastic community living near Lake Mareotis outside Alexandria. An important feature of the community's life was the practice of a communal meal. The members of the Jewish Therapeutic community celebrated a feast that some interpreters take to be Pentecost (*Shavuot*, the feast of weeks), others a feast celebrated every seven weeks as a sabbath of the sabbath, or even two feasts, one celebrated on the forty-ninth day, another on the fiftieth.[17] The precise identity of the meal aside, Philo implies weekly gatherings with prayer, spoken word (including interpretation of the Law), and a communal meal to which may be added his description of another major feast. He writes about the meals of the Therapeutics on three occasions (*Contemplative Life*, 30–37; 67–74; 81–82). Interestingly, the meal follows prayer and spoken word whereas in the symposium tradition, discussion follows the meal. The community consists of both men (Therapeutae) and women (Therapeutrides), though most of the latter are referred to as "aged virgins," all of whom gather together, praying, eating, singing, and drinking until dawn.[18] In his description of the festal gathering, Philo draws a sharp contrast with Greek and Roman meals (*Contemplative Life*, 48–63). Further, in spite of his conventional lower regard for women than for men,

15. Ibid., 51.
16. Ibid., 68–73.
17. See Klinghardt, *Gemeinschaftsmahl*, 189–90.
18. Philo, *Contemplative Life*, 64–82.

he emphatically describes the way both men and women participate in the common meal:

> The feast is shared by women also, most of them aged virgins, who have kept their chastity not under compulsion, like some of the Greek priestesses but of their own free will in their ardent yearning for wisdom. Eager to have her for their life mate they have spurned the pleasure of the body and desire no mortal offspring but those immortal children which only the soul that is dear to God can bring to birth unaided because the Father has sown in her spiritual rays enabling her to behold the verities of wisdom ... The order of reclining is so apportioned that the men sit by themselves on the right and the women by themselves on the left.[19]

Although it is possible to suggest that most of the Therapeutrides—the post-menopausal, childless, unmarried women—were no longer considered as female in the eyes of Philo and others,[20] they nevertheless actively participated in the communal meal with the Therapeutae, and that in spite of sitting on the left apart from the men on the right, they nevertheless assumed a reclining posture at the meal. Given the probability that "women, with few exceptions if any, sat separately from men in ancient synagogues throughout the Roman Empire,"[21] Philo's reference to a similar practice in the Therapeutic meals is hardly surprising. Further, Philo relates that both men and women reclined according to their seniority based on the time of their entry into the community. Although this order of reclining implies some differences in rank among the members, and although there were probably special seats of honor, it is unclear whether such an order determined by seniority represented a hierarchical structure in the community. Philo comments explicitly on the distinctiveness of seniority in the Therapeutic society—the nature of seniority was determined by the degree of maturity "in pursuing the contemplative branch of philosophy," rather than by "the aged and grey headed" (*Contemplative Life*, 87). In addition, in the community meal the simplest and purest food is assigned to the priests. But it is likely that the members of the Therapeutic society did not see such differences in arrangements as an obstacle to the unity of the community.

An additional significant feature in the Therapeutic feast is its striking stance against slavery. Philo writes: "They do not have slaves to wait upon

---

19. Ibid., 68–69.
20. See Kraemer, "Monastic Jewish," esp. 351–56.
21. Mattila, "Where Women Sat," 279.

them as they consider that the ownership of servants is entirely against nature. For nature has borne all men to be free, but the wrongful and covetous acts of some who pursued that source of evil, inequality, have imposed their yoke and invested the stronger (δυνατωτέροις) with power over the weaker (ἀσθενεστέροις)."[22]

Thus, servicing at the banquet was performed not by slave but by free young men chosen for their special virtue: "They give their services gladly and proudly like sons to their real fathers and mothers, judging them to be the parents of them all in common, in a closer affinity than that of blood, since to the right minded there is no closer tie than noble living."[23]

Finally, after the supper, the Therapeutae and Therapeutrides held a sacred vigil which consisted mostly of singing hymns to God. They formed themselves into two choirs, one of men and one of women, performing an enthusiastic and dramatic singing of hymns to God. At the climax of the symposium, having drunk "the strong wine of God's love," they mixed and both became a single choir, "a copy of the choir set up of old beside the Red Sea in honor of the wonders there wrought."[24]

To summarize, the discussion up until now has focused on an important aspect in the Greco-Roman meal tradition, on the basis of evidence from the rhetoric of meals and from actual common meals gleaned from the limited sources. That is, the question of social equality was embedded in or evoked from—implicitly or explicitly—the rhetoric of Greco-Roman meals, especially in its tradition of a "proper meal." Further, we have seen that such an ideal meal did not function merely on the rhetorical level, but was often acted out at actual meals of different social groups. Moreover, it has become clear that the issue of equality at meals is directly linked to the question of difference, that is, how to cope with and negotiate social differences at meals—differences in class, gender, and culture. This leads us to the question: What can we say about differences at Greco-Roman meals? What differences were at stake, and how were they negotiated? These questions are the concern of the following section.

---

22. Philo, *Contemplative Life*, 71.
23. Ibid., 72.
24. Ibid., 85.

2. DIFFERENCE AND MEAL

2.1. Difference in Meal Posture

In the late Republican and early imperial period of Rome, the typical posture at formal meals whatever their settings was reclining on a couch.[25] Reclining at table can be traced as far back as the sixth century BCE, and it became a standardized custom of meals across the Mediterranean world among Greeks, Romans, and Jews.[26] The observation of the common reclining at table has led Dennis Smith, who perhaps initiated the study of early Christian communal meals within the comparative context of the Greco-Roman banquet, to define the social convention of the Greco-Roman banquet as the "common meal tradition."[27] According to Smith, a change in meal posture from sitting to reclining was accompanied by changes in other conventions that also came to be standardized and shared in common.[28] For instance, as Smith observes, reclining at table was "a posture appropriate to a leisurely mean, which the δεῖπνον had become when it was moved to the evening hour."[29]

Although the situation which might have precipitated such a change in meal posture is not clear, the custom of reclining at table reflected an aspect of Greco-Roman aristocratic life, which was not accessible to the majority of lower class people. Reflecting on his life indulged in the table fellowship with his social equals, Cicero explicitly connects reclining at table along with the pleasure of shared friendship and conversation with the convivial ethos of the Roman aristocratic banquet:

> I have always had my club companions . . . I used to dine with these companions—in an all together moderate way, yet with a certain ardour appropriate to my age, which, as time goes on, daily mitigates my zest for every pleasure. Nor, indeed, did I measure my delight in these social gatherings more by the physical pleasure than by the pleasure of meeting and conversing with my friends. For our fathers did well in calling *the reclining of friends at feasts* as a *convivium*, because it implies a communion of life . . . and every

---

25. Smith, "Social Obligation," 33–37; Smith and Taussig, *Many Tables*, 22–23; Corley, *Private Women*, 28.
26. Smith, "Social Obligation," 5–6.
27. Ibid., esp. 38.
28. Ibid., 5–23.
29. Ibid., 6.

day I join my neighbors in a social meal which we protract as late as we can into the night with talk on varying themes.[30]

Noticeably, "the reclining of friends at feasts" to which Cicero referred did not include women, children, and slaves. Slaves prepared the food and served at meals, and in fact reclining requires some people to serve those who recline. In this sense, the Greco-Roman banquet as a social institution was certainly built upon social relations between slaves and their owners and reinforced hierarchical social differences.

In the case of women, Roman customs in the first century shows a somewhat more complicated situation reflecting some changes from earlier practice. It is well known that the earlier Greek customs did not allow women to recline at table. Like children and slaves, women were to sit when they ate. Some change occurred, however, especially during the first century BCE and the first century CE. Roman history during that period evidences some changes regarding the role and status of women in society in general, including their participation, posture, and attitude at formal meals. Indeed some women of higher status participated in formal meals and assumed the posture of reclining.[31] Part of this evidence attesting such a change comes from Cornelius Nepos in the first century BCE: "On the other hand, many actions are seemly according to our code which the Greeks look upon as shameful. For instance, what Roman would hesitate to take his wife to a dinner party? What matron does not frequent the front rooms of her dwelling and show herself in public? But it is very different in Greece; for there a woman is not admitted to a dinner party, unless relatives only are present, and she keeps to the more retired part of the house called 'the women's apartment.'"[32]

Scholars have pointed out that such an enhancement of women's participation at formal meals should be considered as a ramification of the changing atmosphere regarding women's role and status.[33] It seems that more opportunities in the public sphere were accessible to women than before. As Cornelius Nepos's statement above indicates, the Hellenistic ideology which maintained the dichotomy between the public man and the

30. Cicero, *Sen.* 13.45—14.46.
31. Smith, "Social Obligation," 34–35; Corley, *Private Women*, 24–33.
32. Cornelius Nepos, *Praef.* 6–7.
33. Corley, *Private Women*, 24–79 ("in the late Republican and early imperial time, aspects of Greco-Roman meal etiquette were undergoing changes, changes which reflected larger cultural forces throughout Greco-Roman society" [24]).

private woman began to become more relaxed. Gender differences which had long been imposed on and prescribed for women in antiquity were being negotiated precisely within the meal setting. The relatively advanced position for women in the first century, however, was not solidly established; rather it was still very limited and fragile.

With respect to the relationship between women at meals and early Christian communities, Kathleen Corley's *Private Women, Public Meals: Social Conflict in the Synoptic Tradition* deserves particular attention. In the first part of her book, Corley places women in early Christianity and early Christian communal meals within the broad context of Greco-Roman meals, and in the second part she presents a careful investigation of women and meals in the Synoptic Gospels. She seeks to bring together "insights from the fields of Christian feminism, classical social history and social anthropology in order to create a new context within which to understand the portrayal of women in the Synoptic Gospels."[34]

Corley is largely concerned with the social functions of meals, that is, how meal patterns and customs function within the larger society. Drawing on Mary Douglas's work on food and meals, Corley holds that "meal customs reflect and symbolize a culture's social and political relationships."[35] She postulates close correlations between meal structures and the overall structure of society and stresses the social conservatism of meal practice inasmuch as meals function to maintain and stabilize the hierarchical social structure and power relations. Because of such a conservative character of meals, which resist innovation, Corley contends that "innovation in meal practice generally undermines the basic social constructs and relations of a society."[36] She appropriates these two aspects of correlation with social structures and social conservatism into her interpretive framework and focuses on the question of women at Greco-Roman and early Christian meals within a larger Greco-Roman social context, especially in light of Greco-Roman social ideology surrounding women's roles and behavior.

According to Corley, during the Roman period, meal customs were undergoing some changes mainly due to new developments in social and political relationships in Greco-Roman society. These changes affected women's participation in formal meals and meal etiquette itself: ". . . so that women from various social strata began to attend public meals—a behavior

34. Ibid., 21.
35. Ibid., xvi.
36. Ibid.

Difference and Greco-Roman Meals

formerly associated with lower-class women, prostitutes, and slaves."[37] Wives especially participated more in some formal meals. Wives were even allowed to recline at the table with their husbands, which was almost impossible during the former Hellenistic period in Greek society. However, the dominant Greco-Roman social ideology concerning women's role and status in society, according to Corley, was reluctant to accept such an innovative inclusivity, eventuating in social criticism and resistance against it by various means of restricting and excluding women from participation in public meals.

Although some matrons or women as patrons of cultic associations could recline at meals, especially in Rome of the first century CE, the number of women who actually did so is difficult to ascertain. We may surmise that in reality very few reclined at either public or private meals. Moreover, even when they reclined at meals, they hardly seem to have reclined alongside their husbands, especially at public banquets. Rather, a normal expectation would be that they recline with other women or on women's couches separated from the space reserved for men.[38] It was possible for women to recline next to their husbands at meals in the home. But even in that case, most women would not sit next to their husbands in consideration that unexpected guests might come.[39] Furthermore, some women of high status who participated in dinner parties with their husbands did not remain for the drinking part (συμπόσιον) after the meal proper (δεῖπνον) was over, which may be said to constitute an even more important part of the Greco-Roman banquet.[40] Hence, a range of limitations restricted women's participation in and reclining at formal meals.

By contrast, prostitutes, flute girls, or hetaerae, that is, high-class prostitutes were expected, even required, to remain during the συμπόσιον in order to entertain male participants and to enhance the commensality of the men. These women were allowed to recline next to men and were required further to satisfy men's sexual desires.[41] These prostitutes in antiquity, just as in the case of prostitutes today, were actually forced to enjoy freedom to gain access to public space. Like slaves, their freedom to be in public, that

---

37. Ibid., xxi.

38. Ibid., 24–31. For a similar pattern for seating in ancient synagogues see Mattila, "Where Women Sat," 266–86.

39. Corley, *Private Women*, 26.

40. Ibid.

41. Ibid., 25–28.

is, "available to all" was not their choice but the consequence of birth and the product of a social hierarchical economy. These "public" women in contradistinction from public men were differentiated from "private" women, so to say, respectable women. Corley has shown that such a distinction between public women and private women was grounded on the Greco-Roman social ideology which defined the gender difference primarily by the public/private dichotomy and restricted women to the private sphere. Corley has argued correctly that despite some changes that occurred during the early Roman period, such traditional ideology involving women's roles and behavior continued to affect the participation of Roman women in public meals. Furthermore, Corley has attempted to demonstrate that early Christian women at their community meals as reflected in the Synoptic Gospels were not only influenced by the changing cultural ethos of the time but were also restricted by the recurring social ideology against the egalitarian inclusion of women in conviviality in public meals.

As long as social ideology continued to reinforce and stabilize the hierarchical dichotomy between public men and private women, the latter experienced difficulty in crossing boundaries into the public sphere. They could not easily take the risk of being labeled "public" women by reclining next to men at meals and remaining during the συμπόσιον. "Women who had freer access to the 'public' realm were generally courtesans, household slaves, and prostitutes."[42] Therefore, it may not be erroneous to suggest that the number of women who could actually assume the posture of reclining and dining with men was very limited. This would explain how Lucian in the second century CE could still refer to the posture of sitting at table as "womanish and weak" (γυναικεῖος καὶ μαλθακόν).[43]

Meal posture in Greco-Roman banquets was different not only with respect to free men and slaves, and not only with respect to men and women, it varied also among women depending on social class and status. Although changes in posture and negotiations of difference in meals were underway, in Greco-Roman banquets gender and social distinctions persisted in most formal meals. At this point, a hermeneutical issue needs to be raised. Differences that were noticed with respect to the posture of reclining at a meal were socially arranged and hierarchically structured. In most case, those differences were not arranged by women, slaves, and children, i.e., the socially weak, but by the socially strong. Particularly to the latter, difference

---

42. Ibid., 16.
43. Lucian, *Symp.* 13.

Difference and Greco-Roman Meals

mattered for the sustenance of the status quo of the hierarchical society. It is hardly surprising to note that Plutarch makes precisely this point:

> A dinner party is a sharing of earnest and jest, of words and deeds; so the diners must not be left to chance, but must be such as are friends and intimates of one another who will enjoy being together. Cooks make up their dishes of a variety of flavors, blending the sour, the oily, the sweet, and the pungent, but you could not get good and agreeable company at dinner by throwing together men who are different in their associations and sympathies.[44]

The passage clearly shows that along with the emphasis on sharing in a dinner party, there was a tendency to avoid mixing together people of different class, rank, and status. In such a tendency, the same status or homogeneity of the participants at a meal was privileged over differences which were assumed as disturbing the homogeneity or unity of table fellowship. Thus, the question of difference, depending on whose perspective determines difference, is closely linked to the perception of superior/inferior or inclusion/exclusion.

Despite deep concern with respect to the homogeneity of table fellowship that is pervasive in symposia discourses in Greco-Roman literature, there were various situations in which the homogeneity could be disrupted. Matthias Klinghardt especially has drawn attention to the question of homogeneity at both private and association meals, and he challenges the widely accepted hypothesis that association meals in the Greco-Roman period maintained a considerable degree of homogeneity.[45]

With respect to participants at meals, Klinghardt notes the presence of particular types of meal participants of which Plutarch's lengthy discussion is helpful evidence. These three types are named as the uninvited guest, the belated guest, and the secondary guest. First, the uninvited guest (ἄκλητος) is the one who comes to the meal scene without being invited, that is, as a parasite. While the uninvited guest could play a harmless role as an amusing entertainer, that person—as a jester or critical cynic—often disturbed the homogeneous sentiment of the meal. Second, there is the belated guest as a particular type of the uninvited guest. Although Plato and Plutarch do not depict the belated guest as disturbing the general atmosphere of the meal, the probability that such a person would receive a subordinate place in the order of seating could jeopardize the unity of the table fellowship.

---

44. *Quaest. conv.* VII.6.708.
45. *Gemeinschaftsmahl*, esp. 84–97.

Third, there is the secondary guest (ἐπίκλητος) who comes to the meal not by invitation of the host himself but by the invitation of another guest who had been invited by the host. Again, Plutarch's detailed discussion on the matter of the secondary invitation retains a tendency to harmonize some serious problems that the presence of the secondary guests might have caused.[46] Nevertheless, as the other name referring to the secondary guests as "shades" or "shadows" (σκίοι) implies, they were often put into a very odd situation at meals. Furthermore, there accompanied certain tensions and conflicts involved in their coming to the meal and claiming appropriate seating order. This is also hinted at Plutarch's lengthy advice regarding the secondary invitation and the secondary quests. Klinghardt writes: "Diese detaillierten Regeln verdeutlichen, wie sehr man die Gafährdung der Eintracht der Mahlteilnehmer durch die Spannungen zwischen Geladenen und Nachgeladenen empfunden hat. Und es ist gerade der stark an homogener Symposien interessierte Plutarch . . . der durch seine Erörterungen zu erkennen gibt, wie wenig man dieser Gerfährdung entgehen kann, weil sekundäre Einladungen eine feste gesellschaftliche Insitution sind."[47]

Klinghardt elaborates further on the significance of these secondary guests at meals for the often overlook heterogeneous membership of Greco-Roman associations. Women, children, slaves, and freedmen benefited from the "social institution of secondary guests" in gaining access to association meals, including early Christian communal meals. Social differences involving in the inclusion of people differing in class, rank, and status inevitably create a potential threat to the homogeneity of communal meals. Thus, Klinghardt suggests that threat to unity at meals was not merely a problem of individual heterogeneous guests but a structural problem arising from the "social institution of secondary guests."[48]

One can also imagine how the unity at association meals could easily be endangered by looking at detailed lists of regulations concerning communal meals at various associations: "Die Dominanz der Forderung nach Eintracht der Teilnehmer an Privat- und Vereinsmählern indiziert hier also einen gesellschaftsübergreifenden Konflikt . . ."[49] Thus, the prob-

46. Plutarch, *Quaest. conv.* VII.6.706F–710A.
47. *Gemeinschaftsmahl*, 89–90.
48. Ibid. In his introduction to material from Pliny Klinghardt both summarizes Plutarch and anticipates Pliny: "Schließlich zeigen nicht nur die Ausführungen Plutarchs, daß die Gefährdung der Homogenität beim Mahl kein individuelles, sondern ein *strukturelles* Problem darstellten" (91).
49. Ibid., 95.

Difference and Greco-Roman Meals

lem of social differences related to the participants, the order of seating, and meal regulations affirms my thesis that it is above all in the context of meals that members of associations and early Christian groups noticed, experienced, and sought to negotiate social differences in various ways. This too is implicit when Klinghardt discusses how even among homogeneous associations attempts were made to regulate substantial differences by discipline: "Auch sonst treten in Vereinen, deren Mitglieder derselben sozialen Schicht angehören, beim Mahl erhebliche Differenzen auf, die in detaillierten Strafbestimmungen geregelt werden. Diese Konflikte begegnen deshalb bei den Syssitien und Symposien, weil gerade her der Ort ist, an dem unterschiedlich Sozialprestige dargestellt und erworben wird. Und man versteht angesichts dieser Probleme, daß sich Vereine ihrer Homonoia in besonderer Weise versicherten."[50]

Furthermore, in addition to the posture at table, the make-up of the company around the table and the order of seating discussed above, other aspects of communal meals give us glimpses of how the ideal of social equality was in tension with social differences and how the latter were under negotiation in Greco-Roman banquet settings. Social differences among those who participated in Greco-Roman banquets were often noticed in the quality and quantity of food distributed. In other words, who gets what at a meal mattered and made a difference, and it is to these issues that we now turn.

2.2. Difference in the Distribution of Food

Dennis Smith provides an informative overview of "various ways in which the formal meal functioned as an ideal type in philosophical discourse in the Greco-Roman world."[51] He notes that often the literary banquet setting and real-life meal merged in the discussion of meal etiquette. The banquet motif not only functioned as an important literary device for the discussion of ethical categories and principles concerning social relationships, but also served to reflect some aspects of what was widespread and customary at the Greco-Roman formal meals. Thus, the literary discussion of a proper meal and meal etiquette offers a window for us to look at certain discrepancies between the ideal or imaginary meal and the actual meal, and concomitantly between ideal social relationships and actual social

---

50. Ibid., 98.
51. Smith, "Social Obligation," 39.

relationships. In the following, I will seek to show how some differences were noticed, problematized, and discussed in relation to the ways food was ordered and arranged, and distributed according to differing rank and status of participants.

First, we can begin with a rather long passage in Plutarch's Table-Talk in which the topic of the better way of distributing food, either "portion-banquet" (πρὸς μερίδας) or "common sharing" (ἐκ κοινοῦ), is raised and debated. Two different ways of sharing food at meals stand out in the discussion. One is referred to as a portion-banquet and the other as common sharing with emphasis on eating together and drinking together. In the portion-banquet each participant receives a portion of food equal to that of others. The same amount of food is supposed to be distributed to all participants irrespective of social differences. On the other hand, common sharing is broadly defined as "all sharing everything with each other (τῷ κοινωνεῖν ἁπάντων ἀλλήλοις)."[52] In the literary context of this discussion in Plutarch, it is unclear whether the meal of common sharing implies the Greco-Roman *eranos* custom, according to which participants were to bring their own food and put it onto a common table.[53] What is clearly referred to is the custom of sharing together all the provisions on the table. Plutarch provides a good case which indicates how different ways of sharing food at formal meals touch on the question of difference differently:

> When I was holding the eponymous archonship at home, most of the dinners were portion-banquets, and each man at the sacrifices was allotted his share of the meal. This was wonderfully pleasing to some but others blamed the practice as unsociable and vulgar and thought the dinners ought to be restored again to the customary style when my term as archon was over. "For in my opinion," said Hagias, "we invite each other not for the sake of eating and drinking, but for drinking together and eating together, and this division of meat into shares kills sociability and makes many dinners and many diners with nobody anybody's dinner-companion when each takes his share by weight as from a butcher's counter and puts it before himself. Again how does placing a cup before each guest and a pitcher full of wine and his own table (as Demophontidae are said to have done for Orestes) and bidding him drink without heed to the others, differ from entertaining him in the manner

---

52. Plutarch, *Quaest. conv.* II.10.643E.

53. For an interpretation of the problems entailed in the Corinthian community meals from this particular Greco-Roman context, see Lampe, "The Eucharist," 36–49.

Difference and Greco-Roman Meals

which now prevails, serving him meat and bread as though from his individual manger, except that no compulsion to silence lives upon us as upon those who entertained Orestes?[54]

Plutarch initiates the question about the appropriate way of serving food at meals and invites the participants to the discussion by way of recalling the previous discussion which was made over the same issue in the past time. It appears that at the time of Plutarch's writing the common form of distributing food was not the portion-banquet. Hagias, one of the speakers in the literary setting of the symposium conversation, makes his argument in defense of the prevailing custom of sharing common meals at banquets. Hagias grounds his argument on the function of social bonding at the banquet which ties the participants together by emphasizing "not for the sake of eating and drinking, but for drinking together and eating together." Then he tries to develop his argument by saying that at the portion banquet there was unequal distribution of food, especially between the table of each guest and that of the host, as is shown in his reference to the case of Orestes. We may take this point as a hint of an unavoidable aspect of the portion meal. This point, in addition to emphasis on the unsociability of the portion-banquet, was used by Hagias for his defense of common sharing at meals.

The primary point of Hagias's argument, however, seems to have little to do with the enhancement of equality, for he immediately complains about "the distribution of equal portions to men who are actually unequal in their capacities."[55] Or at least we read a different approach to the notion of equality. Although Hagias makes some biological analogy for different food portions to different people such as a sick person, a thirsty or a hungry person, there is no doubt that the category of difference can be extended to other patterns of social relations, that is, differences in rank, status, class, and gender. Hagias's appeal for differentiated portions at the banquet reveals a subtle relationship between difference and equality operating at the common meal, when two of his statements are considered in comparison with each other as follows:

> "When we go to the grocery, we all use the same official measure, but to a dinner-party each man (ἕκαστος) brings his own (ἰδίαν) stomach and it is filled quite full not by the portion equal (ἴσον) to that of others, but by the portion which suffices it.[56]

54. Plutarch, *Quaest. conv.* II.642–43B.
55. Ibid., II.10.643C.
56. Ibid., II.10.643C.

> ... all sharing everything with each other (ἀλλήλοις). That was really like fellowship and communion.[57]

In the first statement, Hagias stresses the meaning of difference by using terms such as ἕκαστος and ἴδιος and interpreting them as conflicting with the notion of equality (ἴσος, ἰσότης). In the second, Hagias deliberately integrates the language of commonality (ἀλλήλοις) into his argument for the custom of "common sharing," which actually values difference over against equality.

Nevertheless, Hagias does not state explicitly the standpoint from which he is arguing for different portions of food at the meal. With this ambiguity, a potential for tension between equality and difference arises. This very ambiguity is picked up by Lamprias who appears as another speaker in the same symposium conversation. Lamprias begins his counterargument by denigrating Hagias's reasoning as if it were simply founded on physical dimensions: "it was not strange for Hagias to experience some irritation at receiving portions equal to those of the rest, for the belly he carried around was so big; and indeed he numbered himself (he added) among those who like to eat their fill, 'for there are no bones in a fish shared with another,' as Democritus says."[58]

Lamprias's criticism of the big bellies of those who want to eat more than their share has much to do with class structure in the context of meal customs, as his following argumentative statements clearly show: "The custom of distributing portions of meat was abandoned when dinners became extravagant; for it was not possible, I suppose, to divide fancy cakes and Lydian puddings and rich sauces and all sorts of other dishes made of ground and grated delicacies; these luxurious dainties got the better of men and the custom of an equal share for all was abandoned."[59]

In Lamprias's view, excessive eating habits of the well-to-do has ruined the practice of equal sharing for all at meals. Further, more often than not the actual practice of common sharing did not meet its ideal, betraying unequal distribution of food, especially with differentiations in the quality of food served at banquets. Lamprias's criticism intimates the difficulty that the men of higher class and status had in sharing food of high quality. From their point of view, differentiation in the quality of food should correspond to the social stratification of those who attend the banquet. The underlying

57. Ibid., II.10.643E.
58. Ibid., II.10.643D.
59. Ibid., II.10.644B.

social ideology may be expressed in the popular slogan: "You are what you eat." Plutarch himself seems to share such a view when he writes: "It is ridiculous for our cooks and waiters to be greatly concerned about what they shall bring in first, or what second, or what middle or last, if those who are invited to the feast are fed at places randomly determined: that arrangement fails to give to age, or rank, or other distinction the position that suits it; it does no honor to the outstanding man."[60]

In addition, Lamprias's argument also helps us to discern that the nature of difference that undergirds Hagias's argument is a tendency toward exclusivism, inasmuch as it depends on demarcating boundaries between persons of higher and lower classes. When governed by the former, the economy of difference at meals reflects the logic of discrimination and exclusion. Interestingly, Lamprias's argument reveals that the custom of equal portions was an effort to negotiate social differences in meals. Indeed, the argument itself can be regarded as a form of negotiation—albeit in a rhetorical form in a literary context (as distinct from the dynamics of actual meals). The same goal of good companionship or unity at the table could be understood by two different approaches to the distribution of food. The equality at the table for which Lamprias argues conflicts with the unity for which Hagias argues, and in effect Lamprias argues for distributive justice in the quantity and quality of food: "But where each guest has his own private portion (τὸ ἴδιον), companionship perishes. This is true where there is not an equitable (ἴσον) distribution."[61] It is also striking that the same phrase τὸ ἴδιον assumes a different value from the two points of view. For Lamprias, when the meal does not follow the custom of equal sharing, τὸ ἴδιον designates a class-specific meal to the advantage of the upper class.[62] By contrast Hagias uses the term to refer to what he takes to be proper for each person.

---

60. Ibid., I.2.616B.

61. Ibid., II.10.644C.

62. See Theissen, *Social Setting*, 145-74. Theissen notes such class-specific and privatizing connotations of ἴδιον δεῖπνον in Greco-Roman banquet customs, and interprets problems and conflicts at the Lord's Supper in Corinth in this light. Theissen, however, arbitrarily separates the Eucharistic meal from regular community meals. This can hardly be justified in that at such an early stage of Corinthian social formation the eucharist entailed a full community meal. Thus, Theissen suggests that Paul's solution to the problem involving social differences in the Corinthian community meal is to confine the ἴδιον δεῖπνον to private homes. "In the face of class-specific social conflicts, Paul moves the sacrament to the center to achieve a greater social integration" (167). Further, Theissen's proposal of love-patriarchalism inadequately explains Paul's perspective as "from below."

Paul and the Politics of Difference

Some other ancient texts, discussed below, also allege that the practice of τὸ ἴδιον at banquets could disrupt the unity of table fellowship in its abusive appropriation of higher quality food and thus accentuating difference. Limited information about such disproportionate distribution comes primarily from critical remarks of some Roman writers in connection with their discussions of banquet customs.

In a passage from one of his letters, Pliny the Younger relates an incident that caught his attention at a dinner party. Corresponding to the discussion above from Plutarch, Pliny observed the deliberate, hierarchical arrangement of food which he called "stingy extravagance." Even wine was divided, Pliny complains, into three categories in accordance with the social rank of the diners: "One lot was intended for himself and for us, another for his lesser friends (all his friends are graded) and the third for his and our freedmen."[63] His neighbor at table also noticed the stingy extravagance. When asked about it, Pliny expressed his opinion and his own practice:

> "I serve the same to everyone, for when I invite guests it is for a meal, not to make class distinctions; I have brought them as equals to the same table, so I give them the same treatment in everything."
> "Even the freedmen?"
> "Of course, for then they are my fellow-diners, not freedmen."
> "That must cost you a lot." "On the contrary."
> "How is that?"
> "Because my freedmen do not drink the sort of wine I do, but I drink theirs. Believe me, if you restrain your greedy instincts it is no strain on your finances to share with several others the fare you have yourself. It is this greed which should be put down and reduced to the ranks if you would cut down expenses, and you can do this far better by self-restraint than by insults to others."[64]

This passage deserves special attention. It is apparent that Pliny values equality in the practice of communal meals. Although the distribution of the same quantity of food goes unmentioned, Pliny apparently promotes the equal treatment of fellow-diners, including the freedmen, in terms of the same quality of food. Pliny stresses that such a principle of equality should be realized at least at a common meal. Nevertheless, it is also clear that the world of the common meal is separated from the outside world. In the meal setting some sort of negotiation is experimented with, perhaps to

63. Pliny, *Ep.* II.vi.2.
64. Ibid., II.vi.3–4.

Difference and Greco-Roman Meals

relax social differences demonstrated in almost every other corner of the public world.

There is no doubt that Pliny belongs to the aristocratic class in the contemporary Roman world. Nevertheless, he attempts to negotiate social differences when he hosts common meals. Instead of adopting the conventional pattern of demonstrating one's social superiority in and by means of the meal, he adjusts "his eating habits to those appropriate to one of a lower social class." Of course, he does not intend to share with his social inferiors the kind of food that he and his social equals would otherwise eat. In fact, he views this accommodation as a tactful economic consideration. The question of cost raised by his neighbor implies that it would have been financially difficult for a member of Pliny's aristocratic class to realize the ideal of equality at a common meal by raising those of a lower class to the level of his own. It is therefore obvious that Pliny's egalitarian practice had its own limitations.[65] In view of these limitations, John D'Arms asks whether "lifting the social level of his low companions" or "descending to theirs"[66] comes closer to the principle of equality—an appropriate question that may not be easy to answer.

It can hardly be denied, however, that Pliny's solution was at least a compromise to dissociate himself from the abusive demonstration of social hierarchy reflected in different quantities and qualities of the food at banquets. Hence, at a common meal hosted by Pliny, one would not expect to hear the same resentment toward him as that which Martial expressed against his host:

> Since I am asked to dinner, no longer, as before, a purchased guest, why is not the same dinner served to me as to you? You take oysters fattened in the Lucrine lake, I such a mussel through a hole in the shell; you get mushrooms, I take hog funguses; you tackle turbot, but I brill. Golden with fat, a turtledove gorges you with its bloated rump; there is set before me a magpie that has died in its cage. Why do I dine without you although, Ponticus, I am dining

---

65. For a critical commentary on Pliny's position in this passage see D'Arms, "Roman Convivium," 308–20. "One cannot resist noting, furthermore, what Pliny seems not to have done on this occasion: he did not protest directly, nor communicate his views to the man responsible for the social arrangements; he did not refuse to eat, nor exchange his own fare for that of one of the less privileged diners; nor did he get up and walk out" (315).

66. Ibid., 315.

> with you? The dole has gone: let us have the benefit of that; let us eat the same fare.[67]

Further, as D'Arms points out, Pliny's accommodating to the lower status of some of his companions would have been possible only in the context of a common meal, the Roman "convivial world" rather than the "public world."[68] Pliny himself was quite aware of the difference between the two worlds. In his letter to the provincial governor, he delivers the following political advice regarding social equality: "but I cannot help sounding as if I were proffering advice when I meant to congratulate you on the way in which you preserve the distinctions of class and rank; once these are thrown into confusion and destroyed, nothing is more unequal than the resultant 'equality.'"[69]

Besides the rearrangement of social differences within Roman banquet settings that we have discussed, this kind of contrast between the convivial and public worlds led D'Arms to question whether the notion of equality itself is applicable to the depiction of the Roman convivial world where "convivial *aequalitas* was a temporary *benedicium* which the great man might (or might not) bestow."[70] By illuminating the broader context of harsher social realities underlying Roman meal customs, especially the institution of patron/client, D'Arms rightly warns us not to overinterpret the convivial principles of equality, friendship, and the relaxation of social barriers which were connected with the "power of the communal meal." These principles were, D'Arms stresses, "a part of the cultural accoutrements of many Roman dignitaries, or at least of those who prided themselves upon being cultivated."[71]

Although D'Arms's critical reading of the Roman world of the symposium takes us quite close to the most plausible reality surrounding and underlying Greco-Roman banquets, the tension between social equality and social stratification at common meals demands yet additional elaboration. First, I will comment briefly on the work of some scholars who deal with this tension with varying agendas and perspectives. Then, in order to elucidate the dynamic power of communal meals in relation to social differences, I will incorporate some recent studies on ritual in the discussion.

67. Martial, *Epigr.* III.60; cf. *Epigr.* I.20; IV.85; VI.11; X.49.
68. D'Arms, "Roman Convivium," 312.
69. Pliny, *Ep.* IX.v.3.
70. D'Arms, "Roman Convivium," 318.
71. Ibid., 317.

3. DIFFERENCE AND RITUAL THEORY

Some fundamental and overlapping questions on the agenda and the context of ritual studies are: What can be said about "differences" we have noticed in Greco-Roman texts on common meals? What can be said about the relationship between Greco-Roman common meals and difference? How can we explain the phenomenon that common meals tend to presuppose or invoke an ideal type of "the proper meal" and at the same time reveal the tense and complex relationship between equality and difference? Although there are various possible approaches to these questions, in this section I intend to demonstrate that some insights and perspectives from modern theories on the nature and function of ritual are especially fruitful in helping to answer these questions.

First, Dennis Smith helps to elaborate the questions at hand by observing not only the tensions between equality and difference in the meals themselves, but also how these tensions are represented in the literature:

> The discussion then raises a fundamental question: whether the meal is going to be defined as a reflection of society or as an institution separate from society with its own rules. In either case, the ethical principles of friendship, pleasure, and joy would function, but in different sense. In a sense, the banquet motif in satire fits into the same discussion, for it presents the meal as a reflection of society, but by ridiculing the society there represented, it implicitly refers to an ideal type of "the proper meal" that places in relief the foibles of society."[72]

In his discussion of the role of communal meals in various philosophical schools during Greco-Roman period, Smith highlights the motifs of friendship and unity at the table as a literary topos inherent in the ideal meal.[73] He also shows that despite special honor and attention given to members of high rank and status at common meals, the communal nature of the meal functioned as an important element of community identity and was further defined by the way in which social obligations extend from the meal to the community which celebrates the meal.[74] Smith discusses in detail the society of *Iobakchoi*, an Athenian religious association of the second century CE and several aspects of the various rules that the community

---

72. Smith, "Social Obligation," 73.
73. Ibid., 52–56.
74. Ibid., 49–51.

had for its community identity and solidarity. Among those rules, those of conduct and penalties in particular are often applied to the meal context of the community. Members had to obey social obligations prescribed for the good order and quietness (εὐκοσμία καὶ ἡσυχία) of the community.[75] Smith contends from this that communal meals fostered social obligations in the community and functioned to control unruly and abusive behavior in ritual, religious, and social contexts. On this basis, as the title of his dissertation indicates, he interprets the problems in the communal meal in Corinth and Paul's arguments with the comparative frame of reference of social obligation.[76] Smith's use of the notion of social obligation sheds light on what early Christian groups might hold in common with Greco-Roman associations, especially with regard to maintaining unity in their communal meals. For my purposes, however, which concern the relationship between social differences and the unity of the community that celebrates the meal, the notion of social obligation needs to be supplemented by consideration of the dynamics of the complex process of dealing with and negotiating social differences.

Kathleen Corley also deals with negotiating social differences but with a very specific agenda. Her main task, as noted above, is to investigate the relationships between some changes in meal customs during the early Roman imperial period and social ideology with respect to women at meals. Above all, Corley endorses Smith's assertion that the customs of Greco-Roman communal meals provide the most appropriate context for understanding not only early Christian meals but also early Christian worship. The consequence for her is to warn against the tendency of scholars to privilege Christian uniqueness in the reconstruction of the beginnings of Christianity.[77] As is now generally acknowledged, a wide variety of social, religious, and philosophical groups, including Jewish and Christian groups, often included women in communal meals. For Corley this is the context for investigating the position of women in early Christianity, particularly with respect to their participation in meals.

According to Corley, the convivial inclusivity of Christian table fellowship, including the presence of women at table, should not be regarded as unique. Rather, such an inclusive ethos is how early Christian groups, including Jewish groups, benefited from changes in the socio-political and

75. Ibid., 149–74.
76. Ibid., 180–220.
77. Corley, *Private Women*, 184–86.

cultural milieu of the early Roman imperial period. Then she argues that despite some changes in meal etiquette with respect to women, Greco-Roman social ideology continued to restrict their activity and behavior at meals by reinforcing the respective dichotomies male/female and public/private by reinscribing the image of the ideal woman over against women who wanted to taste little precious freedom through participating in public meals. The upshot for her is the perpetuation of Greco-Roman ideology in regulating women's position in society upon women's presence at meals. In my approach to issues of difference and equality in relationships involving Jews and Gentiles, I find some affinity with Corley's ideological critical perspective to the extent that she shows how social ideology construes gender difference in order to circumscribe women's participation and behavior in communal meals, thus relegating women to "difference," that is, difference to be marginalized and excluded in society.

Given Corley's focus on meals as primarily a reflection of wider society, it is not surprising that she has appropriated Mary Douglas's socio-anthropological work on food and meals as an important frame of reference. This leads me to comment on Douglas's important contribution to the study on food and meal. Her interpretation of food and meal is summarized in the following succinct statement: "If food is treated as a code, the messages it encodes will be found in the pattern of social relations being expressed. The message is about different degrees of hierarchy, inclusion and exclusion, boundaries and transactions across the boundaries."[78]

According to Douglas, there is the relationship between food categories and social categories. "Food categories therefore encode social events."[79] The seating posture, the seating order, and the quantity and quality of food in the Greco-Roman common meal tradition which we have dealt with can be included in what Douglas considers as food categories. Furthermore, Douglas explains how food meanings encode social boundaries and how the social boundaries are related to the hierarchy of values and the concern about inclusion and exclusion. For example, in Douglas's view, ancient Jewish dietary rules classified categories of animals according to degrees of holiness (purity). The positive value of purity and the negative value of impurity carry the message of the integrity of social boundaries as well as religious and cultural identity. So Douglas asserts: "The meaning of a meal is found in a system of repeated analogies. Each meal carries something

---

78. Douglas, "Deciphering a Meal," 249.
79. Ibid.

of the meaning of the other meals; each meal is a structured social event which structures others in its own image."[80]

Douglas's emphasis on each meal as "a structured social event" confirms what we have discussed above, that is, how differences at a meal, like differences in food categories, are socially structured and arranged. Yet, Douglas seems less concerned about the possibility that a meal as a structured social event can equally function as a deconstructing or reconstructing social event. In other words, although her approach demonstrates how differences at meal encode social values and structures, it gives little attention to the possibility that differences can be problematized, negotiated, and renegotiated at meals.

To a large extent, Jonathan Z. Smith has helped to fill this gap. He has paid particular attention to difference in his work on the nature and function of ritual. Smith's dominant concern about difference centers on the relationship between ritual and place. Three main points that Smith makes about difference and ritual stand out to enable us to grasp better the dynamics of meals, which constantly entail tensions between difference on the one hand and the ideals of equality and unity on the other.

(1) *In ritual, difference is situational or relational, rather than cosmic or substantive.* Focusing on the importance of "place" in the context of ritual, Smith seeks first to decenter the universal symbolism of the "center,"[81] which has generally been imposed on the meaning of place in the understanding ritual. Through detailed comparative analysis of specific forms of ritual in their historical particularities, Smith argues that "place" in ritual should be perceived as "situational" rather than "substantive." For Smith, the duality of sacred and profane, which is tied up with religion and ritual, is dependent primarily on "emplacement" in which ritual objects are located. In other words, ritual objects are differentiated from the same ordinary objects outside of ritual. Ritual objects become or are made sacred simply because they are placed in a sacred place such as a temple. Hence a temple receives a meaning of center, precisely because a temple is the place where kings happen to reside. All of this points Smith to the "arbitrariness of place and placement and replacement" in ritual,[82] though his tone is somewhat

---

80. Ibid., 260.

81. The notion of "center" as a universal symbol was Mircea Eliade's fundamental hermeneutical key to the understanding of "sacred," "transcendence," and "religion." See Eliade, *The Sacred and the Profane.* Cf. Smith, *To Take Place,* 1–23.

82. Smith, *To Take Place,* 104.

Difference and Greco-Roman Meals

exaggerated. Certainly such arbitrariness is recognized without expense of the political and ideological aspects involved in the place like a temple (for instance, priests and kings).

What rivets our attention here is the way Smith comprehends the notion of difference and brings it to understanding of the relationship between place and ritual. Although he uses the notion of "difference" in a broad and elusive way with its multiple meanings, two particular meanings in his use of difference are crucial to his understanding of ritual. To elucidate the paradoxical and complex meaning of difference in place and ritual, Smith challenges Eliade's understanding of sacred and profane (pure and impure) as categories representing essential differences. According to Smith, "there is nothing that is inherently sacred or profane."[83] This constitutes an important starting point in Smith's understanding of "difference" in ritual and his articulation of a general theory about ritual. Such a point enables Smith to perceive what *happens* in and through ritual. Once positioned in a ritual context, certain ordinary objects and activities become extraordinary or "different." This is the sense of difference, above all, that Smith appropriates as the primary meaning of difference and its operation in ritual. Within the emplacement in ritual, difference is created, or to say more precisely, difference is being noticed. This is what Smith means when he says that ritual is "first and foremost, a mode of paying attention."[84]

The longstanding Protestant perspective on ritual has led to an understanding of ritual as "false," "idolatrous," expressive of "emptiness," and "merely symbolic." With emphasis on the "difference marking" role of ritual, Smith offers an understanding of ritual different from "ritual emptiness."[85] In other words, without providing contents that substitute for emptiness, Smith renders the meaning and role of ritual significant precisely in the way it marks difference. "It signals significance without contributing signification."[86] As his reference to Levi-Strauss's linguistic structuralism indicates, this first meaning of difference is preeminently a linguistic—therefore abstract—dimension, namely, the sacred and profane are determined by oppositional duality to each other. Abstract or not, this meaning eluci-

83. Ibid.

84. Ibid., 103.

85. Mary Douglas and Hal Taussig have made similar challenges to such a "Protestant" understanding of ritual. Whereas Smith plays with a different spin on the notion of "emptiness," Douglas and Taussig resist ritual emptiness. See Mary Douglas, *Purity and Danger*, 61–62; Smith and Taussig, *Many Tables*, 11–20.

86. Smith, *To Take Place*, 108.

dates an important aspect of ritual—the situational (relational, contextual) meaning of difference in ritual. I will return to this situational meaning of difference in connection with other theoretical perspectives on difference for the discussion of the contextual and relational meaning of Jew-Gentile difference in communities associated with Paul.

(2) *Ritual provides occasions for reflection and rationalization on difference.* Smith extends ritual's primary role of paying attention to difference to define another aspect of ritual. Here Smith is concerned with what "marking difference" may effect within "a controlled environment" created in and through ritual:

> *Ritual is a means of performing the way things ought to be in conscious tension with the way things are.* Ritual relies for its power on the fact that it is concerned with quite ordinary activities placed within an extraordinary setting, that what it describes and displays is, in principle, possible for every occurrence of these acts. But it also relies for its power on the perceived fact that, in actuality, such possibilities cannot be realized. There is a "gnostic" dimension to ritual. It provides the means for demonstrating that we know what ought to have been done, what ought to have taken place. Nonetheless, by the very fact that it is ritual action rather than everyday action, ritual demonstrates that we know "what is the case." Ritual thus provides an occasion for reflection on and rationalization of the fact that what ought to have been done was not, what ought to have taken place did not.[87]

It is here that we see Smith's second deliberate use of the notion of difference in relation to ritual. He associates the notion of difference with the effect of ritual at the level of social activities. Beyond the ritual effect of marking difference between sacred and profane, the notion of "difference" refers now to the disparity between what happens outside of ritual and what happens in ritual. Thus, the linguistic and structural dimension of difference Smith ascribed to the notion of difference in articulating the issue of ritual and its relation to place is extended to the social realm. In such a way, according to Smith, ritual marks incongruity between what is ideal and what is real. At the same time, this "marking difference" itself allows the participants of ritual to reflect on what ought to be done through ritual activities. In this way ritual functions as a controlled space or "focusing lens" through which a complex process of reflection and rationalization on

---

87. Ibid., 109 (my emphasis).

the difference between what ought to be done and what is not done takes place. In and through such a process of reflection and rationalization, the noticed difference can be negotiated, and the possibility is created what ought to be done can be perfected or improvised in the very context of ritual.

The social effects of ritual in Smith's construct are very significant in that they can be equally applied to the power of meals to negotiate the complex tensions between equality and social status as discussed earlier in this chapter. What I have described regarding the relationship between equality and difference at meals corresponds closely with Smith's assertion that "ritual is a means of performing the way things ought to be in conscious tension with the way things are" (see above), especially if "meal" is substituted for "ritual": "Meal is a means of performing the way things ought to be in conscious tension with the way things are."

It is not difficult to find a kind of correlation between Smith's concept of "the way things ought to be" and what we have seen in the Greco-Roman discourse on the "proper meal." Further, "the way things are" can be correlated to the social reality that meals represent through social differences inside and/or outside meals. Smith's interpretation of ritual, thus, helps us to see that meals, in a ritual manner, provide an occasion for reflection on the kind of social relations that society and meal ought to embody. In a word, meal provides an occasion for reflection on the tension between equality and difference.

(3) *Ritual is an ongoing process through which difference is constantly being noticed, questioned, and negotiated.* In addition to emphasizing perfecting or improvising functions of ritual, Smith also asserts that the tension between what ought to be done ("the now of ritual place") and what is not done ("the now of everyday life") is persistent. Ritual is an ongoing process in and through which diverse groups have to deal with such tension: "Ritual is a relationship of difference between 'nows'—the now of everyday life and the now of ritual place; the simultaneity, but not the coexistence of 'here' and 'there.' . . . One is invited to think of the potentialities of the one 'now' in terms of the other; but the one cannot become the other. Ritual precises ambiguities; it neither overcomes nor relaxes them."[88]

In the final analysis, Smith's theory on difference and ritual has provided a theoretical ground which sheds significant analogous lights on difference and meal. Although Smith did not directly deal with meal settings,

---

88. Ibid., 110.

it would be fair to say that Smith has opened up the potentialities of ritual negation to be more explored regarding the question of social differences at early Christian meals.

Up to now, I limited our discussion about general theory on ritual mainly to the works of Mary Douglas and Jonathan Z. Smith, instead of delving into diverse perspectives and dimensions in the current scholarship of interpreting and revitalizing the meanings of functions of ritual. This is mainly because they have provided some heuristic insights which enable us to take a fresh look at Greco-Roman common meals, in particular early Christian community meals. Mary Douglas's basic theory that meals are socially structured events supports one of my contentions that Jew-Gentile differences manifested in meal practices of particular Christian communities should be defined and interpreted as social constructs. Further, although Smith does not explicitly acknowledge the nature of ritual as social constructs, he has presented a theory that ritual makes possible certain social effects on social differences. By calling more attention to this dynamic process in ritual, Smith invites us to look carefully at what goes on concerning difference in ritual.

Although New Testament scholars have increasingly become aware of the significance of common meals not only in terms of the cultural context of early Christian community meals but also as one of the most important communal activities of early Christianity, the dynamic force of early Christian communal meals as a complex, ongoing process of dealing with and negotiating social, cultural, and gender differences has not been fully appreciated. Therefore, I am giving attention to some specific texts regarding early Christian meals in light of some ritual theory.

In "Dealing under the Table: Ritual Negotiation of Women's Power,"[89] Hal Taussig attempts to demonstrate the power of early Christian meal practice by focusing on its complex process of negotiating the emerging problems of social differences within early Christian communities. As a case study, he investigates the story of the Syro-Phoenician woman in Mark 7:24–30 and Matt 15:22–28 in order to address the issue of gender difference in early Christian meals. With exegetical clarity and historical sensitivity, he traces trajectories in the history of tradition up to the latest version of the story in Matthew. He posits four stages: the chreia in the early

---

89. Taussig, "Dealing under the Table," 264–79.

Difference and Greco-Roman Meals

Jesus movement; its association with a pre-Markan miracle collection; the story in Mark; and Matthew's redaction of Mark.[90]

What is important for my consideration is the way Taussig correlates the textual trajectories (four stages) with distinct social contexts of communal meals in different Christian groups. The formation of different social realities lies behind the development of the trajectories: "Each of the stages of *textual development* corresponds dramatically to a particular first-century community or moment of *social formation*. The unfolding of this contextual trajectory elucidates a *complex set of negotiations* concerning women in particular 'early Christian' communities, especially *at the community meals*."[91]

(1) Taussig posits the form of the initial chreia as follows:

> There was a woman. And a man said to her, "Let the children eat first, for it is not good to take the children's bread and throw it to the dogs." But she answered and said to him, "Sir [Kurie], even the dogs under the table eat from the crumbs of the children."[92]

According to Taussig, this original chreia reflects advocacy for the rights of women at meals. This chreia was then appropriated by the early Jesus movement. Further, debates about the place of women at meals most likely emerged when the early Jesus movement initiated community meals.

(2) The inclusion of the chreia in the miracle collection was hardly fortuitous. Rather, the composition of the miracle collection reflected interest in both women and the topic of meals. Taussig observes that although at this second stage major emphasis fell on the power of Jesus to heal the woman's daughter, women's presence at meals was still—or even more strongly—defended in the name of Jesus. "The concern for women's rights at meals was then a matter of continuity between the chreia composers' community and the miracle chain composers' community."[93]

(3) Some textual changes in the Markan form of the story indicate that the question of women at meals is extended to include and emphasize the question of Jewish-Gentile relationships at meals. In addition, the story is placed inside a home. This indicates for Taussig, that the issue of women at meals was still being debated and actively negotiated in Mark's community.

90. Ibid., 264–66; 266–70.
91. Ibid., 266 (my emphasis).
92. Ibid., 265.
93. Ibid., 269–70.

Here Taussig notes how the elaborations of the story in Mark reflect what was going on with respect to gender issues *in Markan community meals.*

(4) Taussig shows how in the fourth stage the power (equality) of women was renegotiated in the Matthean context with respect to the relationship of women to meals. In particular, Matthew deliberately relocated the controversy over women's presence at meals outside private meals. Taussig's particular contribution is to be found in his interpretation of what he discovered about the significance of meal practice in early Christian social formation in light of ritual theory. Drawing on the work of Jonathan Smith and Mary Douglas, Taussig highlights the dynamic power of ritual as a symbolic framework where differences in communities are marked and negotiated.

In his earlier study of the eucharist, Taussig stressed Smith's emphasis on the social effects of ritual by characterizing and clarifying the effects as "marking or noticing differences," "perfecting or rationalizing differences," and "asserting difference."[94] At this point Taussig was more concerned with ritual identification of differences by drawing attention to the "multivalence" or "emptiness" of ritual symbols: "Ritual symbols allow for groups to recognize these differences without necessarily trying to resolve them. This, of course, is a very effective means of nourishing the group in which differences exist. Rather than try to come up with a common and final solution to the differences, the multivalent symbols of ritual keep allowing for indirect recognition of those differences."[95]

In spite of the emphasis on "ongoing ritual recognition of differences," which Taussig thinks would allow for "valued different perspectives,"[96] what it means to recognize differences in ritual and how this is possible are not fully considered, at least, in his earlier study. "Ritual assertion of differences" can assume quite different meanings depending on the perspective of the one asserting differences. On the one hand, it can mean rearranging and reinforcing hierarchical social differences. On the other hand, it can mean affirmation of otherwise unappreciated, excluded differences. The issue of power relations is again what is at stake here.

To be sure, Taussig takes up the issue of power dynamics in dealing with ritual negotiations of differences within early Christian communities through their meal practice, especially focusing on the perfecting effect of

---

94. *Many Tables,* esp. 99–103.
95. Ibid., 102.
96. Ibid.

Difference and Greco-Roman Meals

ritual. In this connection, he adopts, extends, and enhances Smith's theory of difference in ritual so far as to demonstrate that in the first-century Christian communities there was "a complex process of ritual negotiation of women's power through these communities' meals."[97]

Similar to Smith, Taussig attaches an autonomous role to ritual in terms of "ritual perfection and improvisation." For instance, Taussig points out that "the attention to women at meals stemmed more from the way meals ritually negotiated larger differences than some ideological social vision of equality among the sexes."[98] I think this point very important to the extent that it seeks to avoid the fallacy of a deductive method in reimaging Christian origins in general and early Christian meal practice in particular. Yet, this point should not be taken as to undermine the social realities within and surrounding the first-century Christian groups and their struggles for a more egalitarian, emancipatory community.

This study benefits in several ways from Taussig's valuable contribution to the interpretation of the early Christian meal texts. He clearly shows that early Christian meals, like other Greco-Roman common meals, functions as *loci* for negotiating social difference. He also demonstrates how early Christian groups noticed, problematized, and negotiated social differences in distinct ways depending on their particular social location. Further, on the basis of his correlation of the trajectories of the development of a text with issues of women at meals in specific contexts, Taussig eventually suggests that early Christian meal texts reflect ongoing negotiations of social difference in community meals.

CONCLUSION

In this chapter, I have demonstrated that the Greco-Roman common meal was an important setting for noticing, problematizing, and negotiating social differences over a wide variety of social groups in the first-century Mediterranean world. I have also argued that it was at the common meal practices that social differences within the groups were noticed, problematized, and negotiated.

---

97. Taussig, "Dealing under the Table," 272.

98. Ibid., 275. "the actual hosting of meals by the Jesus movement was probably the occasion for the movement to have to make decisions about women's presence at meals" (269).

Paul and the Politics of Difference

The common meal practice functioned to promote the group identities of various groups bonded together in the meals. It also represented a social structure by replicating hierarchical differences and simultaneously provided the setting for identifying and negotiating differences in the social order. Any effort to negotiate issues of social power would have to deal, implicitly or explicitly, with questions of equality and justice. Thus if the question of difference is seen as the other side of identity, it is also true that identity is the other side of equality. Therefore, it is important to discern power relations involved in and reflected in first-century meal practices, that is, the contextual meaning of difference in dealing with the tension between equality and difference.

This enables me to bring a new perspective to a long-standing debate in Pauline scholarship concerning relationships between Jews and Gentiles in communities associated with Paul. From as far back as Augustine through the Reformation, the understanding of Paul has been dominated by theological agendas, and this is particularly true in dealing with Jewish-Gentile relations. The relationship between Jews and Gentiles in communities associated with Paul has often been discussed as part of Paul's attitude toward the Law. Although inevitably Jewish-Gentiles relationships bring up questions of the Law, too little attention has been directed to the social and practical dimension within socio-historical realities of early Christian communities.

At least in part to the so-called "Lutheran" interpretation of Paul's position toward Judaism, recent studies[99] have emphasized that defense of the equal religious status of Gentiles and Jews played a significant role in Paul's missionary activity and his theological rhetoric. Many scholars have recognized the contextual and contingent character of Paul's diverse, often seemingly inconsistent, statements concerning the Law, and justification by faith as well. Such an advancement in Pauline scholarship, however, has not furthered the discussion on Jewish-Gentile relations within communities associated with Paul beyond a rather abstract level of simply claiming the equality of both Jews and Gentiles as members of the people of God.

A few scholars have worked on the relationship between Jews and Gentiles in early Christian communities by taking into consideration the socio-historical context of first-century Judaism in dealing with matters such as

99. For example, Stendahl, *Paul among Jews and Gentiles*; E. P. Sanders, *Paul and Palestinian Judaism*; E. P. Sanders, *Paul, the Law, and the Jewish People*; Dunn, "Works of the Law"; Dunn, "New Perspective on Paul"; Gaston, *Paul and the Torah*; Räisänen, *Paul and the Law*; Watson, *Paul, Judaism, and the Gentiles*; Segal, *Paul the Convert*.

the so-called Antioch incident in Galatians or the relationship between the Jerusalem Church and the Antiochene Church or the ethnic issues in Romans.[100] Little attempt has been made, however, to understand how the earliest Christian communities as a minority movement might have dealt with the tensions and conflicts related to the differences in their ethno-political and religio-cultural self-identity in the midst of the first-century Roman Empire. Further, little attention has been given to the meal practice of early Christian groups as a very specific context where the ethno-cultural differences between Jews and Gentiles, as well as other social and gender differences, could be recognized, problematized, and negotiated.

The consideration of social and gender differences and the subtly-nuanced relationship between equality and difference in the larger context of Greco-Roman meals in this chapter provides a framework that sheds light on the interpretation of Jew-Gentile difference in early Christian table-fellowship. This further suggests that there is a need to apply "the multiplicity of relatedness"[101] of difference to the category of the Jew-Gentile differences which I shall deal with in the following exegetical chapters. The conventional approach to the question of Jewish-Gentile relations in Paul has often ignored the social constructedness of Jewish-Gentile difference as if "Jewish" difference (identity) is a fixed concept and "Gentile" difference (identity) is an another fixed concept which can be generally applied to all the situations irrespective of the particularity of each community. But the multiplicity of relatedness means that tensions and conflicts at meals, especially what is reflected in Gal 2:11–21 and Rom 14:1—15:13, are relative to complex contexts. In fact, the situations in Galatians and Romans reflect virtually opposite cases of the dynamics in Jewish-Gentile difference.

Further, the ritual theory discussed above also counsels us not to reduce ritual actions to universal or essential meanings, but to attend to the relational or contextual meanings in their particular settings. This can be equally applied to the nature and meaning of the Jew-Gentile differences within early Christian groups. As we shall see in the following chapters, neither Jewish difference (identity) nor Gentile difference (identity) can bear the weight of universal or essential meanings as if they belong to a static system. Rather both display a multiplicity of relatedness, that is, they

---

100. For studies on the Antioch incident in Galatians from a historical perspective see Taylor, *Paul, Antioch and Jerusalem*; Dunn, "Incident at Antioch." On the strong and weak in Romans, Nanos, *The Mystery of Romans*; Walters, *Ethnic Issues*.

101. See Taussig, "Wisdom/Sophia," 264–79, esp. 274–76.

grow out of complex contextual processes in early Christian social formation. In other words, the meaning and nature of Jewish-Gentile difference in Galatians are hardly the same as Jewish-Gentile difference in Romans. In Galatians, as I shall argue, the "Judaizing" tendency becomes a dangerous tendency that would define "Gentile particularity" differentiated from Jewish particularity as a "difference" in the sense of "otherness" to be ignored and excluded. On the other hand, in Romans Paul detects another tendency, virtually the reverse, in which Gentile dominance threatens to define Jewish particularity as an "other" to be devalued and smothered.

With more attention to the complexity involved in questioning Jew-Gentile differences, and with an interpretative framework of the politics of equality and difference that we have considered in examining the social differences at the Greco-Roman meals, in the following exegetical chapters I shall focus on how Jew-Gentile differences were noticed and problematized at the meals reflected in Galatians and Romans, and how Paul and others were engaged in negotiating those troubling differences through their meals. All of this will ultimately eventuate in a politics of equality with difference.

4

Difference and Table-fellowship in Antioch (Gal 2:11–21)

1. THE ANTIOCH INCIDENT AND JEW-GENTILE DIFFERENCE

CONTEMPORARY PERSPECTIVES ON DIFFERENCE and ancient perspectives on meals and difference in the two previous chapters set the stage for the drama in Gal 2:1–21. On the one hand, the issue of difference has become a contested site not only in the postmodern advocacy for pluralism, but also in feminist and postcolonial struggles for social justice on the global scale. On the other, Greco-Roman meals operated as a context in which an egalitarian ethos was not only asserted but also experienced. Such experimentations entailed a complex, ongoing process that had to deal with constant tensions between equality and social hierarchical difference. Indeed meals were among the most prominent and concrete loci in which difference in class, status, gender, and culture were noticed and marked, and negotiated accordingly.

These theoretical and historical perspectives are limelights for comprehending Jewish-Gentile difference in early Christianity as the issue arises in the meal practice of two different congregations associated with Paul, that is, the churches of Galatia and Rome. The limelights elucidate the problem in a particular direction with distinct features. (1) Recent attention to difference exposes the dangers of universalism and essentialism in trying to determine the constituent elements of difference. (2) Difference is properly understood in historical particularities and contingences. (3) An appropriate understanding of difference requires a relational and contextual approach to difference. (4) Negotiating difference is an issue of political commitment depending on the dynamics of difference and the subject (re)claiming difference.

In this chapter and the following chapter, I intend to challenge both the conventional "dejudaized" Paul and the recent emergence of "rejudaized" Paul, by revisiting and reassessing the problems involved in the Jew-Gentile difference in early Christian groups. The conventional picture portrays Paul as transforming the Palestinian Jesus movement into a Hellenistic religion where it ultimately became the Gentile church. Paul was so persuaded by the revelation of Christ to him (Gal 1:15–16) that he moved beyond his Judaism. This is the dejudaized Paul, and in this view Paulinism is the antithesis to Judaism. The so-called "New Perspective on Paul" locates him once again in a Jewish setting but only provisionally in that the notion prevails that Paul set the Jesus movement free from ethnic particularity and made the people of God universal. In both cases Jewish identity is set aside so that E. P. Sanders concludes that the only kind of Judaism that Paul advocated was a messianic Judaism that moved beyond living according to the Law.[1] Especially, the interpretation I offer of the problem of the weak and the strong in Romans 14:1—15:13 in the following chapter shows how much even the New Perspective misses the mark. But to pin everything on Romans would be quite inadequate in that a close reading of Galatians 2:11–21 in its literary and historical context makes it clear that here Paul takes a strikingly different approach to Jewish-Gentile difference.

It is beyond dispute that one of the integral aspects of Paul's thinking and practice was the inclusion of Gentiles and their full participation in the people of God as Gentiles. Not only were they a part of the people of God, their participation was equal to that of the Jews. In fact, Paul's inclusion of Gentile messianists was a part of building up communities envisioning and anticipating the apocalyptic realization of God's covenant promises. In other words, among the varieties of Judaism of the first-century Mediterranean world, Paul's was a particular kind of Judaism that included Gentiles.

It is evident that we can attest to some changes in Paul's own practice of Judaism. He once actively engaged in the Pharisaic movement of his day

---

1. E. P. Sanders, *Paul, the Law, and the Jewish People*, 143–62.

Difference and Table-fellowship in Antioch (Gal 2:11–21)

(Phil 3:5; cf. Acts 22:3–5) and persecuted the Jesus movement (Gal 1:13; 1 Cor 15:9; Phil 3:6). But when Christ, a Palestinian Jew who was executed by crucifixion under imperial Rome, was revealed to him as one whom God raised from the dead (Gal 1:13; 1 Cor 15:9), he took it as a sign of God's fidelity especially to the Abrahamic promises. In other words this was a movement of Jewish apocalyptic hope, to which he not only committed himself, but for which he also became a missionary.

Further, Paul was hardly the only one in Judaism who was concerned with the inclusion of Gentiles in communal life with Jewish people, although he certainly became one of the most controversial figures then as he is now. As some scholars characterize the question of the Gentile inclusion as an "intra-Jewish" or "intramural" or "inter-Jewish and intra-Jewish" issue,[2] there was a wide spectrum of opinion and practice regarding the issue among various Jewish groups.[3] Early followers of Jesus in the diaspora, particularly in Antioch, quickly became open toward the participation of Gentiles. When the heterogeneous character of these communities came to the attention of the *ekklesia* of Jesus' followers in Jerusalem, different—even conflicting—views and strategies emerged with respect to full inclusion of Gentiles. The problem of difference between Jews and Gentiles—thus the questions of unity and equality—surfaced particularly in concrete situations, notably in communal meals in which interaction among members was experienced on a practical level.

Thus, my reading of contextual and dynamic differences between Jews and Gentiles at communal meals aims to problematize two oppositional positions coexistent in current discourse on Paul and the Jew-Gentile difference in the early Christian communities. According to the first position,

---

2. The traditional interpretation treated Paul's attitude toward Judaism as if the issue was about the debate between two separate religions, i.e., Christianity and Judaism. But present scholarship has recognized that the issue was debated among different Jewish groups before the beginning of the Jesus movement, that Christian groups at the least before 70 CE were not separated from Judaism, and that the issue was primarily about the status of Gentile members within the early Christian community. Dunn uses the term "intra-Jewish" referring to all these meanings; Dunn, "Echoes of Intra-Jewish Polemic." Paula Fredriksen treats the question of the inclusion of Gentiles with or without the requirement of circumcision as "an *intramural* controversy, a question of concern and interest only to those already within these groups"; Fredriksen, *From Jesus to Christ*, 152–53. Arguing that "the Galatians whom Paul addresses are members of Christian believing subgroups within larger Jewish communities," Nanos uses both inter-Jewish and intra-Jewish; Nanos, "Inter- and Intra-Jewish Political Context," 146–59.

3. Esp., see S. J. D. Cohen, "Crossing the Boundary"; and S. J. D. Cohen, "Respect for Judaism"; Fredriksen, "Judaism, the Circumcision of Gentiles."

Paul advocates equality between Jews and Gentiles. This is meant to be the abrogation of difference among them, or the elimination of ritual distinction, or at best the indifference to difference. Even the last case alleges that although Paul had the principle of "indifference" *in theory* toward important aspects of Jewish Law such as circumcision, Sabbath observance, and food laws, *in practice* it did not operate and Paul actually expected Christian Jews to give up such Jewish observances.[4]

Segal makes a similar point from his understanding of Paul's experience of conversion as transformation and his commitment to the Gentile Christian communities. He argues that on the basis of his experience of the risen Lord, Paul states the principle of freedom from ritual obligations: "The effect of Paul's preaching and his vision of a new, unified Christian community was the destruction of the ritual distinction between Jew and gentile within the Christian sect. Paul was breaking down a ritual boundary in Christianity, not a boundary between saved and unsaved."[5] On the other hand, on several occasions, Segal maintains that Paul made compromises and accommodations based on magnanimity, for the purpose of maintaining church unity.[6]

The strongest expression of the first position is given by D. Boyarin—from a cultural critical approach—when he interprets Paul and the incident at Antioch: "The crux of the matter . . . is the question of when (or indeed whether) Paul argued that circumcision and observance of such commandments as the laws of kashruth were abrogated *not only for ethnic gentiles but for ethnic Jews as well*. I suggest that for the logic of Paul's theology, which was complete in its entirety from the first moment of his revelation, there was *not the slightest importance* to the observance of such rites for Jews or gentiles."[7] According to Boyarin, Paul's passion for unity led him, for various cultural reasons, to equate equality with sameness which "deprives difference of the right to be different, dissolving all others into a single essence in which matters of cultural practice are irrelevant and only faith in Christ is significant."[8]

---

4. E. P. Sanders, *Paul, the Law, and the Jewish People*, 143–62. See also Räisänen, "Galatians 2.16."

5. Segal, *Paul the Convert*, 202.

6. Ibid., 228–53.

7. Boyarin, *A Radical Jew*, 111 (my emphasis).

8. Ibid., 9.

Difference and Table-fellowship in Antioch (Gal 2:11–21)

On the other hand, recently, some scholars have seriously challenged the above-mentioned position that Paul's insistence on equality between Jews and Gentiles was motivated by and/or resulted in the devaluation of the Law and Jewish cultural practices.[9] Despite differences in method and approach, they stress that Paul's commitment to equality between Jewish and Gentile Christians shows a tolerant attitude toward the pluralism of ethnic differences, in the sense that within the Christian community Jews remain as Jews without giving up their observance of Jewish laws and Gentiles remain as Gentiles without the need to become Jews by means of circumcision and other special observances. This second position grounds its argument in Paul's letter to the Romans. While the first position focuses more on the letter to the Galatians and the relative discontinuity of Pauline Christianity with first-century Judaism, the second focuses more on the letter to the Romans and its relative continuity. The second position postulates also a close affinity between Pauline Christian groups and Jewish communities in the Diaspora. My reading of the Antioch Incident (and the Roman meal practice in the following chapter) will argue for a different interpretation of Paul's politics of difference.

2. ONE GOSPEL OF CHRIST AND THE PROBLEM OF DIFFERENCE (GAL 1:6–9)

It is remarkable that Paul raises the question of difference right at the beginning of Galatians. In the opening address of Gal 1:6–9 Paul explicitly states that he is shocked and deeply troubled, because the Galatians are turning to a different gospel

> I am astonished that you are so quickly deserting him who called you in the grace of Christ and turning to a different gospel (εἰς ἕτερον εὐαγγέλιον) (1:6)

For Paul everything depends on how the phrase immediately following in 1:7 is translated. The dominant interpretation represented for instance by NRSV, NIV, and the majority of commentaries renders the relative clause ὃ οὐκ ἔστιν ἄλλο as "there is no other one." That would mean that Paul starts Galatians with the programmatic denial of difference. If we look at the Greek text more closely, however, the actual translation is "which is

---

9. See especially, Campbell, *Paul's Gospel*; Tomson, *Paul and the Jewish Law*; Nanos, *The Mystery of Romans*, and Donaldson, *Paul and the Gentiles*.

not another one." In fact, this is how numerous English translations render the passage, including KJV, NKJV, NEB. Also the Latin Vulgate phrased it *quod non est aliud* (which is not other).[10] This literal translation still could mean that Paul denies the existence of another *gospel*, suggesting "gospel" is the term Paul wants to be added after "another."[11] As Paul, however, in 2:7 clearly talks about two different gospels, as we will see below, I would propose not to solve the puzzling contradiction between the two statements too quickly. "Don't turn to a different gospel" (1:6) and "The different gospel is not other" (1:7) is a juxtaposition that might indicate Paul is handling the question of identity and difference in a much more dialectical and challenging way than Occidental thought patterns have made us believe.

Paul defines "the different gospel" simply as a gospel contrary to that which Paul and his fellow missionaries preached to the Galatians (παρ' ὃ εὐηγγελισάμεθα ὑμῖν). Again, the meaning of this different gospel is emphasized as the gospel contrary to that which they receive (παρ' ὃ παρελάβετε) and whose representatives are cursed by a double ἀνάθεμα (1:9). If our translation is correct, Paul wants to convince the Galatians not to turn to this different gospel, whose existence is not denied—even if its "difference" is understood differently ("which is not other").[12] I would like to propose an understanding of Paul's polemic opening statement in 1:6–9 in the following way: Paul does not raise his tone to convince the Gentiles of the Galatian churches that there is no other (different) gospel assigned as the gospel of circumcision to the Jews at the Jerusalem conference in 2:7. As they are Gentiles, the Galatians should stay with the gospel of foreskin which initially they received and to which they turned themselves from their pagan gods (Gal 4:8–9). This would mean Paul tries to redefine the meaning of difference. The difference of the other gospel is denied and

---

10. This observation has been made by Brigitte Kahl. Also my following reflections on "one and other" are indebted to her article, "Gender Trouble in Galatia?" 57–73.

11. For example, Dunn, *Theology of Paul's Letter*, 20, 26–28; Betz, *Galatians*, 49; Williams, *Galatians*, 39.

12. The striking contradiction between 1:6–7 and 2:7 would be inevitable if, while denying the existence of another gospel in 1:6 (translated as "there is no other gospel"), Paul himself mentions the other gospel of circumcision in 2:7. This point has been noted by Hans Betz and James Dunn. See Betz, *Galatians*, 58, 96. Dunn's solution to the puzzle is intriguing, but confusing: "And yet Paul denounces the one circumcision gospel (1.6–9) while seeming content to recognize the other (2.7–9). The answer must be that . . . there was a lack of mutual recognition and acceptance: the other missionaries had criticized Paul's gospel as inadequate, and Paul denounced their gospel as no gospel." See Dunn, *Theology of Paul's Letter*, 27.

confirmed at the same time. It is different, yet not other. But if the gospel of circumcision to which the Galatians want to convert is "not another one," why should they not take it over? This requires a further look at Paul's biographical account of the events leading to Antioch.

3. PAUL'S CONVERSION: FROM ONE TO OTHER (GAL 1:11-17)

In telling his personal story, Paul strongly emphasizes that the gospel he preached in Galatia itself is conceived to be "different" by a dominant (Jerusalem) position of Jewish Christians: right from the beginning, it was not "according to human beings," nor based on human tradition, but was received through a revelation of Jesus Christ (1:11-12). Since his life before his call was so different from that of other apostles, Paul tries to explain his call by stressing that it is only God who was able to tremendously change the course of his own life and transform it in a new direction.

In Gal 1:13-15 Paul describes his former life in Judaism as an example of excellent accomplishment and distinguishable commitment with regard to the traditions of his ancestors. He must have been very proud of it at that time. Paul was standing, so to speak, at the top level in Judaism and his extreme zeal was oriented toward the Law-adherent identity of Israel. Paul does not give exact reasons why he became a persecutor of the early Christian communities, but from the context it is quite clear that his rigor toward the traditions of the ancestors was closely linked to his violent opposition against the church (ἐκκλησία) of God.[13] Because Paul states that he "advanced in Judaism beyond many of my people of the same age" (1:14), he must have held an extreme position that not only separated him from his peers in general, but was even more irreconcilable with the theology of the post-Easter Jesus movement.

Even if many details of the whole setting remain unclear and unsaid, three things appear obvious. (1) The whole conflict between Paul and the church of God takes place inside of Judaism, not between two different religions. It is a struggle between a highly conservative stance on the one hand and a position labeled as heretical/dissident "other" on the other hand.

(2) The way Paul describes his conversion shows that he does not merely take over the heretical position of "the church of God," but likely

---

13. On the socio-political dimension of Paul's persecution activity, see Fredriksen, "Judaism, the Circumcision of Gentiles," 541-42; N. Elliott, *Liberating Paul*, 140-80.

goes far beyond it. His divine designation as an apostle of "the gospel for the Gentiles" now seems to have put him into a dissident position himself (1:16), more dissident than the former dissidents he persecuted. This becomes clear at the beginning of the Jerusalem account in 2:1-10, where Paul had to negotiate his different "gospel of foreskin" which was looked at very suspiciously by the Jerusalem authorities (2:2).

(3) Different from the much more comprehensive account of Paul's conversion in Acts 9, Paul's own statement in Galatians does not give any details. Greater importance is attached to the elements he mentions: "But when the one who had set me apart before I was born, and had called me . . . so that I might proclaim him among the Gentiles . . . (1:15-16)." Like the prophets who were called (see Isa 49:1), Paul is also called and sent to preach the gospel among Gentiles. That means that the structure of the argument in Gal 1:13-16 is shaped by the polarity of Jew/Judaism (= Paul's previous position, 1:13) and Gentiles (= Paul's position after his call, 1:16). This suggests that a Jew-Gentile dichotomy underlies the debate on gospel and difference we have followed so far (1:6-9).

4. EQUALITY WITH DIFFERENCE: THE JERUSALEM CONFERENCE (GAL 2:1-10)

Before we hear about what happened in Antioch particularly between Paul and Peter from Paul's own voice in Gal 2: 11-14, Paul himself gives an introduction to the story (Gal 2:1-10), which, along with some fragmentary pieces of evidence preserved in Acts and Josephus, contains invaluable evidence of the situation in the 40s of the first century. Paul's retelling of what New Testament scholarship has referred to as the Jerusalem conference or the Jerusalem council involves the role of Paul and that of the Jerusalem church, the nature of the leadership of the Jerusalem church, and the relationship between the Jerusalem church and the Antioch church during a mostly unknown time in the history of early Christianity.

Although there has been much debate regarding historical problems about the relation of the event described in 2:1-10 to Luke's account of the Jerusalem conference (Acts 15),[14] there is no scholarly consensus on the events surrounding the Jerusalem conference and related issues. Instead of trying to get into historical details in an attempt towards historical

---

14. See Hill, *Hellenists and Hebrews*, 103-47; Bauckham, "James and the Jerusalem Church," 415-80, esp. 467-75; Betz, *Galatians*, 81-83; Segal, *Paul the Convert*, 187-94.

Difference and Table-fellowship in Antioch (Gal 2:11–21)

reconstruction, I will focus on the differences in status and hierarchical relations among major actors in the narratives in Galatians 2 and Acts 15 by considering the broad historical picture underlying the relationship between the community at Antioch and the community in Jerusalem.

4.1. Between Antioch and Jerusalem: Hierarchy Issues

Just before Paul mentions his second visit to Jerusalem with Barnabas (Gal 2:1), he tells of his first encounter with Peter in Jerusalem (1:18–19) which was three years after his conversion. Exactly what motivated his visit and what conversation he had with Peter remains unknown. Likely at that time Peter was exercising the leading role in the community of the followers of Jesus in Jerusalem. Also it is highly probable that the Jerusalem community was assuming the central role in the development of the Jesus movement in Judea after the death and resurrection of Jesus, especially because of the eschatological significance of that community.[15] Compared with Peter's position, Paul's position seems to be a rather marginal one. Peter and other apostles were actually the followers of the historical Jesus since the beginning of Jesus' activities in Galilee, and they were, as Paul says, apostles before him (τοὺς πρὸ ἐμοῦ ἀποστόλους; 1:17), even though for apologetic and polemical reasons Paul is rhetorically so deliberate as to attribute his apostleship to divine authority.[16] Presumably his past activity of persecuting the church contributed to the marginal status in which Paul immediately after his conversion was positioned (1:23; see 1 Cor 15:9). Paul spent some time in Arabia away from Jerusalem, apparently without making direct contact with other people, or with Jerusalem. He was unknown by sight to the churches of Christ in Judea even after his meeting with Peter.

Certainly at the time of his writing to the Galatians, Paul is claiming that his apostleship to the Gentiles depends on divine authority, and thus he is defending his independence from the Jerusalem authority. Yet it is possible to perceive Paul's marginality behind his rhetorical emphasis on independence from the Jerusalem authorities and on the divine authority of his mission to the Gentiles. In other words, Paul retrospectively interprets his lack of authority in relation to the Jerusalem leadership at this

---

15. Dunn, "Relationship between Paul and Jerusalem," 108–28. Bauckham, "James and the Jerusalem Church," 415–80, esp. 467–75.

16. Dunn, "Relationship between Paul and Jerusalem," 108–28; Taylor, *Paul, Antioch and Jerusalem*, 88–122; Betz, *Galatians*, 58–62; Brown and Meier, *Antioch and Rome*, 28.

early post-conversion time as his independence. As the analysis of 1:11–16 already shows, Paul himself was, so to speak, a "difference." Moreover, the very language used in 2:1–10 indicates that Paul could not avoid recognizing the authority of the Jerusalem leadership around the time when he made his second visit to the Jerusalem leadership with Barnabas. Contrary to the conventional image of a "dominant" Paul, which has been partly created by the rhetorical dynamics of Galatians 1–2 itself, this same text of Galatians rather clearly indicates that in reality Paul was in a weak and marginalized position:[17]

- Paul has to go to Jerusalem and submit the gospel he preaches among the Gentiles.
- Without agreement or acceptance by the Jerusalem authorities, he feels that he will have run in vain.
- The practice in the Pauline congregations was subject to observation and inquiry from a superior position of some kind (spies, false-brethren).
- Titus was not forced to be circumcised, but otherwise the Jerusalem leadership apparently was in a position to force the circumcision.
- The Jerusalem authorities (οἱ δοκοῦντες στῦλοι) give Paul the right hand of the community, not vice versa.
- Paul insists that they did not impose an additional requirement,[18] which presumes that technically they were in a position to do so.

This all shows that Paul was not in a dominant position in the context of Jerusalem conference. What is even more important: Paul defends the freedom of Gentile believers (2:4) against a force exercised by dominant Jerusalem leaders (2:3). In brief, Paul acts as an advocate of the "weak" against the "strong."

Excursus: Antioch and Jerusalem according to Acts

In Gal 2:1 Paul says that it was after fourteen years he went up again to Jerusalem with Barnabas. Modern scholarship on Paul has generally tended to exaggerate Paul's active missionary work as an individual, independent,

17. For a similar explanation, see Segal, *Paul the Convert*, 189–91.
18. On this point the account of Galatians differs from that in Acts 15.

Difference and Table-fellowship in Antioch (Gal 2:11–21)

and successful apostle devoted almost exclusively to the conversion of the Gentiles, and as a consequence to the triumphant phase of Gentile Christianity conceived as the Law-free gospel to all the believers (both Jews and Gentiles) in opposition to Jewish Christianity and Judaism in Judea. However, it is surprising that Paul tells us less about what he was doing during those fourteen years. Despite his silence on that matter, the ways in which Paul talks about himself in Gal 1–2 contributed to a certain degree to the conventional image of Paul.

According to Acts 11:25–26, it was on Barnabas's initiative that Paul left Tarsus to begin his lengthy association with the church at Antioch. It seems that Barnabas was closely associated with both the Jerusalem and Antioch churches (cf. Acts 11:22–23) and with the independence of thought and practice in the Antioch community.[19] As Nicholas Taylor remarks, "From the time that Paul joined the Antioch church and derived his dyadic identity from membership of that community, he would have shared corporately in the relationship between his church and the Christians of Jerusalem, even if he was not personally involved in the contact between them."[20] Thus it seems very plausible that Paul was an active member of the community at Antioch, keeping close partnership with Barnabas, and that probably at that church he was commissioned as an apostle—though he tells otherwise in Gal 1:15–16 as we have considered above. According to Acts 13:3 the Antiochene church sent off (ἀπέλυσαν) Barnabas and Paul and, in the following verse, they are described as having been sent off (ἐκπεμφθέντες) by the Holy Spirit. While it may be significant that ἀποστέλλω is not used in this pericope, Barnabas and Paul are nevertheless twice described as ἀπόστλοι in the narrative (Acts 14:4, 14). In view of this, Taylor suggests that Acts 13:4 "represents the commencement of Paul's apostolic ministry, as the delegate of the Christian community in Antioch, accompanying Barnabas on the outreach of that community."[21] Furthermore, there is no indication of direct contact between Paul and the Jerusalem church from his joining the church of Antioch until the Jerusalem conference.[22]

---

19. Taylor, *Paul, Antioch and Jerusalem*, 88.

20. Ibid., 89.

21. Ibid., 90. Taylor goes on to make an interesting and convincing argument that "The close association between Paul's conversion experience and his apostolic vocation was . . . the product of his separation from the church of Antioch" (92).

22. The references in Acts 11:27–30 and 12:25–26 are exceptional in this regard and probably mislocated; cf. Taylor, *Paul, Antioch and Jerusalem*, 89.

Considering the historical plausibility of Paul's long-term socialization within the community in Antioch, scholars have tended to recognize that Paul and Barnabas went to Jerusalem as the representatives of the Antiochene church in order to confer with the leaders of the Jerusalem church about the issue of circumcision of Gentiles within the Antiochene church.[23] On the other hand, the meeting between Paul and Barnabas, the delegates from the Antiochene church, and the leadership of the Jerusalem church represents "the κοινωνία between the churches of Jerusalem and Antioch, not merely between the five individuals named in Gal 2:9."[24]

There is no indication in Gal 2:4 and Acts 15 that the Jerusalem apostles took the initiative to send the Judean men or teachers to Antioch to impose the Law. In that case, there would have been no need for Paul and Barnabas to go to the leadership of the Jerusalem church. Yet, the activity in Antioch of Christians from Judea (Acts 15:1; cf. "false brethren" in Gal 2:4) seems to have caused some problems within the community at Antioch, so that it would therefore have been necessary that Barnabas and Paul reach agreement with the Jerusalem church and its leadership before the controversy became unmanageable.

While the traditional explanation for the reason why the issue of the Gentile circumcision was raised by some men from Judea usually presupposed the dichotomy of liberalism (of Paul and the Antiochene church) versus legalism (of the Jerusalem church), recent studies have sought to offer more nuanced explanations by drawing on the diversity of the first-century Judaism and/or the diverse tendencies within early Jewish Christian movement in terms of attitudes toward Gentiles,[25] along with the historical situation of the Jewish and/or Jewish Christian communities in mid-century Judea.

---

23. Cf. Holmberg, *Paul and Power*, 19; Hill, *Hellenists and Hebrews*, 114; Dunn, "Relationship between Paul and Jerusalem," 121–22. Dunn explains Paul's awkward switching from singular personal terms to plural in Gal 2:9 in terms of Paul's defense of his independent authority after the break of his partnership with Barnabas at the time of his writing to the Galatians.

24. Taylor, *Paul, Antioch and Jerusalem*, 88.

25. Especially Hill's analysis of Galatians 2 and Acts 15 challenges such a dualistic understanding of conservatism versus liberalism and attempts to show the internal diversity of the churches of Antioch and Jerusalem. See also J. J. Scott, "Parties in the Church of Jerusalem," 217–27; Brown and Meier, *Antioch and Rome*, esp. 1–9, 28–44.

4.2. The Jerusalem Conference (Gal 2:1–10)

At any rate, whether Gentiles need to be circumcised in order to be considered as full members equal to Jews was the focus of discussion at the Jerusalem conference. Paul presents Titus, an uncircumcised Greek, as a test case at the Jerusalem conference: "But even Titus, who was with me, was not compelled to be circumcised, though he was a Greek" (Gal 2:3). Without giving some details about the proceedings described in Acts 15, Paul's version of the conference in 2:1–10 highlights the subtle hierarchical dynamics underlying the issues of equality and difference in the relationships between Paul (Antioch) and the Jerusalem church, and between Jews and Gentiles within the Christian communities.

Despite noticeable differences between Paul and Luke-Acts with regard to the Jerusalem conference, both accounts agree on one decisive point. The Jerusalem leadership agreed that Gentiles need not be circumcised (2:6; Acts 15:19). The decision was made essentially in favor of what the Antioch delegation sought. According to Taylor, "The Jerusalem leadership, the effective decision-makers at the conference, affirmed the gospel as lived and preached at Antioch and imposed no further obligations on that community."[26] Yet, while recognizing the authority and primacy of the Jerusalem leadership implicit in the languages of τῶν δοκούντων εἶναί τι (Gal 2:6) and οἱ δοκοῦντες στῦλοι εἶναι (Gal 2:9), in recounting the decision at the conference Paul demonstrates the equality—in spite of difference and hierarchy—between himself and the leadership of the Jerusalem church. According to his argument, such equality with difference is grounded in God's impartiality (πρόσωπον θεὸς ἀνθρώπου οὐ λαμβάνει, Gal 2:6), and God's impartiality is understood not merely as indifference to difference, but as indifference to discriminatory distinction for the sake of equality *with* difference. This inclusive and non-hierarchical definition of difference is what Paul sees as the truth of the gospel (ἡ ἀλήθεια τοῦ εὐαγγελλίου, 2:5) as it is practiced for instance at Antioch and affirmed by the Jerusalem leaders. And this is how the different gospel (1:6) can be understood as not "other."

On the basis of God's impartiality, which guarantees equality between Paul and the Jerusalem pillars, despite their differences, Paul interprets the decision of the conference as the unity of the gospel in terms of the gospel of both foreskin and circumcision (τὸ εὐαγγέλιον τῆς ἀκροβυστίας . . .

---

26. Taylor, *Paul, Antioch and Jerusalem*, 108.

Paul and the Politics of Difference

τῆς περιτομῆς, 2:7). It is not certain whether Paul intentionally avoids the word τὸ εὐαγγέλιον with τῆς περιτομῆς in order to stress the oneness-with-difference of the gospel in Gal 2:7,[27] or simply for syntactical reasons, but arguing for the first option seems not impossible. Moreover, notably Paul deliberately uses the passive πεπίστευμαι in order to define the gospel of both foreskin and circumcision as being derived from the oneness of God, who worked for the mission to the circumcised (through Peter—the Jerusalem church) and to the Gentiles (through Paul—the Antiochene church).

Regarding the agreement at the Jerusalem conference, a number of scholars argue that missionary tasks were divided along ethnic lines.[28] Yet, given that the Antioch community was a mixed group of Jews and Gentiles and that Jews were dispersed throughout the eastern Roman Empire and beyond, a division of missionary work along either racial lines or territorial areas seems untenable. Rather, the agreement more likely was that the gospel of circumcision, represented by James, Peter, and John, would be for Jews, and the gospel of foreskin, represented by Barnabas and Paul, would only apply to Gentiles. And such a mutual understanding was not only grounded on but also reaffirmed the mutual κοινωνία between the church at Antioch and the Jerusalem church. It was expressed by the "right hand" extended to Paul and Barnabas by the Jerusalem leaders on the one hand (Gal 2:9), and it was practiced through the material solidarity of the Gentile toward the poor of the Jerusalem church (2:10)

---

27. Erick Dinkler argues that these notions are not Paul's language, because they contradict his statement in Gal 1:6–7; Dinkler, *Signum Crucis*, 282 (requoted from Betz, *Galatians*, 96). Betz, noticing Paul's use of the first person singular in 2:7, argues that that verse is "Paul's own evaluation of an agreement as it pertains to his own position"; see Betz, *Galatians*, 97. Further, Taylor argues that both Paul and the Jerusalem leadership mutually agreed on such recognition of diversity: "The Jewish community of this period was not unaccustomed to differences of opinion, or incapable of accommodating them within a wider whole, and we have no reason to suppose that the early Christians did not share this capacity for diversity" (Taylor, *Paul, Antioch and Jerusalem*, 112). Stressing that the agreement was made only on the issue of the circumcision of the Gentiles, not the question of Jewish obedience in the context of a mixed congregation, Hill argues that the issue at the Antioch incident was not that of "Judaizing," but "Gentilizing" (Hill, *Hellenists and Hebrews*, 117, 126–42).

28. E.g., Betz, *Galatians*, 100; Conzelmann, *History of Primitive Christianity*, 86; Wilson, *Gentiles and the Gentile Mission*, 72.

5. DIFFERENCE TROUBLE: THE ANTIOCH INCIDENT (GAL 2:11-14)

The conventional interpretation of the Antioch incident sharpens the ideological (or theological) gap between Jewish Christianity, allegedly represented by Peter (and "some people" from James), and Gentile Christianity, allegedly represented by Paul. This gap is replicated in the binary polarity of law-observant and law-free. Over against this conventional interpretation of polar oppositions, I join a growing chorus of scholars who have discovered the diversity of first-century Judaism in general and the diversity of Jewish attitudes toward Gentiles in particular. Early Christianity matches the diversity of Judaism. It too manifests diversity and complexity. Thus, instead of a dualistic schema of Jewish versus Gentile Christianity, we have to recognize multifaceted interrelationships among diverse groups. A major implication of this historical reality for interpreting the Antioch incident is the necessity to avoid generalizing and essentializing Jewish-Gentile difference at table-fellowship as if what happened at Antioch provides a picture of Jewish-Gentile relationships as such. Quite to the contrary, the Antioch incident is a specific case where particular dynamics are at work in Paul's account. In this chapter, I intend to demonstrate that recent interpretation of the Antioch incident still shows several sorts of generalizing and essentializing tendencies in the treatment of the Jew-Gentile difference at table-fellowship in Antioch and as a consequence Paul's politics of difference.

5.1. Historical Considerations

To begin with, it is necessary to comment on some uncertain points about circumstances surrounding the confrontation between Peter and Paul. It is difficult to be certain about the reason why Peter had visited the community in Antioch and about what motivated certain men from James to come to Antioch. And it is not quite certain when this happened, that is, whether it was shortly or years after the Jerusalem meeting.[29] At least it seems rea-

---

29. Despite the difficulties in reconstructing the order of the events on the ground of the accounts in Galatians 2 and Acts 15, the majority of scholars locate the crisis at Antioch during the period shortly after the Jerusalem conference. Especially see Hill's discussion on the chronological problems involved in the Jerusalem conference and the Antioch incident, and the possible alternatives; (Hill, *Hellenists and Hebrews*, 115-22). See also Taylor, *Paul, Antioch and Jerusalem*, 123-27. Reicke assumes that the Jerusalem conference took place in 49 CE and the Antioch incident occurred some years after the

sonable to say that they came to Antioch after the Jerusalem meeting (Gal 2:1–10) we have discussed above and before Paul's writing to the Galatians. At a certain time after the Jerusalem conference Peter visited the Christians of Antioch and joined their table-fellowship of both Jews and uncircumcised Gentiles. Peter ate with the Gentile believers in Antioch (Gal 2:12).

Given that both the Jerusalem church and the Antiochene church agreed that Gentiles need not become proselytes by going through circumcision, it is difficult to explain the motivations and intentions of those who came from James. Furthermore, the question could be asked why the same issue of table fellowship did not become a point of focus at the Jerusalem conference. It is hardly thinkable that the community at Antioch was not yet practicing its mixed table-fellowship at the time of the Jerusalem conference. It is also hard to know the extent of freedom which a significant number of the Jewish Christians of Antioch exercised toward the Gentiles. Yet, what is clear is that the church at Antioch continued the practice of the table fellowship between Jewish and Gentile Christians as it was already practicing before the conference at Jerusalem. "Jewish and gentile Christians in Antioch had found an accommodation whereby they could eat together."[30] But such a practice of mixed table-fellowship has changed with the coming of some men from Jerusalem, who saw the situation differently.

Despite difficulties in reconstructing the situation surrounding the events leading to the incident at Antioch, a number of scholars have tried to interpret the Antioch incident by taking into account a broader historical situation in Judea where the Jerusalem church was located, in order to better understand the position and conduct of the parties involved in the event. In this regard, James Dunn's important article on the incident at Antioch deserves attention.[31]

Dunn observes that during the middle of the first century "many Jews, no doubt a growing proportion within the Jewish territories, must have

---

conference, around 54 CE, arguing that a certain Christian zeal for the law was spread within Christianity specifically during the years 54 to 61 when the notorious Hellenism of Nero caused more violent reaction to Judaism: Reicke, "Judaeo-Christianity," 145–52.

30. Taylor, *Paul, Antioch and Jerusalem*, 127. Cf. Hill, *Hellenists and Hebrews*, 117–22.

31. Dunn, "Incident at Antioch," esp. 129–36. For a different treatment of the persecution of James, the son of Zebedee (Acts 12:2) by King Agrippa, see Horsley and Silberman, *The Message and the Kingdom*, 131–44: "And if we read the account of Acts against his own messianic credentials, it becomes clear that Agrippa's security forces moved against the followers of Jesus as dangerous anti-royal agitators, not as nonobservant Jews" (135).

Difference and Table-fellowship in Antioch (Gal 2:11–21)

believed their distinctive religious and national prerogatives were under increasing threat."[32] As a response to such a threat, according to Dunn, there was a growing "pressure towards conformity with the mainstream of nationalist Judaism" in terms of demand for the loyalty to the Jewish religious and national heritage.[33] A number of incidents reported in Josephus were used as the evidence of such mounting pressures. Suggesting that the followers of Jesus in Palestine, including the Jerusalem church, were not unaffected by such pressure, Dunn interprets events related to the harassment and persecution of the followers of Jesus, e.g., Peter's arrest and the death of James (the brother of John) within that context. Yet, Dunn's consideration of the historical context seems to imply that the Jewish national and religious prerogatives per se function to motivate a certain kind of "conservative" response to the felt threat, rather than perceiving that the Jewish loyalty to religious and cultural traditions as form of resistance against the Roman imperial dominance. Thus, Dunn suggests that the Antioch incident took place during the period in which "Jews had to be on their guard against . . . threats to their national and religious rights."[34] Relating his consideration of the socio-political situation in Palestine to the early Christian community, Dunn draws the following statement: "Indeed we may generalize a fairly firm conclusion from the above review of evidence: *wherever this new Jewish sect's belief or practice was perceived to be a threat to Jewish institutions and traditions its members would almost certainly come under pressure from their fellow Jews to remain loyal to their unique Jewish heritage.*"[35]

Dunn's conclusion is compelling, yet problematic. Apart from the definitional ambiguity in Dunn's use of the term "nationalistic," it is problematic because Dunn presupposes that the potential threat of the early Christian community is primarily related to "Jewish institutions and traditions." What is more problematic is that Dunn interprets the law-observant position of the Jewish Christians as a kind of conservative reaction which was, out of pressure, taken in conformity with nationalistic mainstream Judaism.[36] In other words, the historical context in which Dunn situates the

32. Dunn, "Incident at Antioch," 133.
33. Ibid., 134.
34. Ibid., 135.
35. Ibid. (Dunn's emphasis).
36. Cf. Horsley and Silberman, *The Message and the Kingdom*, 135–44: "The scriptural designation of James as one of the 'pillars' of the Jerusalem community may conceal a clear symbolic allusion of the self-understanding of the Jerusalem community as an alternative to the Temple" (135) (their emphasis).

Antioch incident is compelling, but his interpretation of the historical context is framed in terms of Jewish (Jewish Christian) ethnocentrism versus Christian (Paul's Gentile Christian) universalism, as his interpretation of Paul's position shows.[37] It is not surprising, then, that Dunn's interpretation of the Antioch incident is grounded on the hypothesis that "the open table-fellowship practiced at Antioch was perceived by the Jerusalem church (and perhaps by other Jews) as such a threat."[38]

In a similar way, Taylor considers the deteriorating political situation facing the church in Judea as a historical plausibility for the explanation of the visit to Antioch by the men of James. But Taylor argues that both their visit and demand of a greater degree of conformity to the Jewish law were possible on the ground of the agreed κοινωνία between the churches (with full recognition of the authority of the Jerusalem church) without violating the decision previously agreed at the Jerusalem meeting.[39] Although Dunn's reading of the plausible historical situation behind the account of the Antioch incident is an important contribution, his interpretation of the Antioch incident from the historical perspective seems to be a modification of the traditional understanding of the oppositional dichotomy between Jewish Christianity and Gentile Christianity.[40]

---

37. For a different interpretation, see Horsley and Silberman, *The Message and the Kingdom*, 138–44: "This demand for circumcision—and the wider observance of Israelite ritual laws it implied—has often been viewed by New Testament commentators as narrow-minded retreat from universalism, but it can perhaps be better understood, in its specific historical context, as a call for solidarity" (138).

38. Dunn, "Incident at Antioch," 136.

39. Taylor, *Paul, Antioch and Jerusalem*, 128–31.

40. Neil Elliott critiques against the so-called "New Perspective on Paul," which has become the dominant interpretative tendency of Paul and Judaism after the work of E. P. Sanders and of which a prominent proponent is James Dunn. See N. Elliott, *Liberating Paul*, esp. 66–71; "On the other hand, if we follow other scholars who hold to a 'sociological' explanation, we attribute Paul's 'attack' on Judaism to be his commitments to the gentile Christian church. In this way we may avoid the inaccurate and prejudicial stereotypes of the older 'Lutheran' interpretation. But casting Paul's theology as an effort to justify the status of gentile Christians still assumes a 'background' of tremendous Jewish opposition to the Law-free gentile church. That unproven assumption will involve us in another set of tendentious and prejudicial stereotypes about Jewish 'particularism' and 'ethnocentrism'"(70). I agree with his criticism in the sense that "Paul's effort to justify the status of gentile Christians" should not be used as a totalizing (i.e. without considering the particularity of specific community) interpretative grid. However, my reservation is that Elliott's brilliant criticism should not lead us to underestimate Paul's effort to justify the equal status of both Jews and Gentiles within *different communities*. This point again reminds us of the importance of understanding Paul's position toward

Thus, Dunn summarizes the issue involved in table-fellowship as follows: "The issue of whether the Gentile believers need be circumcised had been settled in favor of the Gentile liberty of action. The issue was now of Jewish believers remaining loyal to their ancestral faith, and in return they might expect the Gentile believers to conform to the sensibilities of their Jewish brothers, in much the same way as they had been willing to 'judaize' when they were 'God-fearers.'"[41]

One of my criticisms of Dunn's argument is that such an assessment of the issue was made without much consideration of the possible hierarchical relationship between Jews and Gentiles within the Antioch community. Furthermore, it does not explain why Paul's position in Gal 2:11–14 is different from that which we see in Rom 14:1—15:13. As Mark Nanos points out, "Another problem with the traditional interpretation of Paul's conviction as revealed in his retelling of the Antioch incident is that it positions Paul in a contradiction of the traditional reading of Romans 14 . . . to tolerate or accommodate Jewish opinions and behaviors."[42]

This leads me to disagree with Dunn's following conclusion regarding Paul's position at table-fellowship in Antioch: "The covenantal nomism of Judaism and of the Jewish believers (life in accordance with the law within the covenant given by grace . . .) was in fact a contradiction of that agreed understanding of justification through faith. To live life 'in Christ' *and* 'in accordance with the law' was not possible: it involved a basic contradiction in terms and in the understanding of what made someone acceptable to God."[43]

Both the historical context and the language of the Antioch incident has certainly been interpreted to mean that "at the center of Paul's thinking was the conviction that when a Jew believed in Jesus as the Christ he or she no longer functioned as a Jew—Torah and *halakhah* should no longer be operative in guiding their faith or behavior."[44] The changing socio-political situation which the Jerusalem church faced in the mid-40s needs to be considered along with not only the relationship between the Jerusalem church and the Antioch church, but also the relationship between the majority of

---

both Jews and Gentiles contextually and relationally.

41. Dunn, "Incident at Antioch," 157.
42. Nanos, "Peter's Hypocrisy," 345.
43. Dunn, "Incident at Antioch," 159 (Dunn's emphasis).
44. Nanos, "Peter's Hypocrisy," 344.

Jewish Christians and the minority of Gentile Christians within the Antioch community.[45]

5.2. Difference at Table-fellowship (Gal 2:11–14)

According to Paul, Peter withdrew from table-fellowship with the Gentile Christians in Antioch on account of some visitors from James (2:12), and his example was followed by other Jewish Christians, and even by Barnabas (2:13). Paul himself stood up against Peter. Although there are gaps to be filled for reconstructing the event, I aim to demonstrate that Paul's attitude toward the table-fellowship with Gentiles in Antioch shows a distinct approach to the Jew-Gentile difference. This enables us to problematize and challenge the conventional universalizing discourses with regard to and Paul's stance toward the Jew-Gentile difference.

Whereas the trouble at meals in Antioch was generated by the unexpected guests from Jerusalem, Paul's criticism was directed at Peter's change of behavior, not at those guests. Further, Paul's description of Peter's change of behavior focused on his withdrawal from mixed table-fellowship. Paul attributes such a change to Peter's fear of the circumcision party (φοβούμενος τοὺς ἐκ περιτομῆς, 2:12). The language in Gal 2:12 shows that Paul is concerned about the unity of table-fellowship between Jews and Gentiles (μετὰ τῶν ἐθνῶν συνήσθιεν)—implying equality and mutuality—which was disturbed and discontinued (ὑπέστελλεν καὶ ἀφώριζεν). Paul described what happened at the mixed table-fellowship by a change from the language of inclusion to that of exclusion. Moreover, the language that Paul uses has implications of power-relations between Jews and Gentiles at the table-fellowship. Let us read the scene (Gal 2:12) again in Greek:

πρὸ τοῦ γὰρ ἐλθεῖν τινας ἀπὸ Ἰακώβου μετὰ τῶν ἐθνῶν συνήσθιεν.

ὅτε δὲ ἦλθον, ὑπέστελλεν καὶ ἀφώριζεν ἑαυτὸν φοβούμενος τοὺς ἐκ περιτομῆς.

Before some visitors came from James, eating together with the Gentiles in equality and mutuality went unquestioned among both Jewish and Gentile Christians. Notice that before the mutual table-fellowship with equality (μετὰ τῶν ἐθνῶν συνήσθιεν) was disturbed, i.e., before the uninvited

---

45. For a treatment of the Jewish community in Antioch, see Meeks and Wilken, *Jews and Christians*, 2–4. Cf. also Brown and Meier, *Antioch and Rome*, 30–32; Segal, *Paul the Convert*, 187–94.

guests came, they were referred to as "some unspecified men" (τινας ἀπὸ Ἰακώβου)—albeit identified as "from James." But whatever happened with their presence, it is characterized by language of exclusion (ὑπέστελλεν καὶ ἀφώριζεν) and power relations (φοβούμενος). At the end of the verse these visitors from James are associated with "those of circumcision (τοὺς ἐκ περιτομῆς)." Thus, the word circumcision stands out as the powerful word of marking a hierarchical difference between Jews and Gentiles that then ruled the ethos of table-fellowship in Antioch. It also represents the tilting balance in equal relationship between Jews and Gentiles in Antioch. This explains why, according to Paul, for fear of "those of circumcision," the rest of the Jews (Ἰουδαῖοι) followed the example of Peter (2:13).

Whether the Jewish Christians acted because of the force of Peter's example or not,[46] the force of persuasion and the hierarchal power relation were such that even Barnabas, who worked together with Paul in Jerusalem in order to ensure the equal standing of uncircumcised Gentiles, sided with the Jewish Christians of Antioch.[47] Paul's use of language (τινας ἀπὸ Ἰακώβου, τοὺς ἐκ περιτομῆς, finally to οἱ Ἰουδαῖοι) highlights the escalating weight of "Jewishness" or Jewish identity on the part of Jewish participants at table-fellowship. Such a rhetorical move seems to prepare for both Paul's rhetorical rebuke of Peter in 2:14 and his argument in defense of equality-with-difference between Jews and Gentiles on the grounds of justification by faith in 2:15–21.

Certainly, Paul's criticism of Peter's change of behavior as it is formulated in Gal 2:14 has been determinative for the dominant interpretation of Paul's principle regarding the Jew-Gentile difference. The issue involved in the Jewish observance of food laws has been placed at the center in the scholarly treatment of the Antiochene practice of table-fellowship, Peter's change of behavior, and Paul's position. If we seek to grasp Paul's approach to the meaning of the Jew-Gentile difference in Christ, i.e. within the nascent Jewish Messianic (Christian) community into which Gentiles are now integrated we need to ask how Paul saw the event. Of course, it should be conceded that we do not know what really happened at the mixed table-fellowship and how exactly it happened. Any reconstruction of historical events can never be free from hermeneutics. Paul's description

---

46. See Taylor, *Paul, Antioch and Jerusalem*, 132; Holmberg, *Paul and Power*, 34.

47. Taylor argues that "any action James was taking in Antioch through the visitors was in terms of, and not contrary to, the agreement, and this would seem to be confirmed by Barnabas and the Antiochene Christians' response to the situation" (Taylor, *Paul, Antioch and Jerusalem*, 134).

of his confrontation with Peter in Antioch certainly leaves several historical questions, no matter how important they are for the reconstruction of the Antioch incident, open to different interpretations depending on the interpreter's historical imagination.

Despite the uncertainly, ambiguity, and contingency entailed in the interpretation of the Antioch incident, Paul makes at least three points explicit. These three points are crucial for a proper understanding of Paul's position toward differences between Jews and Gentiles as well as his understanding and articulation of the gospel in relation to the Jewish-Gentile difference. First, in Antioch, before the arrival of some men from James, the Jewish Christians in Antioch ate with the Gentile Christians. Clearly, the Antioch community not only accepted Gentiles as Gentiles, that is, as (for male Gentiles) the uncircumcised Gentiles, but also practiced table-fellowship together with Gentiles (μετὰ τῶν ἐθνῶν συνήσθιεν, 2:12). While there is evidence that some Jews could have social intercourse with Gentiles by dining with them,[48] the significance of the table-fellowship that the Antioch community was practicing should not be underestimated. In one unified community of Jews and Gentiles, Jews were eating as Jews together with Gentiles and Gentiles were eating as Gentiles together with Jews.[49]

Apparently, Paul saw that such practice of eating together embodies the radical inclusivity of the gospel of Christ in which the differences of foreskin and circumcision remain (τὸ εὐαγγέλιον τῆς ἀκροβυστίας . . . τῆς περιτομῆς, 2:7). Paul's rhetorical and textual emphasis of the double togetherness (i.e., the use of both the preposition μετά and the prepositional suffix συν- in 2:12, μετὰ τῶν ἐθνῶν συνήσθιον) is quite striking. Through the practice of radical inclusivity the differences of circumcision and foreskin are defined as mere differences and remain as such, not differences to be excluded and subordinated as "other." Along with ethno-religious and cultural differences which serve to demarcate and reinforce the boundary between Jews (us) and non-Jews (them), Jewish believers in Antioch, including Paul and Barnabas, regularly ate with Gentile believers. It is hardly questionable that they ate as Jews. When Peter as a visiting missionary came to Antioch, he as a Jew willingly joined the practice of eating together with the Gentile believers.

---

48. See E. P. Sanders, "Jewish Association," 17–88; Tomson, *Paul and the Jewish Law*, 230–36; Nanos, "What Was at Stake?" 282–318.

49. Notice the use of the imperfect form (συνήσθιον) of the verb συνεσθίω, which suggests that the practice was repeatedly enacted.

Difference and Table-fellowship in Antioch (Gal 2:11–21)

Second, with the visit to Antioch by the men from James, the practice of most of the Jews eating with the Gentile Christians was broken. The table-fellowship turned out to be not the same as before. It was, according to Paul, primarily because Peter withdrew and stopped eating with the Gentile believers. Paul's language describing Peter's change of practice strongly suggests that the practice of radical inclusivity recognizing differences as different (or equality with difference) was replaced by separation and exclusion, under the force of persuasion related to the power of circumcision as one of the foremost markers of Jewish self-identity. Peter withdrew (ὑπέστελλεν) from eating together with the Gentiles and separated himself (ἀφώριζεν ἑαυτόν), fearing those of circumcision (φοβούμενος τοὺς ἐκ περιτομῆς).

What was problematic for Paul was the intensifying self-understanding of those of circumcision and the underlying logic behind Peter's fear, eventually leading the practice of table-fellowship embodying equality with difference into a different pattern of practice. Characterizing the practice of μετὰ τῶν ἐθνῶν συνήσθιεν in Gal 2:12, Paul used the prefix συν- symbolizing togetherness or inclusiveness to integrate Gentiles into the one table-fellowship without rendering difference into sameness. To the contrary, in the following verse (2:13), the prefix συν- was linked exclusively to the practice (συνυπεκρίθησαν, συναπήχθη) of the Jewish believers (Ἰουδαῖοι). The oneness of table-fellowship was shattered by the dominance of Jewish table practice, with the implication that Gentiles could not be included in table-fellowship with Jews unless Gentiles became like Jews or the Gentile difference converts to the Jewish sameness. On the one hand, this textual and rhetorical turn may reflect that the Jewish people in Palestine, particularly during the mid-40s, tended to insist upon the observance of Jewish laws and traditions as the only means of resisting against the direct imperial domination of Rome.[50] Thus, perhaps Peter's change of practice with regard to table-fellowship with Gentiles in Antioch was a response to the call for solidarity with Jews and Jewish Christians in Judea. On the other hand, it should be emphasized that Paul's language certainly reflects the changing relationship between Jews and Gentiles in the Antiochene community.

Third, the thrust of Paul's criticism against Peter's change of behavior is concrete and explicit: Peter's refusal to eat with Gentiles was not faithful to the truth of the gospel (ὅτι οὐκ ὀρθοποδοῦσιν πρὸς τὴν ἀλήθειαν τοῦ

---

50. Especially see Horsley and Silberman, *The Message and the Kingdom*, 126–44. In his article "Agitators," Jewett relates such a historical situation to the problems and tensions facing the Galatian congregation.

εὐαγγελίου, Gal 2:14). It should be evident that in reference to the truth of the gospel Paul means the gospel of foreskin and circumcision (Gal 2:7), on which both Paul (the Antiochene community) and Peter (the Jerusalem community) agreed. Peter's withdrawal and separation from the table-fellowship with Gentiles is not the right practice toward the truth of gospel. In other words, Peter's not eating with Gentiles, no matter what issues of Jewish food laws might be involved in such a change, is not the right practice of the gospel which preaches oneness with egalitarian differences. Paul is not saying that Peter's behavior is not the right practice toward the observance of the Jewish laws. It seems hardly conceivable that Paul's criticism was directed toward Peter's observance of Jewish laws or his solidarity with Jewish Christians in Jerusalem.

Paul's criticism against Peter lies in that, influenced by the dominant tendency of privileging the identity/difference of Jewishness, Peter's change of practice at table-fellowship contributes to and promotes a non-egalitarian, hierarchical understanding of the Jew-Gentile difference relegating the Gentile difference to an inferior difference. Its resulting consequence within the context of the Antiochene community would mean, according to Paul, that, unless the Gentile Christians in Antioch become like Jews, they are not equal to the Jewish Christians and they cannot remain as Gentiles within the community. Thus, Paul rebukes Peter: εἰ σὺ Ἰουδαῖος ὑπάρχων ἐθνικῶς καὶ οὐχὶ Ἰουδαϊκῶς ζῇς, πῶς τὰ ἔθνη ἀναγκάζεις ἰουδαΐζειν; (2:14).

Paul's remarks here cannot be interpreted as an objection to the observance of Jewish laws or as the persuasion of Jews to give up Jewish cultural practices. His concern is with Jews who compel Gentiles to "live like a Jew." In his view, Peter's change of behavior contributes to establishing a dichotomy of "living like a Gentile ἐθνικῶς" and "living like a Jew Ἰουδαϊκῶς," with the latter privileged over the former. In such a case, Gentile "difference" becomes the opposite of Jewish identity/difference, and is relegated to difference to be denied and excluded. How can the difference of Gentile marginality be justified?

6. THE RHETORICS OF "JUSTIFICATION BY FAITH" AND THE POLITICS OF DIFFERENCE (GAL 2:15-21)

Thus, at the end of Galatians 1–2, Paul presents his theological understanding of justification by faith in order to explain his disagreement with Peter's position with regard to what happened to the unity with difference at the

Difference and Table-fellowship in Antioch (Gal 2:11–21)

table-fellowship in Antioch. Present New Testament scholarship is divided on the question whether the theological exposition on justification by faith in Gal 2:15–21 should be treated as a summary speech to the episode at Antioch or a separate unit of theological elaboration on justification by faith.[51] Reading Paul's account of the Antioch incident (2:11–14) as well as his articulation of justification by faith (2:15–21) reveals strong elements of literary coherence between the two passages, thus leading me to prefer the first option. The terms of the polarity between Jews and Gentiles clearly link 2:14 and 15. Moreover, Paul's reference to "us" as Jews at the beginning of 2:15 (ἡμεῖς φύσει Ἰουδαῖοι) strongly suggests a continuity with the response of Paul, a Jew, toward the practice of Peter, a Jew, who is criticized in 2:14. Also, Paul's mentioning of "building up again the very thing that I tore down" most naturally refers to the table-fellowship and its subsequent collapse.

Thus, 2:15–21 fits well with the preceding Antioch narrative as the concluding argument recapitulating the significance of the equal standing of Gentiles with Jews at table-fellowship. It further constitutes the climax of Galatians 1–2. Galatians 2:15–21 is not merely theological reflection on justification either by faith or by works of the Law, separated from any concrete community context. Rhetorically and theologically it is tightly linked to the meal practice and the subsequent conflict at Antioch. Having encountered broken table-fellowship and presumably a marginalized status of Gentile believers including his own marginalized position, Paul must have felt a strong need to justify why his position is different from that of Peter and other Jewish believers, and why he defends and sides with Gentile believers at Antioch.

Recapitulating his charge against Peter's change of behavior at table-fellowship, Paul now develops his following rhetorical arguments by focusing on the theological thrust implicated in the latter. First of all, in criticizing Peter's withdrawal from table-fellowship with Gentiles Paul exposes and rejects a Jewish self-identity based on the polarity of (born) Jews/the righteous/pure/superior/the Law versus Gentile/sinners/impure/inferior/sin. According to 1:13–14, Paul knows perfectly well what such a self-understanding is all about. In his pre-Damascus period, he proudly

---

51. For a review of the scholarship on the matter, see Dunn, "Incident at Antioch," 172 n. 117; Betz, *Galatians*, 114.

devoted his life to the same position of extreme Jewishness advocating such a dualistic world-view.[52]

Such a position characterizes and represents an *essentialist* understanding of Jewish identity/difference in the sense that it defines the differences between Jews and Gentiles as two unchangeable essences and oppositional polarities that are inherently different from each other. As a consequence, such a position assumes an exclusive, hierarchical understanding of differences by which Jews and Gentiles are not merely different but the latter are inferior to the former. Stemming from a Jewish insider, i.e., one of the Jews, Paul's criticism of Peter's behavior challenges the emerging exclusive tendency of the politics of identity or "othering," which separates *us*, Jews (ἡμεῖς φύσει Ἰουδαῖοι) from *them*, Gentiles (οὐκ ἐξ ἐθνῶν ἁμαρτωλοί).[53]

Second, as we noted above, Paul established his argument on the common ground with which he assumes Peter agrees. The conviction which Paul and Peter share is stated in 2:16:

> Yet (we Jews) knowing that a man (ἄνθρωπος) is not justified by works of the law (ἐξ ἔργων νόμου) but through faith in/of Jesus Christ, even we have believed in Christ Jesus (διὰ πίστεως Ἰησοῦ Χριστοῦ), in order to be justified by faith in/of Christ, and not by works of the law, because by works of the law all flesh (πᾶσα σάρξ) will not be justified.

As we have seen, the self-identification "we" = Jews (2:15) indicates that the intra-Jewish dialogue regarding how to consider Gentiles within the community continues. Paul introduces the rhetoric of justification in order to problematize a logic of Jewish identity that excludes the full participation of Gentiles as Gentiles unless they become proselytes. He deconstructs the hierarchical framework of "us" as Jews (ἡμεῖς Ἰουδαῖοι) versus "them" as Gentiles and sinners (ἔθνη ἁμαρτωλοί) in 2:15.

Here it is important to distinguish points of agreement and disagreement between Paul and Peter. The point of agreement: Most Jews, Paul says, including Paul and Peter, would agree with the Jewish belief that a man is not justified by works of the law, but by faith.[54] Here his use of ἄνθρωπος

---

52. Cf. Gal 1:14; Phil 3:5–6.

53. On the implications of ἁμαρτωλοί see Dunn, "Incident at Antioch," 150–51.

54. See Segal, *Paul the Convert*, 128: "No other Jews in the first century distinguish faith and law in the way Paul does. For a Jew, faith fundamentally precedes anything as well, but there is no need to distinguish between it and law. Jews perform the commandments because they are commanded by God, not because they guarantee justification."

("man," "person") instead of ἡμεῖς ("we") is noteworthy, presumably because of Paul's intention to disturb the polarity of Jewish-Gentile difference. Furthermore, elaborating on this Jewish belief in justification, Paul emphasizes the common ground on which Paul and Peter are standing as Jews who believe in Jesus Christ, that is, by adding the phrase ἐὰν μὴ διὰ πίστεως Ἰησοῦ Χριστοῦ.[55] Then Paul reasserts the point of agreement, saying that we (Jews) have believed in Christ Jesus, in order to be justified by faith in Christ and not by works of the law. In other words, the doctrine of *justification* is not the point of *disagreement*, but of *agreement*. It is an irony that in the history of interpretation Paul's justification by faith has so long ignored this point and (mis)interpreted the real impetus of the dichotomy of faith-works.[56]

Based upon this common ground, Paul clarifies justification by faith: "Because by works of the law *all flesh* will *not* be justified" (2:16). This shows Paul's difference from Peter's view. Most translations prefer "no one" to "not all" for οὐ . . . πᾶσα σάρξ.[57] However, considering Paul's rhetorical move and the flow of his argument the literal translation, "all flesh will not be justified" is far more appropriate. The first focal point here is that through works of the law, *not* "all the people," that is both Jews and Gentiles, are together justified. Because based on the social and ritual functions of the law, the dichotomy of ἡμεῖς Ἰουδαῖοι versus ἔθνη ἁμαρτωλοί in 2:15 is legitimized. In other words, Gentiles cannot be justified according to those works of the law, thus are excluded from the people of God. Paul seems to use the word πᾶσα σάρξ deliberately to include both Jews and Gentiles in combination with the word σάρξ which carries the connotation of the Jew-Gentile difference in σάρξ of circumcision and foreskin. Hence, it should not be

---

When Betz considers justification by faith in 2:16 as "part of Jewish Christian theology," he misinterprets it as "the denial of the orthodox Jewish (Pharisaic) doctrine of salvation" which claims that "justification by doing and thus fulfilling the ordinances of the Torah" (Betz, *Galatians*, 115–16).

55. Cf. Betz, *Galatians*, 117–18.

56. When read from the close connection to the Antioch incident in Gal 2:11–14, there is no reason that such a point of agreement in 2:17 should be interpreted as meaning that whether one is a Jew or a Gentile is irrelevant. Rather, Paul's argumentative force lies at the emphasis of equality with difference.

57. Cf. Ps 143:2. However I do not fully accept the so-called two covenant theory proposed by Gaston and Gager. My approach differs from those who argue for the two ways of salvation, one (law) for Jews and the other (faith) for Gentiles. I am more concerned with the differences between Jews and Gentiles within the community redefined in terms of faith in Jesus Christ. See Segal, *Paul the Convert*, 125–33.

overlooked that the universalism intended in the use of πᾶσα σάρξ cannot be characterized as the contemporary Hellenistic universalism framed in the dichotomy of πνεῦμα–σάρξ.[58] Rather, it is quite striking that the universalism inclusive of both Jews and Gentiles is advocated on the basis of difference in σάρξ, but by reconstructing the hierarchical relations between different kinds of σάρξ.[59] If through faith in/of Jesus Christ both Jews and Gentiles are justified respectively as Jews and Gentiles with differences, Jewish Christians in Antioch can no longer treat Gentile members of the community as sinners per se.

In 2:17-18, Paul reconsiders how his clash with Peter at the table-fellowship in Antioch is related to the theological dimensions of justification by faith. In Paul's view, eating together with Gentiles in Antioch was done in conformity with the meaning of justification by faith: Jews as Jews were eating together with Gentiles as equals of Jews, not as sinners. Paul interprets this as an effort to build one egalitarian community of Jews and Gentiles: "endeavoring to be justified in Christ" (2:17). Paul does not concede that equal association with Gentiles is equivalent to associating with sinners. Otherwise, this would mean that Christ is a servant of sin (ἁμαρτίας διάκονος).[60] Paul denies this emphatically: μὴ γένοιτο. Why? Paul gives the answer in Gal 2:18-21 by the way in which he identifies himself with the crucifixion event of Christ.

Paul's understanding of the apocalyptical significance of the Christ event categorically precludes any possibility that Christ is a servant of sin. To the contrary, through his crucifixion Jesus Christ has served to deconstruct (ἃ κατέλυσα ταῦτα) the power of sin operating in the negative function of works of the law, in particular the judgmental sin of judging others as sinners, in other words, making others the inferior "others." But, what

58. Against Boyarin, *A Radical Jew*, 57-85, esp. 65-69.

59. It is noteworthy that in dealing with the relationship between Jews and Gentiles Paul uses the term σάρξ in reference to his Jewish people in Rom 9:8 and 11:14.

60. See Rom 15:8: "For I tell you that Christ became a servant (διάκονος) of circumcision for the sake of God's truthfulness, in order to confirm the promises given to the ancestors." It is not accidental that Paul uses the terminology διάκονος in reference to Christ only in Gal 2:17 and Rom 15:8, which are both linked to the context of table-fellowship. I argue that Paul responded differently to the different community situations, which eventually shows his politics of difference from the perspective of solidarity with "the weak." Here in Gal 2:17 by rejecting any possible charge against Gentiles in Christ, Paul sides with the minority of Gentiles in the community at Antioch. On the other hand, Paul's politics of difference leads him to side with Jews in the Roman congregation, as I shall discuss in the following chapter.

is implied here is the conviction that the destructive and divisive power of sin was broken, and therefore the necessity to separate humanity into those doing the works of the law (Jews) and Gentile sinners. The importance of this thought is shown through the fact that Paul mentions it in a very prominent position already in his prescript (Gal 1:4) and makes it the climax of the justification section in Gal 2:21.

To conclude, the key vocabulary Paul adopted for the articulation of justification by faith in 2:15–21, such as works of the law (ἔργα νόμου), grace (χάρις), and sin (ἁμαρτία), are clearly put into the context of the Jew-Gentile polarity in 2:15. This shows that 2:15–21 as the theological key passage of Galatians 1–2 is inseparably linked to the Antioch meal conflict where the differences between Jews and Gentiles appears as the very point of disagreement between Peter and Paul. From all these, it is fair to say that as a theological reflection on the practice of table-fellowship between Jews and Gentiles, the primary concern of the doctrine of justification by faith was about equal relations between Jews and Gentiles within the messianic community of faith. Justification by faith for Paul justifies a new relation of Jews and Gentiles in Christ (2:17), especially at the common table. It is interesting to note that the same linkage between justification and the Jew-Gentile community is made in Rom 3:28–30:

> For we hold that a man is justified by faith apart from works of law. Or is God the God of Jews only? Is he not the God of Gentiles also? Yes, of Gentiles also, since God is one; and he will justify the circumcised on the ground of faith and the uncircumcised through their faith.

This leads us to ask whether Paul's politics of difference toward Jews and Gentiles we have discussed in this chapter can be also discerned in a different community situation. Thus, we now turn to Rom 14:1—15:13, another meal text which reflects tensions and conflicts at the Christian table-fellowship in Rome.

5

The "Weak" and the "Strong" at Table in Romans 14:1—15:13

1. HISTORICAL CONTEXT: THE EDICT OF CLAUDIUS

ALTHOUGH SOME SCHOLARS STILL insist that Romans should be interpreted as a theological treatise written by Paul regardless of its specific historical situation,[1] more scholars have acknowledged that, like other letters Paul wrote, Romans should be read as a letter addressed to the concrete situation of the Roman congregation(s) with specific agenda(s). As the contingent (contextual) nature of the letter of Romans has drawn more attention among scholars, more increasing is a tendency to regard Rom 14:1—15:13 as one of key texts which might shed new light on our understanding of the theological and historical puzzles in the current "Romans debate."[2] Among others, there are problems related to the historical occasion of Romans, the relationship between the theological concerns of the first eleven chapters in Romans and the paraenetic chapters of 12–15, the relationship between Jews and Gentiles within the Roman congregation, and the purpose and message of Romans.

1. Following G. Bornkamm, Robert J. Karris and Victor Furnish are the leading voices for the position. See Karris, "Romans 14:1—15:13," 65–84; Furnish, *The Love Command*.

2. For the letter's "double character" as the fundamental problem of interpreting the letter, see Kümmel, *Introduction to the New Testament*, 305–20; N. Elliott, *Rhetoric of Romans*, 9–43. For the continuing debate, see Donfried, ed., *The Romans Debate*.

The "Weak" and the "Strong" at Table in Romans 14:1—15:13

Who are the "weak," and who are the "strong" in Rom 14:1—15:13? In interpreting Rom 14:1—15:13, scholars have endeavored to answer this question. However, this should include the question of why the "weak" were differentiated as the "weak" from the "strong." In other words, the character and content of the "weakness" of the "weak" and the "strength" of the "strong" are crucial to the understanding of the problems Paul addresses in Rom 14:1—15:13 and his paraenetic intention toward the "strong" and the "weak." How does Paul perceive the relationship between the "weak" and the "strong" in Romans; how does Paul define the meaning of "difference" with regard to meal practice and the formation of early Christian self-identity?

As for the identification of the "weak" and the "strong" in Romans, the prevailing position holds that the "weak" were Jewish Christians (or, Christian Jews) and the "strong" were Gentile Christians (or, Christian Gentiles). Most scholars see especially in the following statements in Romans 14 the theological ground for the identification of the "weak" as Jewish Christians:

> One believes he may eat anything, while the weak man eats only vegetables. (14:2)

> One man esteems one day as better than other, while another man esteems all days alike. Let every one be fully convinced in his own mind. (14:5)

> I know and am persuaded in the Lord Jesus that nothing is unclean in itself; but it is unclean for any one who thinks it unclean (14:14)

However, there have been some objections to the common tendency of regarding the practices referred to in those verses as specifically Jewish. In an attempt to repute the objections raised against the identification of the "weak" in Rom 14:1—15:13 with Jewish Christians in Rome, James C. Walters summarizes them as follows: "(1) Vegetarianism and abstinence from wine were not characteristic Jewish dietary practices; (2) the equations "weak" = Jewish Christians/ "strong" = Gentile Christians do not hold; (3) the passage appears to be a generalized version of a position Paul worked out in relation to a concrete problem in Corinth; therefore it requires no specific historical referent in Rome."[3] As Walters points out, especially the first and third objections find little support in current scholarship.

The first objection that refuses to relate vegetarianism and abstinence to an aspect of Jewish dietary practice is hardly sustainable. It has been

---

3. Walter, *Ethnic Issues*, 85.

noted that Jews in the first century—especially within the context of the Diaspora—often practiced vegetarianism, avoiding meats and wines.[4] The possible motivations for such dietary habits can be referred to Jewish sensitivities to the issue of idolatry and/or kashruth, the specific food laws for Jews. Alan Segal and Peter Gooch, among others, have drawn attention to the problem of idolatry involved in early Christian meal practice, especially in the tensions between the "weak" and the "strong" among Corinthian Christians.[5] While Gooch considers that the problem of the "weak" and the "strong" in Rom 14:1—15:13 was the issue of kashruth, not that of food offered to idols,[6] Segal thinks that Paul is talking about Jewish food laws in general and explaining his strong position to Jewish Christians.[7] Thus, it seems safe to assume that the characterization of the "weak" in Rom 14:2 as those who eat only vegetables is related to Jewish dietary practice and thus the Jew-Gentile problem in the Roman congregation. Following J. Paul Sampley and Wayne A. Meeks,[8] Walters has suggested an alternative explanation which concerns Paul's rhetorical strategy in mentioning vegetarianism and abstinence in Romans 14. Walters argues that in addressing the tensions between the "weak" and the "strong" in Rom 14:1—15:13 Paul deliberately mentioned vegetarianism and special days in an inclusive way. According to this explanation, Paul's rhetorical intention in making such an oblique allusion to Jewish dietary practices was not to polarize the conflicts between Jewish and Gentile Christians in Rome.[9] All this strongly suggests that the dietary practices of vegetarianism and abstinence in Rom14:1—15:13 bear some relation to the Jew-Gentile difference in the Roman congregation. As for the third objection, more scholars tend to emphasize that despite undeniable similarities between the issue discussed in 1 Cor 8–10 and Paul's admonitions toward the "weak" and the "strong" in Rom 14-15, more important differences between them do not seem to allow for a "generalized adaptation" that rendered the specific Roman situation irrelevant.[10]

4. See Segal, *Paul the Convert*, 228–33.

5. Ibid., 228–53; Gooch, *Dangerous Food*.

6. Gooch, *Dangerous Food*, 116–18.

7. Segal, *Paul the Convert*, 234–36.

8. Sampley, "The Weak and the Strong," 40–52; Meeks, "Judgment and the Brother, 290–300.

9. Walters, *Ethnic Issues*, 86–87.

10. Walters, *Ethnic Issues*, 89; Gooch, *Dangerous Food*, 115–19.

The "Weak" and the "Strong" at Table in Romans 14:1—15:13

Much more debated is whether the "weak" in Romans are to be identified with Jewish Christians and the "strong" with Gentile Christians. There are various views regarding this issue: (1) The equation of the "weak"/"strong" with Jewish Christians/Gentile Christians is unacceptable, because Rom 14–15 as "general Pauline paraenesis"[11] does not address a specific Roman situation; (2) The equation is still sustainable, albeit applying strict ethnic categories need to be avoided; (3) Recently Mark Nanos has made the suggestion that the "weak" in Romans should be regarded as "non-Christian Jews" in Rome.[12]

The first position that shows reservation toward any attempt to specify the "weak" and the "strong" by attributing Rom 14:1—15:13 to the general Pauline paraenesis does not seem to hold significant appealing force. The interpretative reading of Romans has swung around to the other direction. Hence, the majority of scholars tend to regard the "weak" in Romans as mostly Jewish Christians (including some Gentile Christians) who continue to practice the Jewish law, and the "strong" as mostly Gentile Christians. However, there is a significant point that should be emphasized regarding this commonly held position, namely, that the problem does not lie in the identification per se, but in the general assumption that scholars have brought to it. In equating the "weak" as Jewish Christian, scholars identified the nature of "weakness" (cf. τὰ ἀσθενήματα; 15:1) of the "weak" with "Jewishness" or Jewish identity itself. In other words, without taking into consideration the relationship between Jews and Gentiles in the Roman community, it has been assumed that the practice of the Jewish law by those who believe in Christ is what characterizes them as the "weak." Their faith accompanied by the practice of the Jewish law is "weak," because faith, it is assumed, means Pauline freedom from the Law.

Mark Nanos has challenged this assumption as the "condescending trap that characterizes almost all interpretations of the 'weaknesses of the weak' as their failure to disregard the practice of the Law, as though the practice of the Law demonstrated a lack of faith," which he also calls "Luther's trap."[13] A further part of his challenge is to suggest that the "weak" in Romans are not Christian Jews but non-Christian Jews, and their "weak-

---

11. Karris, "Romans 14:1–15:13," 65–84.

12. This hypothesis is strongly argued by Nanos in his provocative study titled *The Mystery of Romans*.

13. Nanos, *The Mystery of Romans*, 91, esp. 83–165. A similar challenge has been made by Peter J. Tomson from a different approach; see his *Paul and the Jewish Law*, esp. 221–81.

ness" is the lack of faith in Jesus as the Christ of Israel. Whereas I fully accept Nanos's contention that the weakness in 14:1 has nothing to do with Jewish identity and the practice of the Law, I cannot agree with him regarding the identity of the "weak" as non-Christian Jews in Rome.[14]

On the one hand, some efforts have been made to interpret the tensions between the "weak" and the "strong" in view of the contemporary Roman attitudes toward Jews, including Jewish Christians. In particular, the edict of Claudius against the Jews in 49 CE was regarded as an important reference point of the immediate historical background of Romans. The effect of the Jewish expulsion has been discussed as one of the major historical explanations for the tensions between the "weak" and the "strong" in the Christian community in Rome.

Wolfgang Wiefel, in his influential article entitled "The Jewish Community in Ancient Rome and the Origins of Roman Christianity,"[15] showed that the first Christian congregation in Rome consisted of Jewish Christians and was shaped within the context of Jewish communities in Rome. He noted the importance of the Claudian expulsion of Jews from Rome in its effect on the changing relationship between Jewish Christians and Gentile Christians within the emerging anti-Jewish sentiment in Rome. In view of that context, he suggested the possible emergence of the unequal relationship in which Jewish Christians, who returned to Rome after the death of Claudius (54 CE) and the resultant lapse of the edict, found themselves "only a minority in a congregation which previously they had shaped."[16] In the article, although he tried to reconsider Gentile Christians as the main audience of the letter and Paul's concern toward his Jewish people and Judaism, he did not make specific reference to the "weak" and the "strong."

Some scholars adopted Wiefel's social construction of the early Christian community in Rome, and sought to develop its implications for the tensions between the "weak" and the "strong."[17] Yet, less attention has been given to both socio-historical and hermeneutical problems involved in the "weakness" of the weak. It is, thus, important to note that despite the common emphasis on the historical context, these scholars present different,

---

14. For a very pointed response to Nanos's identification of the "weak," see Reasoner, *The Strong and the Weak*, 131–36.

15. Wiefel, "The Jewish Community."

16. Ibid., 96.

17. In particular, see Walters's above mentioned book and Francis Watson, "Two Roman Congregations," 203–15.

even contrary readings of Paul's purpose and strategy toward the "weak" and the "strong."

Furthermore, it is striking that the conclusions on Paul's purpose toward the "weak" and the "strong" drawn by these "historical" interpretations are not quite different from the conclusions reached by more "theological" interpretations. For example, James C. Walters argues that "Paul's fundamental aim was to create common ground between Jewish and gentile Christians" by relativizing their ethnic differences as well as by "checking the development of separate 'Jewish' and 'gentile' version of Christianity."[18] On the other hand, according to Francis Watson, "Paul's purpose in writing Romans was to defend and explain his view of freedom from the law (i.e., separation from the Jewish community and its way of life), with the aim of converting Jewish Christians to his point of view so as to create a single 'Pauline' congregation in Rome."[19]

All these considerations lead this study to a serious engagement with the following questions: Is it justifiable to say that the "weak" addressed by Paul in Rom 14:1—15:13 were weak because they continued to practice their own Jewish laws, irrespective of the Roman socio-historical context as it was shaped by e.g., "the edict of Claudius?" At the same time, is it equally justifiable to discuss the issue of the "weak" and the "strong" solely on the basis of "the edict of Claudius construct" without paying careful attention to Paul's own rhetorical construct, including his deliberate rhetorical strategy and purpose? Further, is it justifiable to conclude that Paul's purpose toward the "weak" and the "strong" was to create a single, unified community in which Jewish and Gentile differences were irrelevant? In order to answer these questions, I shall turn to the textual dynamics of the "weak" and the "strong" as described and elaborated by Paul. But first we need to draw our attention to the immediate context of Rom 14:1—15:13.

2. LITERARY CONTEXT: "LOVE ONE ANOTHER" IN ROMANS 12–13 AS THE PRELUDE TO THE PARAENESIS ON THE "WEAK" AND THE "STRONG"

Before we encounter the discussion of the "weak" and the "strong" in Romans, what we have is a somewhat lengthy parenesis which Paul presents in Rom 12–13. One may regard it simply as one form of general Pauline

---

18. Walters, *Ethnic Issues*, 91.
19. Watson, "Two Roman Congregations," 206.

paraenesis without any particular connection to the following section on the "weak" and the "strong."[20] However, let us note a couple of key terms and motifs found in both chapters 12–13 and chapters 14–15, which create a strong literary coherence.

At the closing part of chapters 9–11 where Paul engaged in the reciprocal relations between Gentile Christians and Israel, Paul had particularly Gentile Christians in Rome as a target of his instruction, problematizing and warning of the emerging presumptuous, triumphant mind-set on their part. The tendency of rejecting the Jewishness in Jews and/or Jewish Christians has been seriously challenged in the parable of the olive tree (Rom 11:17–24). There seems to be an increasing ethos among the Gentile Christians in Rome that they now replaced the natural (Jewish) branches, albeit they are "grafted in." They consider their position as superior to that of Jews and/or Jewish Christians, the broken-off branches of the olive tree. In such a mind-set, a hierarchical structure of superiority/inferiority is emerging, and concomitantly the balance between differences in identity is tilting. The "identity/difference" of the superior (Gentile) position becomes the dominant "identity" to be associated with, while the "identity/difference" of the inferior position becoming marginalized as "difference" to be dissociated from. Paul's strong point in warning against such a tendency is unmistakably clear: "Do not think you are in higher or superior position" (μὴ ὑψηλὰ φρόνει, 11:20; μὴ ἦτε παρ' ἑαυτοῖς φρόνιμοι, 11:25).

Given that context, Paul begins chapters 12–13 with an appeal for an alternative form or framework (σχῆμα) of life to which Christians in Rome should be conformed (συσχηματίζεσθε) by transforming (μεταμορφοῦσθε) their minds and bodies (12:1–2). A radically different pattern of life is called for, which is non-conformist to this world (μὴ μεταμορφοῦσθε τῷ αἰῶνι τούτῳ). The question is: what is the core of the alternative pattern of life Paul envisions?

First, in Rom 12:3–8 there is a call for the recognition of and mutual respect for differences among members of the Christian body. The unit of the Christian community is characterized in terms of one body which has many different members and functions. Although scholars usually emphasized Paul's understanding of the Christian community as an organic unity, it has been almost neglected that the "oneness" in the image of one body

---

20. See, for example, Käsemann, *Commentary on Romans*, 323: "The arguments of this part of the epistle comprise general exhortation in chapters 12–13 and a clearly separated set of teaching directed to the Christians at Rome in 14:1—15:13."

(ἓν σῶμα) is not explicitly understood as "sameness," (οὐ αὐτὴν ... πρᾶξιν, 12:4), but oneness with difference. There are different "measures of faith," and different "gifts" (cf. μέτρον πίστεως, 12:3; διάφορα χαρίσματα, 12:6)—though the meaning of difference is not related to the Jew-Gentile identity in particular. Moreover, what stands out in this discourse on "oneness (unity) with difference" is Paul's specific urging that every member of the Christian body "not think of himself higher than he ought to think, but to think with sober judgment" (12:3), which serves as a kind of introduction and "headline" to the whole passage.[21] Such an egalitarian mind-set is what makes "oneness with difference" possible. Taking up the key term φρονεῖν already used in 12:3 to describe an egalitarian mind-set, 12:16 redefines loving one another as "love" (ἀγάπη). This leads to the focal topic of love (ἀγάπη).

In Rom 12:9–11, Paul calls for "loving one another" (12:9–10) as the way of "serving the Lord" (12:11). The mutuality of love is highlighted as the center of his paraenesis, with the emphatic repetition of the word "one another" (εἷς ἀλλήλων, 12:5; εἰς ἀλλήλους φιλόστοργοι, ἀλλήλους προηγούμενοι, 12:10). However, the mutuality of love does not remain a theoretical principle, rather, according to Paul, it should work as a praxis for the transformation of the relationship among different members of the community. What is the thrust of such a praxis? Paul makes it clear in 12:16:

> τὸ αὐτὸ εἰς ἀλλήλους φρονοῦντες,
> μὴ τὰ ὑψηλὰ φρονοῦντες ἀλλὰ τοῖς ταπεινοῖς συναπαγόμενοι.
> μὴ γίνεσθε φρόνιμοι παρ' ἑαυτοῖς.
>
> Have the same mind toward/for one another;
> Do not think higher things, but associate with the lowly;
> Do not become those who think (are wise) according to their own selves.

We see that loving one another is redefined as "setting up one's mind for (toward) others" as opposed to "setting up one's mind for (within) one's own self" in equality/sameness (τὸ αὐτό). This opposed (μή) both to a mindset of "upward mobility" (τὰ ὑψηλὰ φρονοῦντες) which dissociates itself from the "lowly" and to a self-mindedness (φρόνιμοι παρ' ἑαυτοῖς). In particular, the mutuality of love, understood as "setting up one's mind for (toward) others in equality," is connected to the practice of "associating

---

21. Cf. Phil 2:3–4.

with the lowly."[22] Such a practice of solidarity with the "lowly" leaves behind one's own perspective/wisdom and self-interest, in other words, the "logic of identity." This is what actually materializes the principle of mutuality. Paul's point is that through such a practice, the vertical, hierarchical social-relations (ὑψηλός–ταπεινός) among different members can be deconstructed and transformed—not reverted—into horizontal, egalitarian social relations towards one another. At this point, it should be pointed out that it is not fortuitous at all that we have the same message in both the preceding chapter (Rom 11:18, 20, 25) and the following one (Romans 15).[23] The importance of Rom 12:16 in Paul's rhetorical strategy of making tight connection between chapters 9–11 and chapters 14–15 should not be ignored.

Furthermore, in Rom 12:17—13:7, Paul's call for such a radical mutuality goes even to its extreme in the sense that it demands loving one's enemies beyond loving one's neighbors: Repay no one evil for evil and never avenge yourselves . . . (12:17). Do not be overcome by evil, but overcome evil with good (ἀλλὰ νίκα ἐν τῷ ἀγαθῷ τὸ κακόν, 12:21). In that context, Paul addresses the issue of obedience to authorities which has been so much debated in the evaluation of Paul's socio-political stance. Here, it is not my intention to engage deeply in the ongoing debate over the interpretation of Rom 13:1–7 which is very crucial to the reassessment of the traditional picture of Paul as a social conservative.[24] What I want to underscore is that even the issue of obedience to authorities is framed and determined by Paul's rhetoric of doing good (τὸ ἀγαθόν, 12:21) and love towards one another (13:8).

Immediately after the passage on obedience to authorities (13:1–7), Paul highlights the imperative to "love one another": "Owe (ὀφείλετε) no one anything, except to love one another; for he who loves his neighbor has fulfilled the law (13:8)." By deliberately connecting the topic of "love one another" to the term τὰς ὀφειλάς referred in the preceding verse (13:7), Paul stresses the priority of "loving one another" and defines that command as the fulfillment of the Jewish law. Again it does not seem accidental that

---

22. See Wengst, *Humility*, 36–57. Commenting on 2 Cor 11:7 in relation to Rom 12:16, Wengst states that "Though he [Paul] originally had the perspective of someone in a high position he adopts the perspective of the insignificant by his life-style" (47).

23. Notice almost verbatim phrases: (11:25; ἵνα μὴ ἦτε παρ' ἑαυτοῖς φρόνιμοι / 15:5; τὸ αὐτὸ φρονεῖν ἀλλήλοις κατὰ Χριστὸν Ἰησοῦν).

24. For an alternative reading to the traditional interpretation, see N. Elliott, "Romans 13:1–7," 184–204.

the same terms used in 13:7 (τὰς ὀφειλάς) and 13:8 (ὀφείλετε) will reoccur right at the beginning of 15:1: We who are strong ought to (ὀφείλομεν) bear with the weaknesses of the weak. It appears not without a rhetorical intention that Paul prepares his paraenesis on the "weak" and the "strong" by reframing the imperative of "love one another" within both its relation to Roman dues and the Jewish law: "Owe (ὀφείλετε) no one anything, except to love one another: for he who loves his neighbor has fulfilled the law . . . . Love does no wrong (κακόν) to a neighbor; therefore love is the fulfilling of the law (13:8–10)."[25]

Finally, Paul ends his paraenesis of love by invoking a sense of eschatological urgency (13:11–14). This section constitutes a counterpart of the very beginning of the paraenesis (12:1–2), as it takes up the key term σχῆμα in 12:2 (Do not be conformed/συσχηματίζεσθε to this world):

> Besides this you know what hour it is, how it is full time now for you to wake from sleep (v. 11) . . . let us conduct ourselves becomingly (εὐσχημόνως, "according to the new pattern of life") as in the day, not in reveling and drunkenness, not in debauchery and licentiousness, not in quarreling and jealousy (13:13).

Certain excessive behaviors such as reveling and drunkenness, quarreling and jealousy are mentioned in contrast to the behavior to be conformed to the new pattern of life. It is important to note that such excessive behaviors are not irrelevant to the meal context, which corresponds to the very context for the tension between the "weak" and the "strong." This point gains further support from Robert Jewett who has suggested the communal meal as the possible locus for the frequent admonitions to "love the brethren," and further "agapaic communalism"—as an alternative to Gerd Theissen's "love patriarchalism"—as the ethical framework suitable for the early Pauline tenement churches.[26]

Jewett has also shown that the words "brotherly love" (φιλαδελφία, 1 Thess 4:9) and "well-doing" (καλοποιέω, 2 Thess 3:13) are referred to in close proximity to the discussion of labor for bread within the common meal context of both communities.[27] Given the context of the common meal practice associated with such words, it is no surprise that alongside the frequent references to "love one another" and "not doing wrong to a

---

25. Cf. Gal 6:2: "Bear one another's burdens, and so fulfill the law of Christ."
26. Jewett, "Tenement Churches," 23–43.
27. Ibid., 33–39.

neighbor" in Romans 12–13, we find the very similar words "brotherly love" (φιλαδελφία, Rom 12:10) and ("doing good") (κακὸν οὐκ ἐργάζεται, Rom 13:10) leading directly into the discussion of the Jewish-Gentile relationships within the common meal setting of the Roman church(es) in Romans 14–15.

All this leads to the conclusion that Rom 12:1—13:4 and Rom 14:1—15:13 should be regarded as a unity, textually and contextually connected to each other as well as the rest of the letter. Paul's appeal to "love one another" through solidarity with the lowly functions as a prelude to his paraenesis on the "weak" and the "strong" in Rom 14:1—15:13. Both interpret each other and support each other.

3. DIFFERENCE BETWEEN THE "WEAK" AND THE "STRONG": ROM 14:1-12

3.1. Difference Trouble: Rhetorical Situation (14:1–5)

Paul begins the last two chapters (Romans 14–15) of his main paraenetic sections in Romans (Romans 12–15) with a word of exhortation: "Welcome the one who is weak in faith, but not for disputes over opinions" (Rom 14:1). This is followed by a very simple description about two different groups: "One believes he may eat everything, while the weak man eats only vegetables" (v. 2). These two groups are described on the basis of their differences in eating practice. One eats (ὁ ἐσθίων) and the other does not eat (ὁ μὴ ἐσθίων). Later, these groups are further contrasted on the basis of their differences in calendar practice. "One esteems one day as better than another, while another esteems all days alike . . ." (v. 5).

Although Paul does not explicitly state the tensions between ὁ ἐσθίων and ὁ μὴ ἐσθίων, what he expects both ὁ ἐσθίων and ὁ μὴ ἐσθίων not to do is given in verse 3. Those who eat are addressed first. It is said that they should not despise those who do not eat. At the same time, those who do not eat should not judge those who eat, because God has welcomed them.

Why should those who do not eat, i.e., the "weak" not pass judgment on those who eat? Why does Paul first take issue with the judgmental behavior on the part of the "weak?" It is important to note that although those who do not eat are addressed as the "weak" (ὁ ἀσθενῶν), they are characterized as the ones who feel entitled to judge those who follow a different eating practice. Although those who eat despise those who do not eat, the

The "Weak" and the "Strong" at Table in Romans 14:1—15:13

former are not characterized as the one who can judge the "weak." How do we explain this? What kind of mind-set is operating in passing judgment by the "weak?" In dealing with the "weak" and the "strong" in Rom 14:1—15:13, what are Paul's intention and rhetorical strategy particularly in this first section of Rom 14:1–12?

It is not surprising, though often unnoticed, that from verse 4 on, Paul uses the term κρίνειν repeatedly with its full connotations and in connection with the term κύριος. The term κρίνειν occurs 8 times in this chapter. It is noteworthy that no other chapter in the entire New Testament reveals such frequent occurrence of the term. This gives an impression that there is a "rhetorical constraint" implying the divisive situation involved in disputes over opinions (μὴ εἰς διακρίσεις διαλογισμῶν, 14:1). The judgmental behavior of κρίνειν seems to contribute to διάκρισις. In order to deal with this, Paul needs to give an explanation of the meaning of "difference" which is related to the self-identity and social formation of the Christian community.

For that purpose, Paul's argumentation begins with an apostrophe: "Who are you to pass judgment on (κρίνων) another servant (ἀλλότριον οἰκέτην)? It is before his own master that he stands or falls. And he will be upheld, for the Master is able to make him stand" (v. 4).

Here we need to pay careful attention to two pairs of relational terms which Paul uses deliberately for his rhetorical argumentation; these are servant/master (οἰκέτης/κύριος) and other/one's own (ἀλλότριος/ἴδιος). The former represents the relation of subjection/domination and the latter represents the relation of difference/identity. Paul placed the problem of judging one another within such a semantic, social structure of relations. As Paul usually uses the term δοῦλος to refer to a servant, the use of οἰκέτης is noticeable. Given that οἰκέτης refers to the house or domestic slave, with the implication of a more immediate relationship between slave and particular master,[28] it is likely that Paul deliberately used the term with the scene of table-fellowship within the household of God in mind, as well as the dynamic relationships between slave and master, and between slave and slave.

Paul describes the status of the person on whom the other person passes judgment as a servant who belongs to another. At the first glance, it is easy to read "another master" from ἀλλότριος as if two masters, instead

---

28. See Käsemann, *Commentary on Romans*, 369; Dunn, *Romans 9–16*, 803. The other references to οἰκέτης are found only in Luke 16:13; Acts 10:7; 1 Pet 2:18. Especially note its occurrence in Acts 10:7 which has a similar context involved in the issue of eating together.

of one master, were implied.[29] However, in that case, Paul's clever use of ἀλλότριος in relation to ἴδιος is missed. According to 14:6, both servants, those who eat as well as those who abstain have one and the same master, whom they honor, yet differently. At the same time, nonetheless, they are different in the sense that each has different (ἀλλότριος) relationship with one's own (ἴδιος) master. That makes one servant different from another servant. Thus, ἀλλότριος not only describes the relation of servant to master, but more importantly establishes a different-but-equal relationship between servants.

The word ἀλλότριος originally denotes "what belongs to an ἄλλος, and therefore 'strange,' also 'alien,' 'unsuitable,' and even finally 'hostile.'"[30] What is implied here is that Jewish Christians should not pass judgment on their "foreign" fellow Gentile Christians who, coming from different origins, have their own different relationship with the Jewish God in Christ. Both Jews and Gentiles, as different-but-equal servants of the household of the Jewish God, are encouraged to welcome one another and eat together at the common table without judging or despising one another. Paradoxically, the metaphor of servant/master here serves to emphasize equality between the servants. "Equality" is not incompatible with difference. Its consequence is that passing judgment on another is not permissible: "And he (= the other/ἀλλότριον) will be upheld, for the Master is able to make him stand" (14:4).

In verse 5, Paul addresses the issue of difference involved in the matter of calendar: "One man esteems (κρίνειν) one day as better than another, while another man esteems (κρίνει) all days alike. Let each one (ἕκαστος) be fully convinced in his own (ἰδίῳ) mind." Given that Paul argued in the previous verses that one should not judge another, it does not seem to be accidental that in this verse Paul applies the verb κρίνω to the different practices of both groups with its neutral meaning and non-personal object. Once again, difference in the observance of special days is fully acknowledged, as the emphatic use of the terms ἕκαστος and ἴδιος shows.

3. 2. Difference in the Lord: Equality with Difference (14:6–9)

Then, in verse 6 Paul moves on to emphasize the Christological significance of the co-existence of different practices within the Christian community

---

29. For example, Dunn translates these words as "the slave of someone else" in Dunn, *Romans 9–16*, 803–804.

30. Büchsel, "ἄλλος, κτλ," *TDNT*, vol. 1, 265.

of Jews and Gentiles. It is important to note how κύριος here functions to integrate differences. Those who eat, eat in honor of the Lord and those who do not eat, do not eat in honor of the Lord. Paul does not say that in the Lord, eating or not eating does not matter as indifference. Eating or not eating does matter to those who eat and those who do not eat. What can be inferred from this is that in the Lord, difference remains. To put it differently, in their equal relationship with the same Lord, Jews remain Jews and Gentiles remain Gentiles.[31] Honoring the Lord is presented as the common ground, or the self-identity of a new community of Jews and Gentiles, and yet such an identity does not invalidate ethnico-cultural differences, nor absorb one into the other. Such a point in Paul's rhetorical argumentation is quite clear in the following statement:

καὶ ὁ ἐσθίων κυρίῳ ἐσθίει, εὐχαριστεῖ γὰρ τῷ θεῷ
καὶ ὁ μὴ ἐσθίων κυρίῳ οὐκ ἐσθίει καὶ εὐχαριστεῖ τῷ θεῷ (14:6).

In verses 7–9 Paul elaborates further on the relationship between the members of the community and the Lord (from a Christological perspective) and articulates it as the core of the self-identity of the Christian community. Living to (for) oneself (ἑαυτῷ) stands in contradiction with acting in honor of the Lord (κυρίῳ, v. 6) and living to (for) the Lord (τῷ κυρίῳ, v. 7). Again the linkage to 12:3, 16 becomes very obvious. By the contrast of ἑαυτῷ with κυρίῳ, a topic of loyalty to one's master is introduced, which has its parallel with the master-servant relations in the contemporary Roman society. Such allegiance to the Lord is expressed to its extreme, that is, to the matter of life and death: "If we live, we live to the Lord (τῷ κυρίῳ), and if we die, we die to the Lord; so then, whether we live or whether we die, we are the Lord's (14:8)."[32]

What immediately follows is that such loyalty is grounded on what Jesus Christ did, i.e., Jesus' death and resurrection (v. 9). For that purpose, Paul emphasizes, Jesus died and returned to life. Here notice a striking focus on the mutual relationship between the Christian members and the Lord.

---

31. Paul's rhetorical force in this respect should be differentiated from Albert Schweitzer's "theory of status quo." According to the theory, if one enters into Christ, the conditions of one's prior state in the world become meaningless. Anyone who regards an alteration in the flesh as necessary to salvation reveals that he or she has not come to recognize existence in Christ. For this reason a Gentile who is circumcised forfeits his salvific union with Christ. Likewise, Jews must not refrain from the observation of Torah. See Schweitzer, *Mysticism*, 177–204.

32. Paul prepares this in Rom 6:1–10; esp. "For if we have been united with him in a death like his, we shall certainly be united with him in a resurrection like his" (6:5).

Would any master or lord be willing to die for his servants in the society that Paul and others knew? Given the conventional subjection/domination relationship between servants and master, the relationship of mutuality which Paul postulates between the members of the Christian community and Christ as the Lord is quite unusual and even subversive, for it protests "the one-sided understanding of loyalty which prevailed in contemporary social and political life."[33] Furthermore, if one maintains and pursues one's loyalty and belongs to the Lord beyond death, one's relationship with the Lord transcends the realm of physical death. The corollary is, at least according to Paul, that such relationship makes the Lord as Lord both of the dead (νεκρῶν) and the living (ζώντων). All of this indicates that eating for the Lord and not eating for the Lord are not matter of indifference;[34] "difference" in the Lord is not indifferent.

3.3. Difference within the Context of Final Judgment (Rom 14:10–12)

Finally, Paul summarizes and restates the debate in 14:1–9 by taking up the two terms "judge" and "despise" of 14:3: "Why do you pass judgment on *your brother*? Or you, why do you despise *your brother*? (v. 10)" Notice the change in language. The word "your brother" (ἀδελφόν σου) replaced the words "the one who eats (v. 3)," as well as "the one who does not eat (v. 3)" and "the servant of another (v. 4)." Paul obviously intends to assure that both Jews and Gentiles, despite their differences, are integrated into the community of Christ the Lord. Then, Paul again brings what he said in the preceding verses to the broader horizon of God's judgment: "For we shall all (πάντες) stand before the judgment seat of God (v. 10)." Certainly, a universal perspective is introduced. But if our reading is correct, this universalism requires no sacrifice of particularism. Rather, as Paul makes it explicit, each

---

33. Georgi, *Theocracy*, 97.

34. In arguing for Paul's oblique approach, Sampley stresses Paul's position here as "indifference." See Sampley's "The Weak and the Strong," 41: "For Paul, keeping or not keeping days and eating and abstaining (14:6) are *adiaphora* (indifferent matters), just as are life and death (14:7–9), because regardless of how different people's preferences and practices are, 'we are the Lord's' (14:8)." Despite his focus on Paul's rhetorical strategy, in my opinion, Sampley seems to miss the exact point of Paul's rhetoric here. A slightly different comment on "adiaphora" is made by William S. Campbell: "It is not the differences in life-style among the Christians that troubles Paul, but rather the attitude to these differences demonstrated on all sides in the disputes (Campbell, "The Rule of Faith," 24).

(ἕκαστος) of the Christian members should give account of himself (περὶ ἑαυτοῦ) to God. Disputes over different practices (διάκρισις διαλογισμῶν), which may result in judging others, each one should be transformed into one's accountability for one's own practice (v. 12) and into an ethos of "not living to oneself" (v. 7).

4. DIFFERENCE AND CONFLICT: PRACTICE OF DIFFERENCE (ROM 14:13-23)

In the discussion of Rom 14:1-12 above, we have seen how Paul laid a rhetorical foundation for the co-existence of different practices among Jews and Gentiles within the Christian community. In dealing with the problem of judging others with respect to the differences in the observances of food laws and special days, Paul addressed the issue of judging one another to the Jews first, even though they were characterized as the "weak." In a very paradoxical way, Paul's rhetoric moved to the point where all, both Jews and Gentiles, should be accountable for their own "difference" before God's judgment.

4.1. Do Not Trouble Your Brothers (14:13-18)

Paul begins this section by calling for mutual acceptance and by introducing a language of mutuality: "Then let us no more pass judgment on one another (ἀλλήλους)." How could this be materialized in practice? "Mutuality (ἀλλήλους)" means a right, reciprocal relation between two different identities.[35] Usually, differences among non-identical groups do not stand in balanced (egalitarian) relations. In real life contexts of human experience, the issue of difference/identity is not a matter of neutral indifference, but of power relations. Paul's particular exhortation in the following verses of this section indicates that the differences between ὁ ἐσθίων and ὁ μὴ ἐσθίων, i.e., Jews and Gentiles in the concrete situation, were leading an

---

35. Brigitte Kahl notes that the Greek term for mutuality/one another ἀλλήλων derives from ἄλλος-ἄλλος (=other-other). She underscores its significance in the Galatian context in terms of a movement that brings the "ones" down to the level of the "others": See Kahl, "No Longer Male," 37–49: (47: ". . . all throughout the parenetic section of Galatians this 'oneness' of the new creation of Israel's God is shown as the movement of the 'ones' going down to the level of the lowly and excluded 'others' of all kinds, to be in solidarity and community with them, to become 'others' themselves").

imbalanced relationship among them. Once again Paul plays with the word κρίνειν, but here we see a change in meaning and shift in audience: "but rather *discern* (κρίνατε) never to put a stumbling block or hindrance in the way of a brother" (v. 13b + 13c). The negative meaning of κρίνειν (passing judgment on others) in verse 13a is rendered into its positive meaning (discern) in verse 13b. The implied audience for this exhortation—though not yet explicit—becomes clear in the following.

In verse 14, Paul speaks with first person singular verbs, which occur only here within Rom 14:15—15:13: "I know and am persuaded in the Lord Jesus that nothing is unclean (κοινόν) in itself; but it is unclean for any one (ἐκείνῳ) who thinks it unclean." This verse, along with verse 20, has been usually and misleadingly taken as unmistakable evidence for Paul's principle of freedom from the Law, or disregard for the Jewish laws. This has been done by isolating the verse from both its rhetorical context and its implied audience. Although Paul appears to identify himself with the position of the Christian Gentiles in Rome, it is important to note that in doing so he has a specific rhetorical and paraenetical strategy in mind. Before Paul delivers negative imperatives toward the Gentile Christians in verses 15-16, he needs to reaffirm their position as Gentiles in Jesus Christ, that is, their difference in Jesus Christ as "difference" which is in itself neither superior nor inferior. The word πέπεισμαι used here is noteworthy in that the same verb stands out in Rom 15:14 where in a quite similar way Paul speaks directly to the Gentile Christians in Rome as his primary audience. At the same time, it should not be overlooked that in verse 14 Paul emphasizes the Jewish Christian position regarding "unclean" (κοινός) food as their Jewish identity in Jesus Christ which should be affirmed and respected.[36]

Then, from verse 15 on Paul's exhortation is directed toward the "strong" ones who think that nothing is unclean in itself, i.e., Gentile Christians in Rome. It is they who are instructed not to let what they eat cause trouble for their Jewish brothers. By using the same word ἐκεῖνος in verse 14 (ἐκείνῳ κοινόν) to refer to those who are injured (ἐκεῖνον) by what the Gentile Christians eat in verse 15, Paul now makes it clear who are in a weak position. Jewish Christians in Rome are in weak position, so their practice is vulnerable to disregard and contempt. In other words, their Jewish identity, because of their socially weak position, becomes "difference" to be despised and destroyed. But, Paul stresses that this is not what love (ἀγάπη) is meant to be among Jews and Gentiles in Christ and what Christ

---

36. See Tomson, *Paul and the Jewish Law*, 249–50.

died for. Otherwise, Gentiles who come to the Jewish God through Jesus Christ and their participation in table fellowship with Jews will incur blasphemy (βλασφημέω, v. 16)[37] from Jews and Jewish Christians.

This leads Paul to remind the Gentile Christians in Rome of the priority of the kingdom of God based on justice, peace, and joy in the Holy Spirit (v. 17). The phrase that "the kingdom of God is not food and drink" is aimed primarily at the Gentile Christian, not the Jewish Christians. Its rhetorical force should not allow one to interpret the verse as the evidence for Paul's disregard for the Jewish law for Jews and Jewish Christians.

4. 2. Mutual Upbuilding of Difference (14:19–23)

This section constitutes a close parallel with the preceding section. As in verse 14, in verse 19 a hortative subjunctive construction appears with the term "one another" (ἀλλήλους). This section is directed toward the positive meaning of "upbuilding" (οἰκοδομή) of different groups within the Roman community. As in the preceding section of Rom 14:13–18, in this section the "strong" continues to be the main audience of Paul's instruction. On the basis of the priority of the "kingdom of God," the members of the Christian community are urged to pursue "what makes for peace and for mutual upbuilding," instead of judging one another and causing one's brother (the "weak") to stumble.

The metaphor "upbuilding" (οἰκοδομή) used here needs special attention. The literal sense of the word, i.e., the meaning of "construction" should not be missed. The meaning of constructing a building or house is tightly connected with the different groups of the community. The impression is given that the Christian community, particularly in the Roman context at the time Paul wrote the letter, is a household built of both Jews and Gentiles.[38] This allows me to suggest that here Paul tries to characterize the identity of the Christian community as a kind of "bridge identity."[39] Viewed in this way, the meaning of mutual upbuiding should not be taken as merely moral

---

37. This word occurs in Rom 2:24; 3:8; 1 Cor 10:30. The last two references convey a similar meaning.

38. Paul has the metaphor οἰκοδομή here explicitly or implicitly to deliver the image and meaning of a household. Note that the term οἰκέτης, specifically referring to "a household servant," is used in Rom 14:4.

39. In appropriating this term, I am in debt to Ann Ferguson's article, "Resisting the Veil of Privilege," 95–113.

edification, but as the practice of radical mutuality. I suggest that this is the rhetorical and ethical force that Paul intends to convey by the elaborate construction of τὰ τῆς οἰκοδομῆς τῆς εἰς ἀλλήλους in verse 19.

Then, in verses 20–21 Paul is more straightforward in revealing the direction of his paraenesis. Paul makes it explicit who are responsible for causing the stumbling of other members of the community. It is the "strong" who let their practice based on the belief that everything is clean (πάντα μὲν καθαρά) jeopardize the unity of the community, or the coexistence of Jews and Gentiles—which Paul depicts as the work of God (τὸ ἔργον τοῦ θεοῦ).[40] One problem is that in the text Paul does not give a clear explanation about how the "strong" with their food consumption are in the position even to destroy the work of God. Although it has been generally explained at the theological level, that is, in terms of the strength (freedom) of their faith (πάντα μὲν καθαρά), the "strong" position of the "strong" in the Roman church needs to be investigated in its social dimension.[41] If the Gentile Christians in Rome were not in a socially privileged position over the Jewish Christians, in that case the faith or freedom of the "strong" alone would not explain their attitudes of despising, or scorning the "weak" and their potential power to destroy the work of God.

It is in this context that we see that Paul puts less weight on the faith claim of the Gentile Christian (only three words are mentioned: πάντα μὲν καθαρά) and reverts his focus to the negative (κακόν), ethical aspect involved in the eating practice of the "strong." In 14:20c Paul clearly states that "it is wrong (κακόν) to eat by making others stumble." An ethical corrective to the abuse from the part of the "strong" is immediately followed in verse 21: "It is right (καλόν) not to eat meat or drink wine or do anything that makes your brother stumble." In this way, the "strong" in Romans, the Gentile Christians in the Roman congregation, are instructed to change their practice. The "weak" are not actually instructed to change their opinions or behavior, except as they relate to their change of attitude from non-acceptance of the "strong" to one of respect and welcome. Paul's instruction directed toward the "strong" in Romans, therefore, actually

---

40. Cf. Käsemann, *Romans*, 378. Reasoner's equation of the work of God with the "weak" is not so convincing; see Reasoner, *The Strong and the Weak*, 192.

41. In this respect, Reasoner's study is an exception. However, despite Reasoner's careful attention to the terms "strong" and "weak" as social status terms in the first-century Roman society and effort to apply them to the situation of the "strong" and the "weak" in Rom 14–15, his argument does not answer the question of why the vegetarian, ascetic "weak" were the social "weak" in the Roman congregation.

runs counter to the conclusion Sanders draws on Paul's attitude toward the Jewish law: "When it came to cases Paul's easy tolerance, which he effortlessly maintained in theory—it is a matter of individual conscience what one eats and whether one observes 'days'—could not work. It was not only a matter of individual conscience, it turned out, but of Christian unity, and he judged one form of behavior to be wrong. The *wrong* form was living according to the law."[42]

Accommodation to the practice of Jewish Christians, according to Paul, does not require a change of conviction on the part of Gentiles. It does not compromise their own belief that they are accepted by God without first becoming Jews or proselytes. Nonetheless, it requires a change of ethical behavior. The faith of the "strong," Paul says in verse 22, should be maintained between them and God, but it should not be abused so as to deny the different faith and practice of the "weak."[43] In the following verse, a different expression of the same meaning is given with respect to the faith of the "weak": "But he who has doubts (ὁ διακρινόμενος) is condemned, if he eats, because he does not act from faith; for whatever does not proceed from faith is sin." If with the term ὁ διακρινόμενος Paul has the "weak" in view,[44] verse 23 makes it clear that the "weak" are not encouraged to change their own conviction or faith in their different practices. In other words, the change of eating practice on the part of the "weak," i.e., the compliance with the eating practice of the "strong" is stated, surprisingly, as lack of faith or weakness in faith; here we encounter a striking reverse of the general reading of Paul's intention.

5. PAUL AND THE POLITICS OF SOLIDARITY: ROM 15:1–13

In this section, Paul recapitulates what he has said in the previous chapter and further articulates his solution to the controversy between the "strong" and the "weak" in relation to Christ and God within a wider theological horizon.

---

42. E. P. Sanders, *Paul, the Law, and the Jewish People*, 178 (my emphasis); for similar views also see Dunn, *Romans*, 811; Watson, "Two Roman Congregations," 205–6.

43. Contra Dunn's comment on this verse: "The 'stronger' the faith (that is, the more unconditional the trust), the less dependent is it on observance of particular traditions; the 'weaker' the faith, the more dependent" (*Romans*, 827).

44. Ibid., 828.

For the first time, Paul uses the label referring to those who disagree with the "weak," with exhortations particularly addressed to them: "We who are strong (οἱ δυνατοί) are in debt to bear the weaknesses of the weak (οἱ ἀδύνατοι) and not to please ourselves (v. 1)." As far as we can tell from the text itself, the term οἱ δυνατοί refers to those who are able to eat anything (14:2), who are able to put a stumbling block in the way of their brothers (14:13), and further who are able to destroy the work of God by what they eat (14:20). It seems most likely that Paul did not invent the terms οἱ δυνατοί (powerful/able/strong) and οἱ ἀδύνατοι (powerless/unable/weak), rather these terms were, as Mark Reasoner argues, "most probably the very labels current in the Roman churches that divided their believing communities."[45] Though it is hard to imagine that any group used the epithet "weak" as a self-designation, the "strong" may well have claimed the label "strong" for themselves. From "we who are strong (ἡμεῖς οἱ δυνατοί)" most exegetes have unduly emphasized Paul's stance as one of the "strong."[46] Although it is true that Paul could identify himself with the position of the "strong," however, this should not lead us to ignore the real thrust of his rhetorical and paraenetic intention. Paul's intention in identifying himself with the position of the "strong" is to be found in his effort to persuade the "strong" in the Roman church.[47]

As labels known in the first-century Roman society and used by the audience of the Romans, the antithetical terms οἱ δυνατοί and οἱ ἀδύνατοι seem to reflect a certain hierarchical power relation underlying the group conflict within the Christian community in Rome. How can mutuality or equal relationship between the "strong" and the "weak" in the household of God be reconstructed and materialized against such a hierarchical situation? Paul presents an answer to that question in Rom 15:1: "We who are strong are in debt to bear the weaknesses of the weak and not to please ourselves."

The "strong" should practice solidarity with the "weak." "To bear with the weaknesses of the weak" is not simply to show sympathy for the latter, but to practice a radical mutuality by "holding up" (βαστάζειν) the "weaknesses" of the weak, not by indulging in self-interest (ἑαυτοῖς ἀρέσκειν). The "weaknesses" (ἀσθενήματα) occurs only here in the entire New Testament. Despite the difficulty of confining the term to one precise meaning, it is misleading to

---

45. Reasoner, *The Strong and the Weak*, 56. For his argument on "strong" and "weak" as terms of social status in first-century Rome, see esp. 45–63.

46. E.g., Dunn, *Romans*, 837; Watson, *Paul, Judaism and the Gentiles*, 96.

47. It is remarkable that Paul's rhetorical statements in Gal 2:15–16 and Rom 15:1–2, despite diametrically oppositional situations of Galatians and Romans, reveal Paul's consistent and committed stance toward the "weak" (others).

The "Weak" and the "Strong" at Table in Romans 14:1—15:13

translate it as "failings" (RSV, NIV) with the pejorative implications of "imperfection" or "deficiency" in faith. On the contrary, Paul seeks to persuade the "strong" to bear the weaknesses of the "weak." In other words, what Paul calls for from the "strong" can be characterized as solidarity with the "weak." Only such a praxis enables them to deconstruct the hierarchical relationship between οἱ δυνατοί and οἱ ἀδύνατοι and to construct (πρὸς οἰκοδομήν) equal relationship (τὸ ἀγαθόν) among neighbors (v. 2).

At the apex of his argument Paul grounds the practice of solidarity with the "weak" on the praxis of Jesus Christ by adducing a text from the scriptures of Israel with a specific paraenetic purpose toward the "strong" (15:3–6). Appealing to the same steadfastness and encouragement of the scriptures and God, Paul explicitly declares his purpose in the form of prayer. That is, Paul hopes that each member of the Christian community in Rome—both Jews and Gentiles—will "with one voice glorify the God and Father of our Lord Jesus Christ." But this is based on a prior petition in his prayer that none other than God will give to members of the "the same prudent mind-set toward one another in accord with Christ Jesus" (τὸ αὐτὸ φρονεῖν ἐν ἀλλήλοις κατὰ Χριστὸν Ἰησοῦν). The most common reading of τὸ αὐτὸ φρονεῖν ἐν ἀλλήλοις as "to live in such harmony with one another" obscures the meaning of this text. The unity, or the oneness (ὁμοθυμαδὸν ἐν ἑνὶ στόματι) of the Christian community Paul envisions is not harmony based on "diplomatic magnanimity"[48] or rational pluralism,[49] but "oneness-in-difference"[50] based on solidarity with the "weak."

Finally, 15:7–13 sums up the entire paraenetic section regarding the "strong" and the "weak" in 14:1—15:13. "Therefore welcome one another" (διὸ προσλαμβάνεσθε ἀλλήλους). Paul once again emphatically appeals to the members of the Christian community in Rome to practice radical mutuality, tightly connecting the latter to the practice of Jesus Christ (v. 7). Then, Paul explains what it means that "Christ has welcomed you, for the

---

48. Segal, *Paul the Convert*, 234–53. Segal argues that for the unity of one community Paul is making an accommodation or a compromise, though Paul does not have to compromise his principle about the irrelevance of food laws. "From Paul's perspective the accommodation is a kind of magnanimity. He outlines two axioms, an ideological position of strength and a diplomatic principle of conciliation" (236). Paul's purpose was, according to Segal, "to make a single community by accommodation in ritual but not in principle" (239).

49. Tomson, *Paul and the Jewish Law*, esp. 236–58. Although Tomson rightly emphasizes Paul's "pluralist position" in terms of "coexistence of Jews and gentiles" and "tolerance and pluralism as to Jewish dietary delicacy," his explanation of Paul's "rational pluralism" deriving from a wide range of intellectual sources puts less weight on the ethical hermeneutic underlying Paul's argument in Rom 14:1—15:13.

50. I borrowed this term from Kahl, "Gender Trouble in Galatia?" 57–73.

glory of God." 15:8–9 not only gives an elaborate description of the practice of Jesus Christ in relation to the problem with the "strong" and the "weak," but it actually constitutes a well-articulated summary of the whole letter of the Romans:

> For I tell you that Christ became a servant to the circumcised to show God's truthfulness, in order to confirm the promises given to the patriarchs, and in order that the Gentiles might glorify God for his mercy (15:8–9).

For the first time in this whole paraenetic section regarding the "strong" and the "weak," the ethnic terms περιτομή and ἔθνη are explicitly mentioned. This is another clear indication that the problem of the "strong" and the "weak" in Romans is an essential part of Jewish-Gentile difference. It is striking that Paul describes Christ as a servant (διάκονος) to the circumcised. Apart from Gal 2:17, this is the only occasion in which Paul speaks of Christ as διάκονος. Both texts have the table-fellowship between Jews and Gentiles as their common context. Along with προσλαμβάνομαι, διάκονος here fits well with the context of table fellowship. Furthermore, Paul's characterization of Christ as a servant has a double referent. On the one hand, the practice of solidarity with the weak follows the practice of Jesus Christ. The Lord (κύριος) of the table-fellowship community in 14:1–12 is characterized as a servant to the weak, correspondingly here the circumcised. At the same time, the characterization of Christ as servant is for the inclusion of the Gentiles in God's mercy. This summary of the exhortation shows dramatically that the inclusion of the Gentiles through Christ does not compromise the priority of the Jews, a main theme which runs through the whole letter.

As far as the relationship between Jews and Gentiles in Romans is concerned, Paul wants his audience to understand that the purpose of Christ's becoming a servant to the circumcised is to confirm the promises given to the ancestors. Again, it should not be overlooked that Paul understands the role of Christ thoroughly within the Jewish covenantal context, and that the fulfillment, or confirmation of the promises is made possible through the servanthood of Christ. How does such covenantal fulfillment relate to Gentiles? To the Jews what is the fulfillment of the promises (God's truthfulness) is understood as God's mercy (ἔλεος) to Gentiles. This underlines the theme of "to Jews first, also to Gentiles." The term ἔλεος recalls one of the principal motifs in chapters 9–11 (9:15–16, 18, 23; 11:30–32). As in chapters 9–11, especially in the parable of the olive tree, Paul reasserts that the integration of Gentiles into the people of God is based on, and derivative from the priority of the Jews. At the same time, it is significant to note that the practice of Christ as a servant is understood as what brings together the circumcised/God's faithfulness and the Gentiles/God's mercy.

At this point, Paul draws on some of the Jewish scriptures which are relevant to the present context. There is a progressive movement in Paul's rhetorical arrangement of Rom 15:9–12. Because of the Jewish people, the possibility of knowing the God of Israel is open to Gentiles (ἐν ἔθνεσιν, v. 9). Then, Gentiles are coming together with (μετά) the people of God and praise the one God: "Rejoice, O Gentiles, with his people" (ἔθνη, μετὰ τοῦ λαοῦ αὐτοῦ). With μετά, the hostile and different categories of people are integrated, yet into the one God of Israel (v. 10). This will bring about, it is hoped, the integration of all the nations (v. 12). At this point, the climax follows:

> The root (ῥίζα) of Jesse shall come, he who rises to rule (ἄρχειν) the Gentiles; in him shall the Gentiles (ἔθνη) hope.

Through the Jewish Messiah (= the priority of the Jews), not through the Roman Caesar, all the Gentiles along with the Jewish people shall have hope in the Jewish Messiah, for he rules through his subversive practice of servanthood (= solidarity with the "weak"). For Paul, in Romans, the issue of the "strong" and the "weak," that is, the issue of difference/identity is tied up with the problem of "Jews" and "Gentiles," and further with the question of global justice (δικαιοσύνη), hope (ἐλπίς) and peace (εἰρήνη).[51]

CONCLUSION

In this chapter, I have sought to uncover the meaning of unity in Paul's reshaping Christian identity by focusing on Paul's dealing with the "weak" and the "strong" within the meal context of the Roman Christian community. The original thrust of unity Paul emphasizes and envisions in the letter to the Romans has been concealed, undermined, and distorted mainly due to the long history of the Western Christian tradition that has tended to

---

51. Georgi shows that in Romans Paul uses these terms for his critical engagement with the dominant political theology of the Roman Empire. See his *Theocracy*, 79–104: "If the terms chosen by Paul for his Roman readers have associations with the slogans of Caesar religion, then Paul's gospel must be understood as competing with the gospel of the Caesars. Paul's gospel enters into critical dialogue with the good news that universal peace has been achieved by the miracle of Actium" (87).

identify its exclusivisitc, imperialistic triumphalism with its misinterpretation of Paul's theological universalism.

Any theological universalism including the one we see in Paul's theological articulations in Romans cannot be properly understood when it is interpreted in separation from the concrete socio-historical context in which such a kind of universalism is advocated and formulated. Table-fellowship, or early Christian meal practice, is one of the most important and appropriate contexts in which the members of the early Christian community, like members of various associative groups in the first-century Greco-Roman society, seem to experience and experiment with the most intimate and public social interaction. My concern in this chapter lay at the issue of the relationship between difference and equality at the table fellowship of the Roman Christian community.

I have tried to show that in spite of an ongoing debate about the identification of the "weak" and the "strong" in Romans, the prevailing position that regards the "weak" as Jewish Christians and the "strong" as Gentile Christians can be still sustained. But, most scholars have failed to question the inherited assumption that Paul's gospel or faith is fundamentally antithetical to the observance of Jewish laws, and that ethnic, cultural, and social differences do not count in Paul's sense of being a Christian. Further, a kind of modern assumption on universalism and equality was operative in the majority of Pauline scholarship. In other words, the modern mind has been taught to assume a priori that universalism and equality are incompatible, respectively, with particularism and difference.

Quite differently, I have argued that at the core of Paul's paraenesis on the "weak" and the "strong" in Rom 14:1—15:13 is presented a solidarity politics which advocates pluralism of differences on the basis of solidarity with the "weak." First, we have seen that the groups of the "weak" and the "strong" are Jewish Christians and Gentile Christians, not because those who follow the Jewish laws are weak by definition, but because the historical and rhetorical contexts involved in the controversy between the "weak" and the "strong" in Romans are suggestive of the marginalized status of the "weak." As Jewish Christians they are facing a repressive behavior towards their Jewish identity on the side of their "strong" Gentile Christian brothers.

Secondly, I have tried to uncover Paul's understanding of "difference" primarily from the textual and contextual analysis of Rom 14:1—15:13, underscoring Paul's rhetoric on difference, the implied audience of his paraenesis, and the paraenetical intention. The power of Paul's rhetoric on difference lies in the ways Paul prepares and allows for the differences and co-existence among Jews and Gentiles by reconstructing the different-but-equal relations among the brothers or fellow-servants.

Thirdly, I have demonstrated that Paul's politics of difference, or the pluralism Paul pleads for toward the "weak" and the "strong" in Romans is grounded on one radical aspect of his Christology, that is, Christ's solidarity with the "weak," the solidarity with the "circumcised." Therefore, the "strong" are urged to respect the difference of the "weak," and even to accommodate to the practice of the "weak." This is the most concrete content of the "obedience of the faith" among the Gentiles that Paul explicitly states as one of his reasons for writing the letter to the Romans (Rom 1:5; 16:26).

6

Equality with Difference
Solidarity with the "Weak"

1. POLITICS OF DIFFERENCE AND/OR PAUL'S UNIVERSALISM

IN THE PRECEDING TWO chapters, I have examined Paul's stance toward the differences between Jews and Gentiles, which were the focal points of tensions and conflicts at table-fellowship in two particular Christian communities, in Antioch and Rome respectively. The main reading strategy for this task centered on contextualizing the rhetorical statements, arguments, or discourses preserved in Paul's letters in order to discern his understanding of "difference," in particular Jewish-Gentile difference within the context of early Christian social formation in the first-century Greco-Roman world. I have tried to stress that Paul's understanding of "difference" itself was shaped contextually and formulated in relation to particular situations. In other words, Paul perceived the meaning of difference differently depending on particular situations in the communities, and his rhetoric on difference responded to the different hierarchical relations between Jews and Gentiles in each community.

Thus, it may not be surprising that some scholars have attributed Paul's attitude toward the Law and Judaism to idiosyncrasy or inconsistency.[1] Yet,

---

1. For example, Richardson, "Pauline Inconsistency," 347–62.

Equality with Difference

I did not posit my question within the framework of Paul's attitude toward the Law and Judaism in general, nor of Paul's position about the observance of Jewish laws. In fact, in regard to Paul and Judaism, recent New Testament scholarship has tended to acknowledge that Paul's criticism against Judaism or the Law is tightly linked to the question of how Gentiles are related to Jews and Judaism. The focus of this study is not, however, to investigate the origin and nature of Paul's (and early Christianity's) mission to the Gentiles, nor is it concerned with questions of equality between Jews and Gentiles, although I have partly discussed these issues when necessary. In this study my concern was directed rather toward more practical questions such as how Paul understands the difference between Jews and Gentiles within the mixed communities of early Christianity, and how Paul relates himself to both Jews and Gentiles in terms of difference, and particularly within relationships of social hierarchy between Jews and Gentiles.

The question I have constantly raised in this study is how to understand the problem of difference in relation to equality and/or unity. Recognizing that such a question was not only pertinent to the Greco-Roman Jewish world of the first century but also to the bewildering contemporary world, in chapter 2 I situated the overall theoretical concerns in this study into a range of current theoretical discourses and politics on difference—from postmodern, feminist, and postcolonial critical theories to Korean *minjung* perspectives. I discerned that the category and meaning of difference as a political struggle for identity among marginalized people is a valuable point of intersection among these critical approaches.

In chapter 3, I considered the meal practice in Greco-Roman societies as the cultural milieu for social and religious activities of various groups, clubs, and associations, including Jewish and early Christian gatherings. I also discussed meal settings as one of the concrete contexts where tension and conflicts arose in relation to social differences. This enabled me to approach the theme of Paul and difference by focusing on the practice of table-fellowship in early Christian communities. Two points converge in eating practices in Antioch and Rome. One is the Jewish-Gentile difference in relation to table-fellowship; the other is the egalitarian ethos promoted and accompanied by the practice of communal meals.

Thus, considering both the broader context of Greco-Roman meal practice and the shifting historical situation confronting Jewish people in Palestine of the mid-to-late 40s, in chapter 4, I reassessed Paul's understanding of and stance toward the differences between Jews and Gentiles by rereading the incident at Antioch (Gal 2:11–21). I demonstrated that Paul's dealing with the differences between Jews and Gentiles in Antioch was motivated primarily by his concern with emerging hierarchical, oppositional relations between Jews and Gentiles in that particular setting.

Such concern, I argue, was not determined by some kind of Jewish ethnocentric or particularistic essentialism but was rather conditioned contextually by the perception of the situation in which Jewish identity or Jewishness becomes an aspect of social dominance. According to Paul's understanding of difference, such a tendency may subject Jewish identity to the logic of identity which renders Gentile identity into "difference," an inferior difference devalued as "other." Paul did not confront Peter because Peter wanted to observe Jewish practices nor because Paul regarded keeping the Jewish Law as irrelevant or incompatible with faith in Jesus Christ. Rather Paul criticized Peter because Paul construed Peter's change in practice or inconsistency as conducive to the potential danger of making Gentiles "them" in opposition to "us." Such a politics of difference was governed by the paradigm of inclusion versus exclusion, not by that of Jewish particularism versus Christian universalism.

Then, by means of my exegetical work on the relationship between the "weak" and the "strong" in Rom 14:1—15:13, I showed how Paul's understanding of difference between Jews and Gentiles, and his stance toward the weak and the strong, were governed by the same kind of politics of difference that we saw in Paul's rhetoric in Galatians. Whereas I accept the position of the majority of scholars that the weak and the strong in Rom 14:1—15:13 roughly represent Jews and Gentiles respectively in the Christian community in Rome, I offered a different characterization of them. I identify the weak with Jewish Christians in Rome not simply because of their sensitivity to Jewish dietary regulations and observance of specific days but because of their minority social status and their marginalized position in the community. Correspondingly the identification of the strong in Rom 14:1—15:13 is not based merely on their belief that they are allowed to eat anything (14:2) but also on their socially dominant position in relation to the Jews of the community. This characterization of the weak and the strong is supported by the effort to take into account the effect of the edict of Claudius (49 CE) on the historical situation of the early Christian community in Rome, in particular the shifting of social relationships between Jews and Gentiles in the community.[2]

2. See chapter 5, 136–41.

Equality with Difference

Consequently, I demonstrated how in the letter to the Romans as a whole, and particularly in 14:1—15:13, Paul was aware of an emerging dominant tendency among Gentile Christians to devalue and marginalize the identity of Jewish Christians and the Jewish identity of the Christian community as well. In diametrical contrast to the situation in Galatia, Paul perceived another potential in Rome for the logic of identity to establish Gentile identity as a superior position and to push Jewish identity into an inferior position to be devalued as "other." In the situation of the Roman community, Jews needed and wanted to assert their Jewish identity (difference) over against the dominance of Gentile identity. To the contrary, in Antioch Gentiles were under the pressure of a dominant Jewish identity.

Thus, from reading Gal 2:11-21 and Rom 14:1—15:13 in relation to each other, it becomes clear that in Galatians Jews ("us"—Ἡμεῖς φύσει Ἰουδαῖοι, Gal 2:15) manifested the tendency the make Gentiles "other" ("them"—οἱ ἁμαρτωλοί, Gal 2:15) on the one hand, and in Romans Gentiles ("us"—ἡμεῖς οἱ δυνατοί, Rom 15:1) showed a tendency to consider Jews "other" ("them"—οἱ ἀδύνατοι, Rom 15:1). Whereas Paul perceived Gentiles as "different" in Galatians, he perceived Jews as "different" in Romans. This provides formidable evidence that Paul understood the meaning of difference in contextual and relational ways rather than in essentializing and universalizing ways. Further, it explains why Paul sided with Gentiles in the Antioch incident in Galatians and with Jews in Romans. In this way, Paul endeavored to put into practice his conviction of equality of Jews and Gentiles so that Jews maintain their Jewish identity and Gentiles their Gentile identity, that is, equality with difference. In Galatians, Paul became as one outside the Law in order to win Gentiles (see 1 Cor 9:21), while in Romans he practiced being a Jew in order to win Jews (see 1 Cor 9:20). In other words, Paul's stance toward equality and difference between Jews and Gentiles in terms of a politics of difference may resonate with Paul's statement in another context:

> To the weak I became weak, that I might win the weak. I have become all things to all, that I might by all means save some. I do it all for the sake of the gospel, that I might share in its blessings (1 Cor 9:22-23).

On the basis of Paul's politics of difference as I have shown in this study, I challenge the prevailing scholarly view of Paul's universalism. The typical construal of Paul's universalism is undoubtedly linked with Paul's concern for the Gentiles and the Gentile mission. A number of scholars have insisted that Paul's understanding of formulation of the gospel, faith, and its relation to Torah leads to the corollaries that faith eradicates any fundamental ethnic distinction between Jews and Gentiles; the value of historical Jewish identity markers is denied; and historical Israel as God's people according to the flesh has been superseded by spiritual Israel, i.e., the church.

Especially during the last two decades a paradigm shift has occurred in Pauline scholarship. This has precipitated attempts to reconsider several aspects crucial to the old interpretation of Paul, in particular with respect to Paul's discourse on faith and works, his experience of conversion or call, and his view of the relationship of Israel and the church. Nevertheless, the traditional understanding of Paul's universalism in terms of "no distinction between Jews and Gentiles" remains intact. Numerous scholars have explained such a Christian universalism of no difference between Jews and Gentiles by relating Paul's concern for the Gentiles and the Gentile mission to his conversion experience with the resultant convictions about faith, Christ and Torah, and Israel and the church. This universalism, however, has not been accounted for. Rather, it has been axiomatically assumed that Paul's concern for the Gentiles naturally leads to the elimination of Jew-Gentile difference, and consequently any ethnic identities.

Terence L. Donaldson has called into question the basic framework operating with the scholarly insistence on Paul's universalism as making irrelevant particularistic distinctions between Jews and Gentiles.[3] He rightly calls such an interpretive framework itself "a universalistic paradigm" within which "humankind as such—individually or collectively, but always generically and without further ethnic differentiation—is taken to be his [Paul's] fundamental soteriological category."[4] Donaldson clearly observes how this framework has been working for the older interpretation of Paul:

> For if Paul's basic concern is how humanity, generically considered, can find justification with God, and if his conversion was essentially a conversion away from an ethnic and particularist religion centered on the Torah to a Christ who is the universal savior of all, then it follows that "Israel" can be retained as a positive category only if it is redefined in a nonethnic manner.[5]

---

3. Donaldson, *Paul and the Gentiles*.
4. Ibid., 3.
5. Ibid., 7.

Equality with Difference

In other words, Donaldson problematizes the unquestioned assumption among interpreters of Paul that if salvation is through Christ, not through Torah, then the Torah-based difference between Jews and Gentiles is irrelevant. I consider Donaldson's criticism, along with that of others,[6] against the universalistic paradigm not only appropriate but also timely, inasmuch as along with him, we are witnessing a growing interpretive and hermeneutical move to unearth the tenacity of Christian universalism and its manifold dangers. In this regard, Donaldson's critique should be taken as an important contribution, because it starts with a critical evaluation that the framework in which the majority of Pauline scholarship has viewed Paul's universalism turns out ironically to be a universalistic approach. He cautions that in order to reapproach, reevaluate, and wrestle with Paul's universalism, interpreters need to be self-critical of a "'universalistic' paradigm that held sway over Pauline interpretation from the emergence of Gentile orthodoxy in the second century until comparatively recently and that continues to be influential into the present."[7]

This leads me to make some further comment on the problem of Pauline universalism particularly in reference to Daniel Boyarin's work. First, although Boyarin says that he regards Paul as a Jewish cultural critic criticizing Judaism from within, his reading of Paul's discourse basically presupposes a new religious formation separate from Judaism. Accordingly, the question of Jewish difference in Paul was set up within the later (and present) framework of the debate between Jews (Judaism) and Christians (not Gentiles at Paul's time but Christianity). Therefore, it is hardly surprising that Boyarin identifies Western Christian universalism with Paul's universalism without distinguishing between the two.

Second, this enables Boyarin further to identify Paul's Jewish difference with the contemporary view of Jewish difference. Boyarin's essentialist understanding of difference is clearly reflected in his statement: "The quintessentially 'different' people for Paul were Jews and women."[8] Boyarin seems to impose a different category and agenda on Paul's dealing with equality and difference, since for Boyarin the question is "*not the relative*

---

6. For example, N. Elliott, *Liberating Paul*, esp. 69–72: "The only theological principle to be celebrated in the 'new perspective' is a 'universalism' that effectively excludes Torah-observant Jews (who are by definition, 'exclusivistic')" (70). See also Tomson, *Paul and the Jewish Law*, 1–30.

7. Donaldson, *Paul and the Gentiles*, 8.

8. Boyarin, *A Radical Jew*, 17.

statuses of Jewish and gentile Christians but the statuses of those—Jews and others—who choose not to be Christians."[9]

Third, Donaldson's critique, noted above, of the universalistic framework that scholars have axiomatically assumed for Paul's universalism as the erasure of difference, that is, equality with sameness, can be appropriately applied to Boyarin's view. Boyarin says, "I suggest that for the logic of Paul's theology, which was complete in its entirety from the first moment of his revelation, there was not the slightest importance to the observance of such rites for Jews or gentiles."[10] Such an assertion categorically denies any possibility that Paul might have approached the question of Jew-Gentile differences contextually by taking into account particular community situations with which he was engaged.

Finally, if Boyarin's Pauline universalism were an appropriate interpretation of Paul, Boyarin would have the right to object to that universalism. If Boyarin's interpretation is actually about the universalism developed by later Christianity when it became a dominant religion rather than by Paul, then Boyarin would be liable for depriving a first-century Jew of the right to speak for himself from his own peculiar context. At the end of his book, addressing the present troubling question about identity and difference as an answer to Paul's question, Boyarin offers an alternative to Paul's solution (as perceived by Boyarin) of equality with sameness: "A dialectic that would utilize each of these as antithesis to the other, correcting in the 'Christian' system its tendencies toward a coercive universalism and in the 'Jewish' system its tendencies toward contemptuous neglect for human solidarity might lead beyond both toward a better social system."[11]

Interestingly and ironically, that statement is equivalent to what I have argued for Paul's politics of difference in this study, if the word "Gentile" is substituted for "Christian." I have demonstrated such a dialectical dimension in Paul's understanding and treatment of Jew-Gentile difference not only by reassessing Paul's texts regarding meals but also by further elaborating on the logic and dynamics of Greco-Roman meal practice relative to difference.

9. Ibid., 9 (emphasis original).
10. Ibid., 111.
11. Ibid., 235.

2. DIFFERENCE IN MEAL AND RITUAL, AND PAUL

In what ways does the discussion of Greco-Roman meal practice of the first century facilitate my approach to the problems involved in the meal practices featured in Gal 2:11–21 and Rom 14:1—15:13? What kind of connection is to be made between Greco-Roman meal practice and Paul's politics of difference? Do the logic and dynamics of Greco-Roman meals have something to tell us about Paul's (and others') dealing with differences at meals? Moreover, what light does the study of "difference" in ritual shed on the understanding of Paul's politics of difference within the context of Greco-Roman meals? In this section I put these questions together in a summarizing way.

As discussed in chapter 3 above, Dennis Smith's study on Greco-Roman meals has established that Greco-Roman meal customs represent common practices and shared understandings of meals over a wide range of social and religious groups, including Jewish and early Christian groups, spanning the Mediterranean world extensively, both geographically and chronologically. By presenting a comprehensive review of the nature and forms of the common meal tradition as a social institution, Smith has compelled us to see that the common meal tradition was embedded pervasively in the cultural milieu of Greco-Roman societies and accommodated to various situations and interpretations. In adopting, accommodating, and interpreting the common meal tradition for specific purposes and interests of the group, the early Christian community was not an exception to that tradition at all. Smith, followed by others, has demonstrated that the early Christian communities were accustomed to the general customs and practices of the common meal tradition, adapting it to their own situations. Along with the meal practice in 1 Corinthians, scholars have recently paid special attention to the meal settings in the Synoptic Gospels.[12] This has enabled me to see a new possibility in considering the problems involved in table-fellowship in the Christian communities in Antioch and Rome in light of the Greco-Roman tradition of communal meals. In other words, I have considered the Greco-Roman common meal tradition as an important setting for the communities with which Paul deals in Galatians and Romans.

---

12. For the study of Corley, see chapter 3, 80–82 and see 100–103 for the work of Taussig.

2.1. The Logic and Dynamics of Greco-Roman Meals and Difference

The importance of meals as a setting for social interaction in Galatians and Romans can be elaborated by paying attention to the logic and dynamics underlying and governing Greco-Roman meal tradition in general. Dennis Smith and Matthias Klinghardt have noted that one of the prominent features of the Greco-Roman meal was the constant concern for the horizontal or egalitarian ethos at meals. Descriptions of table-fellowship in Greco-Roman literature, in particular "proper meal" (συμποτικά) discourse, clearly show that the meal functioned both as a rhetorical symbol and as a practical setting for building and maintaining the unity of table-fellowship by promoting social equality, the sense of social bonding, and social obligations among participants. As a rhetorical symbol, proper meal discourse presents an ideal picture of community by adopting a series of horizontal concepts, ethical principles, and unifying motifs.

Moreover, it is important to note that even the rhetorical topos of an ideal meal derived from and reflected the actual practice of the common meal tradition. This means that discourse concerning equality as it is inscribed in the proper meal had social implications and ramifications. Thus, the logic of equality underlying Greco-Roman meals is a significant factor that helps to explain the social phenomenon that during the first century BCE and the first century CE various subaltern associations in the Roman world were engaging in social experiments at their common meals.

On the other hand, scholars have observed that alongside the underlying logic of equality at meals, the problem of difference became another significant aspect governing the logic of Greco-Roman meals. Dennis Smith notes how symposium literature reflects the ways in which differences in social status, class, and gender were arranged and displayed at meals.[13] Meals as a social institution often represented and reinforced the hierarchical structure of society by providing differently for participants according to differences in status, class, and gender. Furthermore, claiming that the various voluntary associations in Roman society comprised heterogeneous members, Klinghardt illustrates the diverse ways and the variable situations in which tensions and conflicts at meals were occasioned and the unity at meals was often disrupted by social differences represented among the heterogeneous membership.[14]

---

13. See chapter 3, 78–83, 93–94.
14. See chapter 3, 83–85.

Equality with Difference

Thus, it has been acknowledged that the Greco-Roman meal was also a site of difference. It was a site of potential social conflict relative to the hierarchical placement of social differences. The Greco-Roman meal functioned as a site of difference to be placed and at the same time as a site of difference to be replaced. This dialectical valence of equality and difference lies at the core of the logic and dynamics of the Greco-Roman meal. Conflicts at meals in early Christian communities are related to and reflective of such logic and dynamics of the Greco-Roman meal. Relying on Mary Douglas's study on meals, Kathleen Corley considers the Greco-Roman meal tradition to be a window through which to look at the way early Christian communities took different stances toward the dominant ideology of gender in Roman society. Taking another tack by integrating theories on ritual from both Douglas and Jonathan Smith, Hal Taussig argues that social differences, particularly gender difference in his study of the Syro-Phoenician woman (Mark 7:24–30; Matt 15:22–28) were noticed, problematized, and negotiated at actual meals of communities within the ongoing process of early Christian social formations.

As we have discussed in chapter 3, the debate between Hagias and Lamprias, as it is described in an episode of Plutarch, and Pliny's self-defense for his equal treatment of social differences at meals are good examples of how the dynamic logic of Greco-Roman meals was operating in meal settings on both rhetorical and practical levels. Viewed within this wider context of the Greco-Roman meal with its dynamic ethos, the confrontation between Peter and Paul in the setting of the community meal at Antioch (Gal 2:11–21) and the tensions between the "weak" and the "strong" in table-fellowship in Rome (Rom 14:1—15:13) share commonalities with the cases from Plutarch and Pliny. In its table-fellowship the community in Antioch is not unfamiliar with the same kind of general tension between social equality and social difference, and neither is Paul. Although the specific issues related to Jew-Gentile difference complicated the matter in both Antioch and Rome, the logic and dynamics of the Greco-Roman meal were operating under the tables of these early Christian communities. From this it is possible to infer that the logic and dynamics of Greco-Roman meals were also implicit in Paul's treatment of difference between Jews and Gentiles. This leads to the point where the logic and dynamics of the Greco-Roman meal intersect with the logic and dynamics of ritual in general.

2.2. The Logic and Dynamics of Ritual

Approaching early Christian meal texts within the comparative framework of the Greco-Roman common meal tradition provides two hermeneutical vantage points. First, early Christian common meals are viewed in relation to the practices that these communities were sharing in common with other groups and associations in Roman society. It underscores that the practice of Christian table-fellowship is accounted for as comparable to other practices rather than as uniquely Christian. This implies a perspective that is far more horizontal and relational. Second, at the initial stages of Christian social formation, common meals and ritual meals (eucharist or sacramental meals) were not separated. There was no strict distinction between common and sacred. What was called "the Lord's supper" was a communal meal (ritual) imbued with distinct significations. This might be taken as an intersecting point which brings together theories of Greco-Roman (and early Christian) meals and theories of ritual.

So how can the understanding of difference in ritual theory be correlated to the logic and dynamics of the Greco-Roman meal as noted above? I discover a heuristic approach in the way Taussig deals with early Christian meals by integrating the insights of both Mary Douglas and Jonathan Smith. By bringing together Douglas's emphasis on the structural ordering of *social hierarchical difference* at meals and Smith's focus on the process of *ritual negotiation of difference* and placing this combination into the context of early Christian communities, Taussig has demonstrated that at early Christian meals, social differences were not only noted and marked, but also negotiated in various ways in distinct situations, and further, that such a process of negotiating difference continued through different stages of early Christian social formation, particularly within the setting of community meals. Here the concept of negotiation implies multiple ways of dealing with social differences by the community and the members.

Appropriating the linkage between difference, meal, and ritual negotiation that Taussig has elaborated, I have extended the category of difference in order to deal with the difference between Jews and Gentiles as they are reflected in two different communities. Thus, I approached the question of Jew-Gentile difference within the larger cultural context of the Greco-Roman meal and within the local situation of meals in particular communities. Further, this facilitated my ability to see Paul's politics of difference as a way of negotiating differences between Jews and Gentiles at meals within the logic and dynamics of the Greco-Roman meal.

Equality with Difference

3. PAUL AND THE POLITICS OF DIFFERENCE: TOWARD A KOREAN CHRISTIAN IDENTITY.

In this final section, I wish to relate the significance of Jewish-Gentile difference in early Christian social formation and Paul's politics of difference to the specific context of present Korean Christianity and suggest some further implications for the development of Korean biblical hermeneutics. How is my particular focus on issues of Jew-Gentile difference in Paul's epistles to Galatia and Rome in the Roman Empire of the first century related to an Asian Gentile context in the globalizing world of the twenty-first century? What does Paul's understanding of difference as I construe it tell us about Korean "difference"? What relevance does Paul's politics of difference have for any significant effort committed to the ongoing process of (re)making identity/difference? Why should one argue for "equality with difference" with an emphasis on justice, rather than simply celebrate "difference"?

3.1. Recontextualizing the Jew-Gentile Difference

In recontextualizing the issue of Jew-Gentile difference within the context of Korean Christianity, an analogous phenomenon draws particular attention. Western Christianity has taught us Asian Christians that there is neither "Occidental" nor "Oriental" in Christ, in other words, in Gentile Christianity. By preaching that there is no Occidental-Oriental distinction, Occidental Christianity has been successful in persuading us to believe that any ethnic specificity, whether Korean, Jewish, Indian or African, is irrelevant or *adiapheron* to the essence of Christian faith. It is not difficult to see that in the effort to eliminate distinction, Western Christianity tactfully deployed the Pauline discourse of "no distinction between Jews and Gentiles" as one of the main proof texts for the purposes of its own missionary and imperial universalism. The discourse of "no distinction between Jews and Gentiles" was used by powerful Western Christianity to exercise its hegemony under the guise of universalism. I am saying this because it is important to distinguish who uses such a logic of identity and who imposes it on whom. Just as Jewish difference was deprived of its own ethnic specificity and historical memory in the later development of Gentile Christianity,[15] the ethnic, historical, and cultural values of Korean identity were suppressed by the universal discourse and imperialistic move of

---

15. Boyarin, *A Radical Jew*.

Western Christianity. In this sense, it may not go too far to say that despite differences in historical specificity, Korean difference has much affinity with Jewish difference. Thus I am also in agreement with the hermeneutical and cultural standpoint of Boyarin and Elizabeth Castelli in their sharp criticism of the "coercive" universalism in Christianity.[16]

The process, however, through which Korean identity has become a denied and alienated identity in the history of Korean Christianity is a very complex one. The process has been one-sided from Western Christianity, but there was an interdependent complicity as well, in which Korean Christianity has actively participated from the beginning of its acceptance of Western Christianity up to the present. Above all, a "syncretistic complicity" of Western Christianity and Korean Confucian traditions occurred in terms of domination and hierarchical dualism. Within such a system of dualistic thinking and perspective adopted by Korean Christianity, the polarity of otherworldly-worldly occupies a central position, and is supported by sets of binary oppositional notions, such as spirit-body, male-female, free-slave, public-public, and Christian-heathen (Jewish).

Historically speaking, what we encounter during Second Temple Judaism before 70 CE is Jewish-Gentile (pagan) polarity. But within Christian circles since the second century CE and throughout Christian history, that polarity has been largely replaced by the binary opposition Christian-Jewish (and all others). Its implication is that now heathen (non-Christian) difference has become parallel to Jewish difference. To put this differently, the exclusive tendency of Western Christianity toward Jewish difference has been replicated in the exclusive tendency of Korean Christianity toward other cultural and religious traditions in Korea.

Undoubtedly and unfortunately, most Korean Christians are socialized—religiously and culturally—to privilege one side of the sets of binary oppositions over the other side. Moreover, it is ironical that Korean Christianity has been zealous to imitate and identify itself with Western Christianity without knowing that Korean Christianity cannot and should not be the "same" as Western Christianity, and on the other hand has never been treated as equal to Western Christianity. It is so unfortunate that Korean Christianity has been endeavoring to imitate Western Christianity and its universalism. It is as if the closer Asian Christians imitate the content and patterns of Western Christianity, the closer they get to the (soteriological) core of the Christian faith. In this way, Korean Christianity is not only fully

16. On Boyarin and Castelli, see the Introduction above, 15–20.

assimilated to but also deeply colonized by Western cultural imperialism. This is true to the extent that most Korean Christians have slight awareness of how blind they are to their own Korean identity which has been neglected and suppressed by a Western universal identity, which is not "ours." In this regard, I consider that as a Western self-reflective criticism, the postmodern critique of the logic of identity of Western cultural hegemony is valuable for our own self-reflective deconstruction of what we have constructed with the numerous bricks of binary, hierarchical oppositions in dealing with difference. Nonetheless, the issue of the politics of identity/difference within the Korean Christian context requires a critical and discreet appropriation of Western postmodern criticism.

There is another aspect which needs to be included in a project of deconstructing the legacies of Western cultural universalism within the Korean Christian context. As I indicated in the Introduction,[17] the predominant understanding of the Christian faith in Korean Christianity is characterized by personal piety centered on the dichotomy of otherworldly-worldly. Particularly, Pauline discourse on justification by faith, on neither Jew nor Gentile, and on spirit and flesh has been interpreted as integral to an *a*political, *a*historical, and *a*cultural Christianity. As such, faith has been understood as if the impartiality of faith has nothing to do with differences and domination in the framework of class, gender, race, and empire. Pauline texts have been interpreted and used as proof texts for such an understanding of "universal faith." A notable development in current Pauline scholarship is that in recognition of various forms of violence legitimated by Christian universalism, scholars seriously interrogate Paul's texts and the scholarly interpretation from postmodern, feminist, and postcolonial contexts. Like other biblical texts, Paul's discourse—on several issues—has been contested for both oppression and liberation. Placed in the hermeneutical framework of a politics of identity/difference, Pauline discourse is once again becoming a bone of contention. I situate my own work in the context of such a paradigm shift in Pauline studies.

3.2. Paul and Difference in the Context of the Korean Minjung

Up to this point minjung theology in Korea has not engaged Paul's discourse and practice critically and creatively, primarily because of the universalist and imperial reading patterns discussed above. Minjung theologians have

17. See the Introduction above, 2–3.

tended to regard Paul and his theological discourse as scarcely conducive to or even as an impediment to the construction of a Korean liberation theology from the perspective of the minjung. Minjung theologians, following the dominant reading patterns in the West, have taken Paul's universalism and social conservatism for granted, and they have not seriously challenged such a dominant position relative to Paul. Nor have they tried to reinterpret Paul as an important frame of resource for their task. They have tended simply to avoid referring to Paul. In other words, they did not know what to do with Paul. For minjung theology, Paul was part of the problem rather than a part of the solution and was consequently ignored. Paul has been pressed into the service of the hegemonic logic of identity rather than adopted for an emancipatory politics of difference. Compared with minjung theology's enormous efforts devoted to the historical Jesus during the last two decades, almost no attention has been paid to Paul. Within the framework of liberation of the minjung, Paul himself has been rendered a marginalized difference, i.e., the "other."

Such a marginalization of Paul in minjung theology is fundamentally grounded in the following questionable assumptions.

(1) The context of Paul's theology and praxis has been treated under the umbrella of Hellenism instead of first-century Roman imperial *pax Romana*. A certain social assimilation and/or conservatism has been assumed as natural on Paul's part. The essentializing divide between Judaism and Hellenism has been operating as a major explanatory category for Paul's context.

(2) Paul's discourse has generally been assumed to be unrelated to his concerns for the people of specific communities. Paul's theological and discursive reflection has been separated from his politics and praxis. The divide between theology and praxis has been presupposed.

(3) The gap between the historical Jesus in the Gospels and Paul at the historical, literary, and theological levels has been unquestioned by most minjung theologians. The divide between the historical Jesus and Paul has facilitated minjung theology to justify taking its distance from Paul.

(4) Although minjung theologians emphasize the significance of the Galilean oppressed, i.e. the minjung, in focusing on the study of the historical Jesus, it has assumed that Paul and his message have nothing to do with the oppressed minjung under Roman imperial domination.

Equality with Difference

Paul has been viewed as an "individual" theologian rather than a person who lived in the midst of people and in solidarity with the "weak," occasionally spending his life in prison and finally being executed.[18]

These assumptions induced minjung theologians to separate Paul not only from the concrete interests and needs of the oppressed—Jew and Gentile, male and female, slave and free—but also from ordinary people of today, most of whom are disenfranchised and alienated under the cultural politics of globalization. Neil Elliott is on the mark when he states, "The ultimate horizon of any effort to liberate Paul from his metaphorical chains must be the liberation of men and women who suffer very real opposition and violence in our own day."[19]

3.3. Reconfiguring the Significance of the Minjung for the Politics of Difference

In chapter 2 of this study, I discussed postmodern, feminist, and postcolonial perspectives on the problem of difference with the intention of reconsidering the significance of Korean minjung theology by taking into account its similarities and dissimilarities with other comparable discourses on difference. Since the appearance of minjung theology in Korea, the concept of minjung has been a focal point of controversy. Because of the socio-political situation in Korea during the 1980s, minjung theologians were reluctant to give substance to the concept of minjung, particularly avoiding the category of social class. Instead, minjung was defined in a rather oblique way as a concept inclusive of all oppressed people. Minjung theologians have received criticism that they are romanticizing or mystifying the concept. Whether such criticism is valid or not, minjung theology's inclusive gesture shown in its definition of minjung became problematic because it did not pay proper attention to the issue of gender difference, that is, the significance of women who constitute an integral part of the minjung as marginalized and as those who are denied the subject position in hierarchical and oppressive Korean society. The divide between class and gender was implicit in the formative shape of minjung theology, and this has been problematized especially by Korean feminists and feminist

---

18. For this neglected aspect of Paul's praxis, see especially Tamez, *The Amnesty of Grace*, 47–64.

19. N. Elliott, *Liberating Paul*, 23.

theologians. As one way of my appropriation of the postmodern critique of the logic of identity, I emphasize a continuing need for the development of a proper theory on the notion of minjung within the specific Korean historical context and the global imperial context as well.

My review of Western feminist approaches to gender differences in chapter 3 helps us to recognize the importance of critical engagement with the problems and dangers of essentialism, universalism, and pluralism which continuously evolve within the politics of difference with respect to gender, race, class, and empire. Drawing on feminist perspectives on the issue of difference, I accentuate that despite and because of differences in historical specificity and subjectivity, one instance of identity/difference, for example, gender difference, cannot be treated separately from its relation to and interdependence on other instances of class, race, and empire. This is the case because each human being, each group, and each society as a "subject" is situated within a specific historical context, and therefore, the issue of identity/difference is about relations, *par excellence*, social power relations. Thus, any move toward "the play of difference" in terms of valorizing difference in postmodernism or in other social criticisms should be problematized. At the same time, it explains why any insistence on essential identity in terms of romanticizing identity or nativism should raise an alert.

In the vicissitudes of Korea's long history the word *minjung* refers to the people who have been oppressed, rendered powerless, marginalized, and made invisibile as "others" under multiple forms of social injustice— economic, socio-political, religio-cultural, patriarchal, and colonial. As such minjung stands for an individual subject as well as a collective subject. The thrust of minjung theology's understanding of minjung aims at the subversive declaration that despite and in the very midst of suffering, marginality, invisibility, and the otherness of the minjung, the minjung have actually been the subject of Korean history. Recognizing that the term minjung signifies the marginality of identity related to the multiple faces of social injustice and oppression, I would suggest that the notion incorporates the plurality of differences in itself. Minjung is the notion which most appropriately includes the second terms in constructs of binary dichotomy, such as women, slaves, the poor, the weak, people of color, Asian, Jews, non-Christians, the colonized—any who are marginalized as other. In a word, minjung is "difference."

In appropriating postcolonial perspectives on difference, I wish to reflect on a further implication of refocusing the significance of minjung as "difference." Because the term pertains to the majority of Korean people, its meaning cannot be separated from that of the Korean nation (*minjok*). From the beginning of the last century, the Korean nation had to endure Japanese colonization for thirty-six years. After independence from Japanese rule, the Korean nation was forced into a divided nation of north and south by foreign powers, especially by the United States with its imperialistic and hegemonic interests and strategies. For more than a half century since, the Korean nation and people have been suffering from the division of land, history, family, and national identity. At the very heart of the oppression and suffering of the Korean minjung lies the tragic reality of the divided nation. Any discourse on difference within the Korean context cannot avoid the issue of Korean difference as a divided identity.

The most violent repression and denial of Korean identity, including Korean Christian identity, is executed by the imperial force of dividing the Korean nation and people into two oppositional differences. During the last half century, the people of both North and South Korea have been socialized to see each other as oppositional difference, that is, as the other whose difference should be suppressed, denied, and ultimately eliminated. A dominant form of Korean Christianity functioned as part of an ideological machine to maintain and reinforce this exclusive politics of identity. Korean Christians have surrendered their Korean identity to Western universal Christian identity under the logic of faith.

A new way of thinking difference between North and South Korea is finally emerging in the hearts and minds of the Korean minjung on both sides of the 38th parallel. Awareness is growing that the unity of the Korean people and nation cannot be accomplished by the logic of one side absorbing the other—a reunification that would mean sameness—but a new pattern of confederated reunification—equivalent to unity with difference. This radical unity which includes difference is to be grounded on the power of sharing differences with the persistent praxis of solidarity with the weak. Furthermore, this paradigm shift may suggest a new avenue toward the global politics of difference as well. It promotes a new mode of globalization in which difference (the other) occupies the subject position—a courageous challenge to the present mode of globalization in which sameness turns out to be a logic of domination.

A liberative hermeneutics of inclusion in Paul's interpretation of faith in Jesus Christ has almost been stifled in Western Christianity, and consequently in Korean Christianity. Over the centuries, in the name of theological universalism Western Christianity has superimposed its own imperial identity, which resulted in the denial of non-Western difference/identity. The faith that Western Christianity brought to the Korean people replicates the exclusivist logic of identity which Paul opposed. As a way of redefining Korean Christian identity as well as decolonizing the hegemony of Western universalism and globalization, the inclusive hermeneutics of faith Paul articulated within the concrete context of table-fellowship between Jews and Gentiles needs to be recovered and appropriated anew. I hope this study may serve as a catalyst for further elaboration of a biblical hermeneutics in minjung theology.

Bibliography

Ahn, Byung Mu. "The Body of Transmission of the Jesus Event." In *The Development of Korean Minjung Theology in the 1980s*, edited by The Korea Theological Study Institute, 229–55. Seoul: The Korea Theological Study Institute, 1990.
———. "The Jesus Movement and *Mul*." In *The Development of Korean Minjung Theology in the 1980s*, edited by The Korea Theological Study Institute, 348–65. Seoul: The Korea Theological Study Institute, 1990.
———. "Jesus and the Minjung in the Gospel of Mark." In *Minjung Theology as the Subjects of History*, edited by the Commission on Theological Concerns of the Christian Conference of Asia, 138–52. Maryknoll, NY: Orbis, 1983.
Alcoff, Linda. "Cultural Feminism versus Poststructualism: The Identity Crisis in Feminist Theory." *Signs* 13 (1988) 405–36.
Alföldy, Geza. *The Social History of Rome*. Translated by David Braund and Frank Pollock. London: Croom Helm, 1975.
Applebaum, S. "The Social and Economic Status of the Jews in the Diaspora." In *The Jewish People in the First Century*, Vol. 2, edited by S. Safrai and M. Stern, 701–27. Assen: Van Gorcum, 1974.
Armour, Ellen T. *Deconstruction, Feminist Theology, and the Problem of Difference: Subverting the Race/Gender Divide*. Chicago: University of Chicago Press, 1999.
Aune, David. "Orthodoxy in First Century Judaism?" *Journal for the Study of Judaism* 7 (1976) 1–10.
Bassler, Jouette M, ed. *Pauline Theology*. Vol. 1, *Thessalonians, Philippians, Galatians, Philemon*. Minneapolis: Fortress, 1991.
Bauckham, Richard. "James and the Jerusalem Church." In *The Book of Acts in Its Palestinian Setting*, edited by Richard Bauckham, 415–80. Grand Rapids: Eerdmans, 1995.
Benko, Stephen. "The Edict of Claudius of AD 49 and the Instigator Chrestus." *Theologische Zeitschrift* 25 (1969) 406–18.
———. *Pagan Rome and the Early Christianity*. Bloomington: Indiana University Press, 1984.
Berquist, Jon L. "Postcolonialism and Imperial Motives for Canonization." *Semeia* 75 (1996) 15–35.
Betz, Hans Dieter. *Galatians: A Commentary on Paul's Letter to the Churches in Galatia*. Hermeneia. Philadelphia: Fortress, 1979.
Bhabha, Homi K. *The Location of Culture*. New York: Routledge, 1994.

Bibliography

Bible and Culture Collective; George Aichele et al. *The Postmodern Bible*. New Haven: Yale University Press, 1995.

Bordo, Susan. "Feminism, Postmodernism, and Gender-Scepticism." In *Feminism/Postmodernism*, edited by Linda J. Nicholson, 133–56. New York: Routledge, 1990.

Boyarin, Daniel. *A Radical Jew: Paul and the Politics of Identity*. Berkeley: University of California Press, 1994.

Brett, Mark G. "The Ethics of Postcolonial Criticism." *Semeia* 75 (1996) 219–40.

———, ed. *Ethnicity and the Bible*. Biblical Interpretation Series 19. Leiden: Brill, 1996.

Briggs, Sheila. "The Politics of Identity and the Politics of Interpretation." *Union Seminary Quarterly Review* 43 (1989) 163–80.

Brown, Raymond E., and John P. Meier. *Antioch and Rome: New Testament Cradles of Catholic Christianity*. New York: Paulist, 1983.

Büchsel, Fredrich. "ἄλλος, κτλ." In *Theological Dictionary of the New Testament*, edited by Gerhard Kittel and translated by Geoffrey W. Bromiley, 1:264–67. Grand Rapids: Eerdmans, 1987.

Burtchaell, James Tunstead. *From Synagogue to Church: Public Services and Offices in the Earliest Christian Communities*. Cambridge: Cambridge University Press, 1992.

Butler, Judith. *Bodies that Matter: On the Discursive Limits of "Sex."* New York: Routledge, 1993.

———. *Gender Trouble: Feminism and the Subversion of Identity*. Thinking Gender. New York: Routledge, 1990.

Campbell, William S. "The Freedom and Faithfulness of God in Relation to Israel." *Journal for the Study of the New Testament* 13 (1981) 27–45.

———. *Paul's Gospel in an Intercultural Context: Jew and Gentile in the Letter to the Romans*. Frankfurt: Lang, 1992.

———. "The Rule of Faith in Romans 12:1—15:13: The Obligation of Humble Obedience to Christ as the Only Adequate Response to the Mercies of God." Unpublished SBL paper, 1992.

Castelli, Elizabeth A. *Imitating Paul: A Discourse of Power*. Louisville: Westminster John Knox, 1991.

Chossudovsky, Michel. *The Globalization of Poverty: Impacts on IMF and World Bank Reforms*. London and Atlantic Highlands, NJ: Zed, 1997.

Cohen, Shaye J. D. *The Beginnings of Jewishness: Boundaries, Varieties, Uncertainties*. Berkeley: University of California Press, 1999.

———. "Crossing the Boundary and Becoming a Jew." *Harvard Theological Review* 82 (1987) 13–33.

———. "Respect for Judaism by Gentiles according to Josephus." *Harvard Theological Review* 80 (1987) 409–30.

Cohen, Norman J. "Judaism and Christianity: The Parting of the Ways." *Thought* 67 (1992) 409–19.

Collins, John J. *Between Athens and Jerusalem: Jewish Identity in the Hellenistic Diaspora*. New York: Crossroad, 1983.

Connolly, William E. *Identity/Difference: Democratic Negotiations of Political Paradox*. Ithaca: Cornell University Press, 1991.

Conzelmann, Hans. *History of Primitive Christianity*. Translated by John E. Steely. Nashville: Abingdon, 1973.

Corley, Kathleen. *Private Women, Public Meals: Social Conflict in the Synoptic Tradition*. Peabody, MA: Hendrickson, 1993.

Bibliography

Craffert, Pieter F. "The Pauline Movement and First-Century Judaism: A Framework for Transforming the Issues." *Neotestimentica* 27 (1993) 233–62.

Crossan, John Dominic. *The Birth of Christianity: Discovering What Happened in the Years Immediately After the Execution of Jesus*. New York: HarperSanFrancisco, 1998.

Cummings, Bruce. *The Origins of the Korean War*. Princeton: Princeton University Press, 1981.

Daly, Mary. *Beyond God the Father: Toward a Philosophy of Women's Liberation*. Boston: Beacon, 1973.

———. *Gyn/Ecology: The Metaethics of Radical Feminism*. Boston: Beacon, 1978.

Dahl, Nils Alstrup. *Studies in Paul: Theology for the Early Christian Mission*. Minneapolis: Augsburg, 1977.

D'Arm, John. "The Roman Convivium and Equality." In *Sympotica: A Symposium on the Symposion*, edited by Oswyn Murray, 308–20. Oxford: Clarendon, 1990.

Davis, Angela. *Women, Race, and Class*. New York: Random House, 1981.

Derrida, Jacques. *Margins of Philosophy*. Translated by Alan Bass. Chicago: University of Chicago Press, 1982.

———. *Of Grammatology*. Translated by Gayatri Chakravorty Spivak. Baltimore: Johns Hopkins University Press, 1976.

———. *Writing and Difference*. Translated by Alan Bass. Chicago: University of Chicago Press, 1978.

Di Stefano, Christine. "Dilemmas of Difference." In *Feminism/Postmodernism*, edited by Linda J. Nicholson, 63–82. New York: Routledge, 1990.

Donaldson, Laura E. "Postcolonialism and Biblical Reading: An Introduction." *Semeia* 75 (1996) 1–14.

Donaldson, Terence L. *Paul and the Gentiles: Remapping the Apostle's Convictional World*. Minneapolis: Fortress, 1997.

———. "Proselytes or 'Righteous Gentiles'?: The Status of Gentiles in Eschatological Pilgrimage Patterns of Thought." *Journal for the Study of the Pseudepigrapha* 7 (1990) 3–27.

———. "Zealot and Convert: The Origin of Paul's Christ-Torah Antithesis." *Catholic Biblical Quarterly* 51 (1989) 655–82.

Donfried, Karl P. ed. *The Romans Debate*. Rev. ed. Peabody, MA: Hendrikson, 1991.

Douglas, Mary. "Deciphering a Meal." In *Implicit Meanings: Essays in Anthropology*. London: Routledge & Kegan Paul, 1975.

———. *Purity and Danger: An Analysis of Concepts of Pollution and Taboo*. London: Routledge & Kegan Paul, 1966.

Dube, Musa W. "Reading for Decolonization (John 4:1–42)." *Semeia* 75 (1996) 37–59.

Dunn, James D. G. "Echoes of Intra-Jewish Polemic in Paul's Letter to the Galatians." *Journal of Biblical Literature* 112 (1993) 459–77.

———. "The Incident at Antioch (Gal. 2.18–21)." In *Jesus, Paul and the Law: Studies in Mark and Galatians*, 129–82. Louisville: Westminster John Knox, 1990.

———. "The New Perspective on Paul." In *Jesus, Paul and the Law: Studies in Mark and Galatians*, 183–214. Louisville: Westminster John Knox, 1990.

———. "The Relationship between Paul and Jerusalem according to Galatians 1 and 2." In *Jesus, Paul and the Law: Studies in Mark and Galatians*, 108–28. Louisville: Westminster John Knox, 1990.

———. *Romans 9–16*. Word Biblical Commentary 38B. Dallas: Word, 1988.

Bibliography

———. "The Theology of Galatians." In *Pauline Theology*, Vol. 1, *Thessalonians, Philippians, Galatians, Philemon*, edited by Jouette M. Bassler, 125–46. Minneapolis: Fortress, 1991.

———. *The Theology of Paul's Letter to the Galatians*. New Testament Theology. Cambridge: Cambridge University Press, 1993.

———. "Works of the Law and the Curse of the Law." *New Testament Studies* 31 (1985) 523–42.

During, Simon. "Postmodernism or Postcolonialism?" *Lindfall* 39 (1985) 366–80.

Eliade, Mircea. *The Sacred and the Profane: The Nature of Religion*. Translated by Willard R. Trask. New York: Harcourt Brace Jovanovich, 1959.

Elliott, John H. "Jesus the Israelite was neither a 'Jew' nor a 'Christian': On Correcting Misleading Nomenclature." *Journal for the Study of the Historical Jesus* 5.2 (2007) 119–54.

Elliott, Neil. *Liberating Paul: The Justice of God and the Politics of the Apostles*. Maryknoll, NY: Orbis, 1994.

———. *The Rhetoric of Romans: Argumentative Constraint of Strategy and Paul's Dialogue with Judaism*. Journal for the Study of the New Testament Supplements 45. Sheffield: Sheffield Academic, 1990.

———. "Romans 13:1–7 in the Context of Imperial Propaganda." In *Paul and Empire: Religion and Power in Roman Imperial Society*, edited by Richard Horsley, 184–204. Philadelphia: Trinity, 1997.

Esler, Phillip Francis. *Community and Gospel in Luke–Acts*. Society for New Testament Study Monograph Series 57. Cambridge: Cambridge University Press, 1987.

———. *Conflict and Identity in Romans: The Social Setting of Paul's Letter*. Minneapolis: Fortress, 2003.

Fantham, Elaine. "Aequabilitas in Cicero's Political Theory, and the Greek Tradition of Proportional Justice." *Classical Quarterly* 67 (1973) 285–90.

Fargu, M. la. "Socio-historical Research and the Contextualization of Biblical Theology." In *The Social World of Formative Christianity and Judaism*, edited by Jacob Neusner et al., 3–15. Philadelphia: Fortress, 1988.

Feldman, Louis H. *Jew and Gentile in the Ancient World: Attitudes and Interactions from Alexander to Justinian*. Princeton: Princeton University Press, 1993.

Ferguson, Ann. "Resisting the Veil of Privilege: Building Bridge Identities as an Ethico-Politics of Global Feminisms." *Hypatia* 13.3 (1998) 95–113.

Foucault, Michel. *The Archaeology of Knowledge*. Translated by A. M. Sheidan Smith. New York: Pantheon, 1972.

Fraser, Nancy and Linda J. Nicholson. "Social Criticism without Philosophy: An Encounter between Feminism and Postmodernism." In *Feminism/Postmodernism*, edited by Lind J. Nicholson, 19–38. New York: Routledge, 1990.

Fredriksen, Paula. *From Jesus to Christ: The Origins of the New Testament Images of Jesus*. New Haven: Yale University Press, 1988.

———. "Judaism, the Circumcision of Gentiles, and Apocalyptic Hope: Another Look at Galatians 1 and 2." *Journal of Theological Studies* 41 (1991) 532–64.

Furnish, Victor. *The Love Command in the New Testament*. Nashville: Abingdon, 1972.

Gager, John. *The Origins of Anti-Semitism: Attitude toward Judaism in Pagan and Christian Antiquity*. New York: Oxford University Press, 1983.

———. *Reinventing Paul*. Oxford: Oxford University Press, 2000.

———. "Some Notes on Paul's Conversion." *New Testament Studies* 27 (1981) 697–704.

Bibliography

Gallagher, Susan. "Mapping the Hybrid World." *Semeia* 75 (1996) 229–40.

———. *Postcolonial Literature and the Bible Call for Justice*. Jackson: University Press of Mississippi, 1994.

Gaston, Lloyd. *Paul and the Torah*. Vancouver: University of British Columbia Press, 1987.

Georgi, Dieter. *Theocracy in Paul's Praxis and Theology*. Minneapolis: Fortress, 1991.

Gooch, Peter D. *Dangerous Food: 1 Corinthians 8–10 in Its Context*. Waterloo, ON: Wilfrid Laurier University Press, 1993.

Gordon, Linda. "The Trouble with Difference." Unpublished paper, 2–8.

Grant, Jacquelyn. *White Women's Christ and Black Women's Jesus: Feminist Christology and Womanist Response*. American Academy of Religion Academy Series 64. Atlanta: Scholars, 1989.

Hann, Robert R. "Judaism and Jewish Christianity in Antioch: Charisma and Conflict in the First Century." *Journal of Religious History* 14 (1987) 341–60.

Hartin, Patrick J. "Jewish Christianity: Focus on Antioch in the First Century." *Scriptura* 36 (1991) 38–50.

Hill, Craig. *Hellenists and Hebrews*. Minneapolis: Fortress, 1992.

Holmberg, Bengt. *Paul and Power: The Structure of Authority in the Primitive Church as Reflected in the Pauline Epistles*. Philadelphia: Fortress, 1980.

hooks, bell. *Ain't I a Woman: Black Women and Feminism*. Boston: South End, 1981.

Horsley, Richard A. "1 Corinthians: A Case Study of Paul's Assembly as an Alternative Society." In *Paul and Empire: Religion and Power in Roman Imperial Society*, 242–52. Harrisburg, PA: Trinity, 1997.

———, ed. *Paul and Empire*. Harrisburg, PA: Trinity, 1997.

———, ed. *Paul and Politics*. Harrisburg, PA: Trinity, 2000.

———. "Submerged Biblical Histories and Imperial Biblical Studies." In *The Postcolonial Bible*, edited by R. S. Sugirtharajah, 152–73. Sheffield: Sheffield Academic, 1990.

Horsley, Richard, and Neil Asher Silberman. *The Message and the Kingdom: How Jesus and Paul Ignited a Revolution and Transformed the Ancient World*. 1997. Reprinted, Minneapolis: Fortress, 2002.

Hutcheon, Linda. "Circling the Downspout of Empire." In *Past the Last Post: Post Colonialism and Post-Modernism*, edited by Ian Adam and Helen Tiffin, 167–89. Calgary, ALB: University of Calgary Press, 1990.

———. *The Politics of Postmodernism*. New York: Routledge, 1989.

———. "A Postmodern Problematics." In *Ethics/Aesthetics: Post-Modern Positions*, edited by Robert Merrill. Washington DC: Maisonneuve, 1988.

Huyssen, Andreas. "Mapping the Postmodern." In *Feminism/Postmodernism*, edited by Linda J. Nicholson, 234–77. New York: Routledge, 1990.

Jaggar, Alison. *Feminist Politics and Human Nature*. Philosophy and Society. Totawa, NJ: Rowman & Allanheld, 1983.

Jameson, Fredric. *Postmodernism, or the Culture of Logic of Late Capitalism*. Durham, NC: Duke University Press, 1991.

Jewett, Robert. "The Agitators and the Galatian Congregations." *New Testament Studies* 17 (1970–71) 198–212.

———. "Tenement Churches and Communal Meals in the Early Church: the Implications of a Form-Critical Analysis of 2 Thessalonians 3:10." *Biblical Research* 38 (1993) 23–43.

Johnson, Luke Timothy. "The New Testament Anti-Jewish Slander and the Conventions of Ancient Polemic." *Journal of Biblical Literature* 108 (1989) 419–41.

Bibliography

Joubert, S. J. "A Bone of Contention in Recent Scholarship: The 'Birkat Ha-Mim' and the Separation of Church and Synagogue in the First Century AD." *Neotestamentica* 27 (1993) 351–63.

Judge, E. A. "Cultural Conformity and Innovation in Paul: Some Clues from Contemporary Documents." *Tyndale Bulletin* 35 (1984) 3–24.

Judge, E. A., and G. S. R. Thomas. "The Origin of the Church at Rome." *Reformed Theological Review* 25 (1966) 81–93.

Kahl, Brigitte. "Gender Trouble in Galatia? Paul and the Rethinking of Difference." In *Is There a Future for Feminist Theology?*, edited by D. Sawyer and D. Collier, 57–73. Studies in Theology and Sexuality 4. Sheffield: Sheffield Academic, 1999.

———. "No Longer Male: Masculinity Struggles behind Gal 3:28." *Journal for the Study of the New Testament* 2 (2000) 37–49.

Kang, Won Don. "A New Search for Theological Hermeneutic." In *The Development of Korean Minjung Theology in the 1980s*, edited by The Korea Theological Study Institute, 256–95. Seoul: Korea Theological Study Institute, 1990.

———. *The Theology of Mul*. Seoul: Han Wool, 1992.

Karris, Robert J. "Romans 14:1—15:13 and the Occasion of Romans." In *The Romans Debate*, edited by Karl P. Donfried, 65–84. Rev. ed. Peabody, MA: Hendrikson, 1991.

Käsemann, Ernst. *Commentary on Romans*. Translated by Geoffrey W. Bromiley. Grand Rapids: Eerdmans, 1980.

Katz, Steven T. "Issues in the Separation of Judaism and Christianity after 70 C.E.: A Reconsideration." *Journal of Biblical Literature* 103 (1984) 43–76.

Kee, Howard Clark. "The Transformation of the Synagogue after 70 C.E.: Its Import for Early Christianity." *New Testament Studies* 36 (1990) 1–24.

Kim, Chang Nack. "The Significance of Minjung in Doing Theology." In *The Development of Korean Minjung Theology in the 1980s*, edited by The Korea Theological Study Institute, 108–31. Seoul: Korea Theological Study Institute, 1990.

Kim, Jin Ho. "A Genealogical Understanding of Minjung Theology." *Time and Minjung Theology* 4 (1997) 6–29.

———. "Minjung as the Subject of History: Reappraisal on 'Minjung' of Minjung Theology." *The Theological Thought* 80.1 (1993) 21–47.

Kittel, Gerhard, ed. *Theological Dictionary of the New Testament*. Vol. 1. Translated by Geoffrey W. Bromiley. Grand Rapids: Eerdmans, 1987.

Klinghardt, Matthias. *Gemeinschaftsmahl und Mahlgemeinschaft: Soziologie und Liturgie Frühchristlich Mahlfeiern*. Texte und Arbeiten zum neutestamentlichen Zeitalter 13. Tübingen: Francke, 1996.

Kloppenborg, John S., and Stephen G. Wilson, eds. *Voluntary Associations in the Greco-Roman World*. London: Routledge, 1996.

Kraabel, A. T. "The Roman Diaspora: Six Questionable Assumptions." *Journal for the Jewish Studies* 33 (1989) 445–64.

Kraemer, Ross S. "Monastic Jewish Women in Greco-Roman Egypt: Philo Judaeus on the Therapeutrides." *Signs* 14 (1989) 342–70.

Kümmel, Werner Georg. *Introduction to the New Testament*. Translated by H. C. Kee. Nashville: Abingdon, 1975.

Kwok, Pui-Lan. "Response to the *Semeia* volume on Postcolonial Criticism." *Semeia* 75 (1996) 211–17.

La Piana, George. "Foreign Groups in Ancient Rome." *Harvard Theological Review* 20 (1927) 183–403.

Lampe, Peter. "The Eucharist: Identifying with Christ on the Cross." *Interpretation* 48 (1994) 36–49.
Lategan, Bernard. "Is Paul Defending His Apostleship in Galatians?" *New Testament Studies* 34 (1988) 411–30.
Leon, Harry Joshua. *The Jews of Ancient Rome*. Philadelphia: Jewish Publication Society of America, 1960.
Lieu, Judith et al., eds. *The Jews among Pagans and Christians in the Roman Empire*. London: Routledge, 1992.
Longenecker, Bruce W. *Eschatology and the Covenant: A Comparison of 4 Ezra and Romans 1–11*. Journal for the Study of the New Testament Supplements 57. Sheffield: JSOT Press, 1991.
Lüdemann, Gerd. *Paul: Apostle to the Gentiles*. Translated by F. S. Jones. London: SCM, 1984.
Lyotard, Jean-François. *The Postmodern Condition*. Translated by Geoff Bennington and Brian Massumi. Minneapolis: University of Minnesota Press, 1984.
Mack, Burton L. *Who Wrote the New Testament? The Making of Christian Myth*. San Francisco: HarperSanFrancisco, 1995.
MacDonald, Margaret Y. *The Pauline Churches: A Socio-historical Study of Institutionalization in the Pauline and Deutero-Pauline Writings*. Society for New Testament Studies Monograph Series 60. New York: Cambridge University Press, 1988.
McKnight, Scot. *A Light among the Gentiles: Jewish Missionary Activity in the Second Temple Period*. Minneapolis: Fortress, 1991.
McMullen, Ramsey. *Roman Social Relations*. New Haven: Yale University Press, 1974.
Malina, Bruce J. "Jewish Christianity or Christian Judaism: Toward a Hypothetical Definition." *Journal for the Study of Judaism* 7 (1976) 46–56.
Marcus, Joel. "The Circumcision and the Uncircumcision in Rome." *New Testament Studies* 35 (1989) 67–81.
Marxsen, Willi. *The Beginnings of Christology*. Translated by Paul J. Achtemeier and Lorenz Nieting. Philadelphia: Fortress, 1979.
Mattila, Sharon Lea. "Where Women Sat in Ancient Synagogue." In *Voluntary Associations in the Greco-Roman World*, edited by John S. Kloppenborg and Stephen G. Wilson, 268–86. London: Routledge, 1996.
Meeks, Wayne A. "Breaking Away: Three New Testament Pictures of Christianity's Separation from the Jewish Communities." In *"To See Ourselves as Others See Us": Christians, Jews, "Others" in Late Antiquity*, edited by Jacob Neusner and Ernest S. Frerichs, 93–116. Scholars Press Studies in the Humanities Series. Chico, CA: Scholars, 1985.
———. "Judgment and the Brother: Romans 14:1—15:13." In *Tradition and Interpretation in the New Testament: Essays in Honor of E. Earle Ellis for His 60th Birthday*, edited by Alan T. Davies, 1–26. New York: Paulist, 1987.
Meeks, Wayne A., and Robert L. Wilken. *Jews and Christians in Antioch in the First Four Centuries of the Common Era*. Sources for Biblical Study 13. Missoula, MT: Scholars, 1978.
Miles, Angela. "Feminist Radicalism in the 1980's." *Canadian Journal of Political and Social Theory* 9 (1985) 16–39.
Mishra, Vijay, and Bob Hodge. "What is Post(-)colonialism?" In *Colonial Discourse and Post-Colonial Theory: A Reader*, edited by Patrick Williams and Laura Chrisman, 276–90. New York: Columbia University Press, 1994.

Bibliography

Mohanty, Chandra Talpade. "Under Western Eyes: Feminist Scholarship and Colonial Discourses." In *The Post-Colonial Studies Reader*, edited by Bill Ashcroft, Gareth Griffiths, and Helen Tiffin, 259–63. New York: Routledge, 1995.

Mosala, Itumeleng J. *Biblical Hermeneutics and Black Theology in South Africa*. Grand Rapids: Eerdmans, 1990.

Myers, Ched. *Binding the Strong Man: A Political Reading of Mark's Story of Jesus*. Maryknoll, NY: Orbis, 1988.

Nanos, Mark D. "The Inter- and Intra-Jewish Political Context of Galatians." In *Paul and Politics: Ekklesia, Israel, Imperium, Interpretation: Essays in Honor of Krister Stendahl*, edited by Richard Horsley, 146–59. Harrisburg, PA: Trinity, 2000.

———. *The Mystery of Romans: The Jewish Context of Paul's Letter*. Minneapolis: Fortress, 1996.

———. "Peter's Hypocrisy (Gal 2:11–21) in the Light of Paul's Anxiety (Rom 7)." In *The Mystery of Romans: The Jewish Context of Paul's Letter*, 337–71. Minneapolis: Fortress, 1996.

Neusner, Jacob, and Ernest S. Frerichs, eds. *"To See Ourselves as Others See Us": Christians, Jews, "Others" in Late Antiquity*. Scholars Press Studies in the Humanities Series. Chico, CA: Scholars, 1986.

Nicholson, Linda J. "Introduction." In *Feminism/Postmodernism*, edited by Linda J. Nicholson, 1–16. New York: Routledge, 1990.

Nolland, J. "Uncircumcised Proselytes?" *Journal for the Study of Judaism* 12 (1981) 173–94.

Oduyoye, Amba (Mercy). "Reflections from a Third World Woman's Perspective: Women's Experience and Liberation Theology." In *Irruption of the Third World: Challenge to Theology: Papers of the Fifth International Conference of the Ecumenical Association of Third World Theologians, August 17–29, 1981, New Delhi*, edited by Virginia Fabella and Sergio Torres, 246–55. Maryknoll, NY: Orbis, 1983.

Overman, J. Andrew. "The God-fearers: Some Neglected Features." *Journal for the Study of New Testament* 32 (1988) 17–26.

Park, Andrew Sung. *The Wounded Heart of God: The Asian Concept of Han and the Christian Doctrine of Sin*. Nashville: Abingdon, 1993.

Park, Soon Kyung. "National Reunification and Minjung Theology: Toward A New Development of Minjung Theology." *The Theological Thought* 80 (1993) 56–83.

Perkinson, Jim. "A Canaanitic Word in the Logos of Christ; or The Difference the Syro-Phoenician Woman Makes to Jesus." *Semeia* 75 (1996) 61–85.

Pieris, Aloysius S. J. *An Asian Theology of Liberation*. Maryknoll, NY: Orbis, 1988.

Price, S. R. F. *Rituals and Power: The Roman Imperial Cult in Asia Minor*. Cambridge: Cambridge University Press, 1984.

Räisänen, Heikki. "Galatians 2.16 and Paul's break with Judaism." *New Testament Studies* 31 (1985) 543–53.

———. *Paul and the Law*. Philadelphia: Fortress, 1986.

Rajak, Tessa. "Jews and Christians as Groups in a Pagan World." In *"To See Ourselves as Others See Us": Christians, Jews, "Others" in Late Antiquity*, edited by J. Neusner and E. S. Frerichs, 247–62. Scholars Press Studies in the Humanities Series. Chico, CA: Scholars, 1985.

———. "Was There a Roman Charter for the Jews?" *Journal of Roman Studies* 74 (1984) 107–33.

Reasoner, Mark. *The Strong and the Weak: Romans 14:1—15:13 in Context*. Society for New Testament Studies Monograph Series 103. Cambridge: Cambridge University Press, 1999.

Reicke, Bo. "Judaeo-Christianity and the Jewish Establishment, A.D. 33–66." In *Jesus and the Politics of His Day*, edited by Ernst Bammel and C. F. D. Moule, 145–52. Cambridge: Cambridge University Press, 1984.

Richardson, Peter. "Pauline Inconsistency: 1 Corinthians 9:19–23 and Galatians 2:11–14." *New Testament Studies* 26 (1979) 347–62.

Rich, Adrienne. *Of Woman Born: Motherhood as Experience and Institution*. New York: Norton, 1976.

Ruether, Rosemary. *New Woman/New Earth: Sexist Ideologies and Human Liberation*. New York: Seabury, 1975.

———. *Sexism and God-Talk: Toward a Feminist Theology*. Boston: Beacon, 1983.

Ruggini, Lellia Cracco. "Intolerance: Equal and Less Equal in the Roman World." *Classical Philology* 82 (1987) 187–205.

Rutgers, Leonard Victor. "Roman Policy Towards the Jews: Expulsions from the City of Rome during the First Century CE." *Classical Antiquity* 13 (1994) 56–74.

Said, Edward. *Culture and Imperialism*. New York: Vintage, 1994.

Sampley, J. Paul. "The Weak and the Strong: Paul's Careful and Crafty Rhetorical Strategy In Romans 14:1—15:13." In *The Social World of the First Christians: Essays in Honor of Wayne A. Meeks*, edited by L. Michael White and O. Larry Yarbrough, 4–52. Minneapolis: Fortress, 1995.

Sanders, Cheryl J. "Womanist Theology/Feminist Theology: A Dialogue." *Daugthers of Sarah* 15 (1989) 6–7.

Sanders, E. P. "The Covenant as a Soteriological Category and the Nature of Salvation in Palestinian and Hellenistic Judaism." In *Jews, Greeks, and Christians: Religious Cultures in Late Antiquity*, edited by Robert Hamerton-Kelly and Robin Scroggs, 11–44. Studies in Judaism in Late Antiquity 21. Leiden: Brill, 1976.

———. "Jewish Association with Gentiles and Galatians 2:11–14." In *The Conversa-tion Continues: Studies in Paul and John, In Honor of J. Louis Martyn*, 170–88. Nash-ville: Abingdon, 1990.

———. *Paul and Palestinian Judaism: A Comparison of Patterns of Religion*. Philadelphia: Fortress, 1977.

———. *Paul, the Law, and the Jewish People*. Minneapolis: Fortress, 1983.

Sanders, Jack T. *Schismatics, Sectarians, Dissidents, Deviants: The First One Hundred Years of Jewish-Christian Relations*. Harrisburg, PA: Trinity, 1993.

Sawicki, Jana. "Foucault and Feminism: Toward a Politics of Difference." *Hypatia* 1.2 (1986) 23–36.

Schüssler Fiorenza, Elisabeth. *In Memory of Her: A Feminist Theological Reconstruction of Christian Origin*. New York: Crossroad, 1984.

———, ed. *Searching the Scriptures: A Feminist Introduction*. Vol. 1. New York: Crossroad, 1993.

Schweitzer, Albert. *The Mysticism of Paul the Apostle*. Translated by William Montgomery. Baltimore: Johns Hopkins University Press, 1998.

Scott, Joan W. "Deconstructing Equality-versus-Difference: Or, The Uses of Poststructuralist Theory for Feminism." *Feminist Studies* 14.1 (1988) 38–62.

Scott, J. Julius, Jr. "Parties in the Church of Jerusalem as seen in the Book of Acts." *Journal of the Evangelical Theological Society* 18 (1975) 217–27.

Segal, Alan F. *Paul the Convert: The Apostolate and Apostasy of Saul the Pharisee*. New Haven: Yale University Press, 1990.

Bibliography

———. "Universalism in Judaism and Christianity." In *Paul in His Hellenistic Context*, edited by Troels Engberg-Pedersen, 1–29. Minneapolis: Fortress, 1994.

Segundo, Juan Luis. *The Liberation of Theology*. Translated by John Drury. Maryknoll, NY: Orbis, 1975.

———. "The Shift within Latin American Theology." *Journal of Theology for Southern Africa* 52 (1985) 17–29.

Seifrid, Mark A. *Justification by Faith: The Origin and Development of a Central Pauline Theme*. Novum Testamentum Supplements 68. Leiden: Brill, 1992.

Slemon, Stephen. "Modernism's Last Post." In *Past the Last Post: Post-Colonialism and Post-Modernism*, edited by Ian Adam and Helen Tiffin, 1–12. Calgary: University of Calgary Press, 1990.

Smallwood, E. Mary. *The Jews under Roman Rule: From Pompey to Diocletian*. Studies in Judaism in Late Antiquity 20. Leiden: Brill, 1976.

Smith, Dennis E. *From Symposium to Eucharist: The Banquet in the Early Christian World*. Minneapolis: Fortress, 2003.

———. "Social Obligation in the Context of Communal Meals: A Study of the Christian Meal in 1 Corinthians in Comparison with Greco-Roman Communal Meals." ThD diss., Harvard Divinity School, 1980.

———. "What Do We Really Know About the Jerusalem Church?" *Westar Institute Seminar Papers* (Spring 2000).

Smith, Dennis E., and Hal Taussig. *Many Tables: The Eucharist in the New Testament and Liturgy Today*. Philadelphia: Trinity, 1990.

Smith, Jonathan Z. "Fences and Neighbors: Some Contours of Early Judaism." In *Approaches to Ancient Judaism*, edited by William Scott Green, 1–25. Brown Judaic Studies. Chico, CA: Scholars, 1980.

———. *To Take Place: Toward Theory in Ritual*. Chicago Studies in the History of Judaism. Chicago: University of Chicago Press, 1987.

———. "What a Difference a Difference Makes." In *"To See Ourselves as Others See Us": Christians, Jews, "Others" in Late Antiquity*, edited by Jacob Neusner and Ernest S. Frerichs, 3–48. Scholars Press Studies in the Humanities Series. Chico, CA: Scholars, 1985.

Spelman, Elizabeth V. *Inessential Woman: Problems of Exclusion in Feminist Thoughts*. Boston: Beacon, 1988.

Stendahl, Krister. "The Apostle Paul and the Introspective Conscience of the West." In *Paul among Jews and Gentiles*, 78–98. Philadelphia: Fortress, 1976.

———. "Paul among Jews and Gentiles." In *Paul among Jews and Gentiles*, 1–77. Philadelphia: Fortress, 1976.

———. *Paul among Jews and Gentiles*. Philadelphia: Fortress, 1976.

Stowers, Stanley Kent. *A Rereading of Romans: Justice, Jews, and Gentiles*. New Haven: Yale University Press, 1994.

Sugirtharajah, R. S. *Asian Biblical Hermeneutics and Postcolonialism*. The Bible & Liberation Series. Maryknoll, NY: Orbis, 1998.

———. "Biblical Studies after the Empire: From a Colonial to a Postcolonial Mode of Interpretation." In *The Postcolonial Bible*, edited by R. S. Sugirtharajah, 12–22. Sheffield: Sheffield Academic, 1990.

———, ed. *The Postcolonial Bible*. Bible and Postcolonialism 1. Sheffield: Sheffield Academic, 1998.

Suh, Kwang Sun. "A Biographical Sketch of an Asian Theological Consultation." In *Minjung Theology: People as the Subjects of History*, edited by the Commission on Theological Concerns of the Christian Conference of Asia, 15–37. Maryknoll, NY: Orbis, 1983.

Suh, Nam Dong. *In Search of Minjung Theology*. Seoul: Hangil, 1984.

———. "Toward a Theology of Han." In *Minjung Theology: People as the Subjects of History*, edited by the Commission on Theological Concerns of the Christian Conference of Asia, 55–69. Rev. ed. Third World Studies. Maryknoll, NY: Orbis, 1983.

Tamez, Elsa. *The Amnesty of Grace: Justification by Faith from a Latin American Perspective*. Translated by Sharon H. Ringe. Nashville: Abingdon, 1993.

Taussig, Hal E. "Dealing under the Table: Ritual Negotiation of Women's Power in the Syro-Phoenician Pericope." In *Reimagining Christian Origins*, edited by Elizabeth Castelli and Hal E. Taussig, 264–79. Vallley Forge, PA: Trinity, 1996.

———. *In the Beginning Was the Meal: Social Experimentation & Early Christian Identity*. Minneapolis: Fortress, 2009.

———. "Jerusalem as Occasion for Conversation: Examining the intersection of Acts 15 and Galatians 2." *Westar Institute Seminar Papers* (Fall 2000) 217–28.

———. "Wisdom/Sophia, Hellenistic Queens, and Women's Lives." In *Women and Goddess Traditions: In Antiquity and Today*, edited by Karen L. King, 264–79. Studies in Antiquity and Christianity. Philadelphia: Fortress, 1977.

Taylor, Joan E. "The Phenomenon of Early Jewish-Christianity: Reality or Scholarly Invention?" *Vigiliae Christianae* 44 (1990) 313–34.

Taylor, Nicholas. *Paul, Antioch and Jerusalem: A Study in Relationships and Authority in Earliest Christianity*. Journal for the Study of the New Testament 66. Sheffield: Sheffield Academic, 1992.

Theissen, Gerd. "Social Integration and Sacramental Activity: an Analysis of 1 Cor 11:17–34." In *The Social Setting of Pauline Christianity: Essays on Corinth*, 145–74. Edited and translated by John H. Schütz. Philadelphia: Fortress, 1982.

———. "The Strong and the Weak in Corinth: A Sociological Analysis of a Theological Quarrel." In *The Social Setting of Pauline Christianity: Essays on Corinth*, 121–44. Edited and translated by John H. Schütz. Philadelphia: Fortress, 1982.

Tiffin, Helen. "Introduction." In *Past the Last Post: Post-Colonialism and Post-Modernism*, edited by Ian Adam and Helen Tiffin, vii–xvi. Calgary, ALB: University of Calgary Press, 1990.

———. "Post-Colonialism, Post-Modernism and the Rehabilitation of Post-Colonial History." *Commonwealth Literature* 23.1 (1988) 169–81.

Tomson, Peter J. *Paul and the Jewish Law: Halakha in the Letters of the Apostle to the Gentiles*. Compendia rerum Iudaicarum ad Novum Testamentum. Section 3: Jewish Traditions in Early Christian Literature 1. Minneapolis: Fortress, 1990.

Urbach, E. E. "Self-Isolation or Self-Affirmation in Judaism in the First Three Centuries: Theory and Practice." In *Jewish and Christian Self-Definition*. Vol. 2, *Aspects of Judaism in the Greco-Roman Period*, edited by E. P. Sanders et al., 269–98. Philadelphia: Fortress, 1981.

Verneput, D. J. "Paul's Gentile Mission and the Jewish Christian Community: A Study of the Narrative in Galatians 1 and 2." *New Testament Studies* 39 (1993) 36–58.

Walters, James C. *Ethnic Issues in Paul's Letter to the Romans: Changing Self-Definitions in Earliest Roman Christianity*. Valley Forge, PA: Trinity, 1993.

Bibliography

Watson, Francis. *Paul, Judaism and the Gentiles: A Sociological Approach.* Society for New Testament Studies Monograph Series 56. Cambridge: Cambridge University Press, 1986.

———. "The Two Roman Congregations: Romans 14:1—15:13." In *The Romans Debate*, edited by Karl P. Donfried, 203-15. Rev. ed. Peabody, MA: Hendrickson, 1991.

Wengst, Klaus. *Humility: Solidarity of the Humiliated: The Transformation of an Attitude and Its Social Relevance in Graeco-Roman, Old Testament-Jewish, and Early Christian Tradition.* Translated by John Bowden. Philadelphia: Fortress, 1988.

———. *Pax Romana and the Peace of Jesus Christ.* Philadelphia: Fortress, 1986.

West, Cornel. "The New Cultural Politics of Difference." In *The Cornel West Reader*, 119-39. New York: Basic Civitas, 1999.

———. "Race and Modernity." In *The Cornel West Reader*, 55-86. New York: Basic Civitas, 1999.

West, Gerald O. *Biblical Hermeneutics of Liberation: Modes of Reading the Bible in the South African Context.* Pietermaritzburg: Cluster, 1991.

———. "Finding a Place among the Posts for Post-colonial Criticism in Biblical Studies in South Africa." *Old Testament Essays* 10.2 (1997) 322-42.

Wiefel, Wolfgang. "The Jewish Community in Ancient Rome and the Origins of Roman Christianity." In *The Romans Debate*, edited by Karl P. Donfried, 85-101. Rev. ed. Peabody, MA: Hendrickson, 1991.

Williams, Delores S. "The Color of Feminism." *Christianity and Crisis* 45 (29 April 1985) 164-65.

———. "The Color of Feminism: Or Speaking the Black Woman's Tongue." *Journal of Religious Thought* 42/1 (1986) 42-58.

———. *Sisters in the Wilderness: The Challenge of Womanist God-talk.* Maryknoll, NY: Orbis, 1993.

Williams, Patrick, and Laura Chrisman. "Colonial Discourse and Post-Colonial Theory: An Introduction." In *Colonial Discourse and Post-Colonial Theory: A Reader*, 1-20. New York: Columbia University Press, 1994.

Williams, Patrick, and Laura Chrisman, eds. *Colonial Discourse and Post-Colonial Theory: A Reader.* New York: Columbia University Press, 1994.

Williams, Sam K. *Galatians.* Abingdon New Testament Commentaries. Nashville: Abingdon, 1997.

Wilken, Robert L. *The Christians as the Romans Saw Them.* New Haven: Yale University Press, 1984.

Wilson, Stephen G. *The Gentiles and the Gentile Mission in Luke–Acts.* Cambridge: Cambridge University Press, 1985.

Wimbush, Vincent L., ed. *African Americans and the Bible: Sacred Texts and Social Textures.* New York: Continuum, 2000.

———. "Historical/Cultural Criticism as Liberation: A Proposal for an African American Biblical Hermeneutic." *Semeia* 47 (1989) 43-56.

Whittaker, Molly. *Jews and Christians: Graeco-Roman Views.* Cambridge Commentaries on Writings of the Jewish and Christian World, 200 BC to AD 200 6. Cambridge: Cambridge University Press, 1984.

Young, Iris Marion. "Humanism, Gynocentrism and Feminist Politics." *Women's Studies International Forum* 8 (1985) 173-83.

———. *Justice and the Politics of Difference.* Princeton: Princeton University Press, 1990.

www.ingramcontent.com/pod-product-compliance
Lightning Source LLC
Chambersburg PA
CBHW051740230426
43670CB00012B/2103